praise for

Radical Transformation

Kevin MacKay forges an inspiring and empowering repertoire of new ways to think and act collectively to defend our social and ecological life systems. *Radical Transformation* offers an honest, fresh perspective on the most pressing question of our time: how ordinary people working together on the basis of solidarity, cooperation, and direct action can rescue the future from the destructive systems and corrupt oligarchs that threaten it. MacKay's arguments deserve a wide audience and a lively debate.
— Stephen D'Arcy, associate professor of philosophy, Huron University College, author of *Languages of the Unheard: Why Militant Protest is Good for Democracy*

Kevin MacKay has produced an eyes-wide-open account of our civilizational crisis. With rare honesty and integrity, his *Radical Transformation* embodies a radicalism in the best sense of going to the root of the matter and its implications for our embattled species. MacKay moves effortlessly from the local to the universal and back again to tease out our human foibles and possibilities. A *cri de ceour* for sense and sanity in the face of the bulldozers of mindless growth.
— Richard Swift, author of *SOS: Alternatives to Capitalism*

Radical Transformation provides a lucid overview of a central issue of our times: the potential collapse of industrial civilization and the political changes needed to avoid it. Kevin McKay argues convincingly that an egalitarian, democratic political culture, which reigned for much of human history, is a prerequisite for avoiding cataclysm. Read this important book and join the movements working for radical transformation.
— Yves Engler, co-author of *Stop Signs: Cars and Capitalism on the Road to Economic, Social and Ecological Decay*

Techno-industrial society is in a perilous state of ecological overshoot and decaying social order but seems paralyzed to inaction. Fatal implosion seems inevitable. Kevin MacKay traces this conundrum to a drearily repeating historical cycle in which economic and political elites establish oligarchic control of moral authority. Meanwhile, ordinary citizens conspire in their own demise through misplaced fealty to the hegemonic powers that rule them. In a gut-wrenching analysis of this Death System's pathology and consequences MacKay shows why mere reform is no remedy – any real solution resides in society's radical transformation. The question is whether modern society is already too far gone to reinvent itself. Let the reader ponder the odds that we can yet establish an eco-centric social democracy – a Life System – that truly reflects humanity's unique high intelligence, moral vision, and cooperative nature.

— William E. Rees, PhD, FFSC, human ecologist, originator of the Ecological Footprint concept and professor emeritus of planning and ecological economics, University of British Columbia

Radical Transformation is a brilliant, provocative book. It argues that today's "Death System" of oligarchic power is promoting global economic and ecosystem collapse. Before it is too late, Kevin MacKay calls on us to create a new "System of Life" based on cooperative, moral communities and a genuinely democratic, socialist, and ecological politics. This book can play an important part in helping to make this alternative politics of life and hope a reality.

— Don Wells, professor emeritus of labour studies and political science, McMaster University

In its power to reframe our contemporary problems – borrowing from left analysis, for example, while helping us to see through a simplistic left-right dichotomy – Kevin MacKay's extremely thoughtful book helps us discern what "Life System revolutionaries" are and how they can recognize the path they must take.

— Dr. Graeme MacQueen, author of *The 2001 Anthrax Deception*

Radical Transformation
Oligarchy, Collapse, and the Crisis of Civilization

Kevin MacKay

Between the Lines
Toronto

Radical Transformation: Oligarchy, Collapse, and the Crisis of Civilization

© 2017 Kevin MacKay

First published in Canada in 2017 by
Between the Lines
401 Richmond St. W., Studio 277
Toronto, Ontario M5V 3A8
1-800-718-7201
www.btlbooks.com

All rights reserved. No part of this publication may be photocopied, reproduced, stored in a retrieval system, or transmitted in any form or by any means, electronic, mechanical, recording, or otherwise, without the written permission of Between the Lines, or (for photocopying in Canada only) Access Copyright, 56 Wellesley Street West, Suite 320, Toronto, Ontario, M5S 2S3.

Every reasonable effort has been made to identify copyright holders. Between the Lines would be pleased to have any errors or omissions brought to its attention.

Library and Archives Canada Cataloguing in Publication

MacKay, Kevin, 1972–, author
Radical transformation : oligarchy, collapse, and the crisis of civilization / Kevin MacKay.
Includes bibliographical references and index.
Issued in print and electronic formats.
ISBN 978-1-77113-260-2 (softcover). – ISBN 978-1-77113-261-9 (ePub). – ISBN 978-1-77113-262-6 (PDF)

1. Social change. 2. Social history. 3. Democracy. 4. Oligarchy. 5. Civilization. I. Title.
HM831.M32 2017   303.4   C2016-907424-2
                                                                                                            C2016-907425-0

Cover design by Jennifer Tiberio
Cover image © YouWorkForThem/RuleByArt
Text design and page preparation by Steve Izma
Printed in Canada

We acknowledge for their financial support of our publishing activities the Government of Canada through the Canada Book Fund, the Canada Council for the Arts, which last year invested $153 million to bring the arts to Canadians throughout this country, and the Government of Ontario through the Ontario Arts Council, the Ontario Book Publishers Tax Credit program, and the Ontario Media Development Corporation.

 Canada Council   Conseil des Arts
for the Arts   du Canada

Contents

Acknowledgements / vii

Introduction: Welcome to the Apocalypse / 1

Part I The Crisis of Civilization

1 Collapse / 34

2 Dissociation / 46

3 Complexity / 58

4 Stratification / 67

5 Overshoot / 77

6 Oligarchy / 97

Part II Radical Transformation

7 The Death System / 136

8 Toward a System of Life / 178

Notes / 217

Index / 242

Acknowledgements

This book would not have been possible without the insight, support, and contributions of many people.

A number of friends provided both encouragement and critical feedback on early drafts. Dr. Graeme MacQueen, Dr. Jolen Beccaria, Leanne Forsythe, and Martyn Kendrick all helped shape the first version of *Radical Transformation* and spurred the project onward at its inception. Their patience and generosity in reading early chapter drafts were invaluable.

Matt Adams and Amanda Crocker at Between the Lines took a chance on an ambitious book and gave critical and helpful direction during the editing process. Mary Newberry provided excellent editorial suggestions that strengthened the manuscript and clarified my arguments. Her firm, yet collaborative editorial hand helped make this a much better book.

My comrades and colleagues in labour and social movements have helped me understand civilization's crisis and provided me countless inspiring examples of how this challenge might be met. My fellow executive at OPSEU Local 240 – Geoff Oncercin-Bourne, Heather Giardine-Tuck, Gaspare Bonomo, and Mary Allen – continually demonstrate what principled social unionism can accomplish.

Co-workers and sustainers in the Sky Dragon Community Development Co-operative – Dan Smith, Marg Ann Roorda, Don Wells, Graeme MacQueen, Rashne Baetz, Philippa Tattersal, Lauren Olson, Karen Burson, Todd Bulmer, Susan Moore, Dana Fisher, Mark Ellerker, Ray Cunnington, Tom Bernacki, Dave Gould, Gordon Odegaard, Steven Lake, George and Lenore Sorger, Don MacLean, Dean Carriere, Irina Aoucheva, Caroline Fram, Javad Khansalar, Gordon Guyatt, Trish Beddows, Ed Mallon, Simon DeAbreau, Melanie Skene, and Sandra Preston – have taught me that radically transformative models of economy and community can be practically realized.

Finally, my mother Sharon MacKay, father Donald MacKay, and sister Kathleen MacKay have provided me with the unconditional love and support that keeps me working toward a better world. None of this would be possible without them.

Introduction:
Welcome to the Apocalypse

> The world is not being destroyed because of a lack of information: it is being destroyed because we don't stop those doing the destroying.
> — Derrick Jensen

People of the Valley

Radical Transformation is about human civilization – about its present crisis, its conflicted and contradictory development, and should the current narrative not drastically change, about its impending collapse. It's also a story of change, and of the challenges facing us today should we seek to alter our society's fateful course. A story this broad needs to be grounded within local events and direct experiences, in the problems of civilization as they manifest in our daily lives. Throughout the book I reference many such individual struggles, with the intent of making larger themes and conflicts clearer.

In this spirit, I begin with the tale of a singular place and time – a beautiful swath of wild nature in the heart of a North American industrial town. This green space, the Red Hill Valley, became the site of an over fifty-year conservation battle. The struggle to save the valley from destruction presents a microcosm of civilization's looming crisis, and reflects a scene repeated over and over again in communities worldwide.

The Red Hill Valley is situated in the east end of Hamilton, a mid-sized Canadian city on the shores of Lake Ontario. Hamilton, like any number of rust-belt cities in the United States, such as Buffalo, Cleveland, or Baltimore, is a gritty town, with a history of steelmaking and manufacturing, and a tough, but creative working-class culture. In its heyday, Hamilton deemed itself the Ambitious City, and vied with its larger neighbouring city, Toronto, for the role of primary port and civic centre. Stelco and Dofasco, two major steel mills, were the backbone of the local economy, and companies like Firestone,

Radical Transformation

Westinghouse, International Harvester, National Steel Car, Proctor and Gamble, and Otis Elevator made it the area's industrial capital.

Labour struggles were an integral part of Hamilton's past, and in 1946 the members of United Steel Workers of America (USWA) Local 1005 went on a historic eighty day strike, staring down the owners of Stelco and the federal government, and helping win job security and full federal recognition for unions. The improved wages and working conditions, coupled with a post-war economic boom, gave rise to a prosperous and growing working class.[1] In the 1950s 60s and 70s Hamilton was a shining example of industrial capitalism's success, with a robust economy and vibrant cultural life.

Like most North American manufacturing centres, the golden era of Hamilton was short lived, and began to unravel in the 1980s. The heads of industrial corporations started pushing back against the gains made by trade unions and enacted a devastatingly effective strategy on several fronts. Neoliberal governments were elected – Ronald Reagan in the United States, Brian Mulroney in Canada – and tax, trade, investment, and employment laws began changing. Economic sectors were de-regulated, foreign ownership encouraged, and large manufacturers began to offshore their production to states with cheaper workforces, lower environmental standards, and weaker labour laws. At the same time, newly concentrated media mega corporations began a systematic attack on unions, social movements, and the political left, and the new language of free trade and global competition became dominant.

By the mid-1990s, Hamilton was a ghost of its former industrial glory. Most of the large industry had left, taking tens of thousands of good paying jobs that never returned. The economic shock was massive, and entire neighbourhoods were thrown into poverty and foreclosure. The downtown, once a vibrant business and entertainment district, became a hollowed-out wasteland of abandoned buildings, dollar stores, and strip clubs. The homeless appeared in greater and greater number, shelters were filled to capacity, and crack cocaine infected the downtown streets. It was as if the city had imploded, and the political and money elites had neither plan, nor great concern, for the collapse. They either moved out of town, or simply stayed away from the areas of concentrated blight. The Ambitious City, once Steeltown, had become Hamilton the Broken – a community in deep crisis.

While the major manufacturers that had employed so many Hamiltonians departed for more profitable shores, they left behind the toxic legacy of industrialization. The beautiful harbour that the industrial sector sprawled along was declared one of the most toxic areas in North America. Once it had been known for clean water, with excellent swimming and fishing. Now scientists warned against both, and the harbour became dead to recreational use. In warehouses all through the industrial district, toxic waste was left to fester, and countless properties were fenced off due to dangerous levels of contamination. The two main steel mills – Stelco and Dofasco – remained, both operating with drastically reduced workforces, and both filling the air with toxic pollutants. Hamilton's air quality became a serious public health issue, and scientific studies declared the city an asthma hot-spot.[2]

In the midst of this bleak economic and environmental situation, Hamilton retained some breathtaking natural treasures. There were botanical gardens and preserves of wild nature, with idyllic hiking trails, overwhelmingly located in high-income areas near the university, or in the wealthier outlying towns. The one exception to this was Red Hill Valley – home to the meandering Red Hill Creek, and at one point one of North America's largest urban parks.

Red Hill was part of unique geological features that had long defined Hamilton and its surrounding villages. The city rests against the northwest shore of Lake Ontario and is bisected by the Niagara escarpment, an over 400 million year old forested ridge that runs from New York state, through Ontario, and into Michigan, Wisconsin, and Illinois.[3] Originally, fourteen rivers flowed from the escarpment down into Hamilton Harbour in Lake Ontario. These valleys were home to runs of salmon, now-endangered Carolinian forest, and hundreds of species of wildlife.[4] The rivers combined to make Hamilton the City of Waterfalls, with over one hundred falls within city limits.[5] However, due to urbanization, by the 1960s the only viable river remaining was Red Hill Creek, which flowed through a large wooded valley in the east end of the city. Red Hill Valley existed for years as an incredible urban nature preserve for the people of Hamilton.

In 1956 it also caught the eye of developers, who thought the lush valley and living creek a perfect place to locate an expressway. Years of community struggle, led by CHOP (Clear Hamilton of Pollution), succeeded in swaying local government toward conservation. In 1974 Hamilton city council promised "to retain the natural character of the Red Hill Creek Valley and to maintain permanently its present natural state."[6]

Twenty years later, a 1995 wildlife inventory identified 24 species of fish in Red Hill Creek, along with 25 species of mammal, 78 species of breeding birds and over 600 plant species.[7] Five nationally and provincially designated rare species were also recorded, further buttressing the argument that the Red Hill ecosystem was environmentally significant, sensitive, and worthy of conservation. In 1976 the City of Hamilton declared the Red Hill Valley an

Environmentally Significant Area in its official plan. In 1990 it was designated by UNESCO as one of 564 World Biosphere Reserves.

Unfortunately, for Red Hill the respite was to be short lived. Under intense pressure from local development interests, the city once more put the valley on the table as the site of a north-south expressway. This move set off more than thirty years of continuous struggle by numerous community organizations, grassroots movements, and even governments to protect the sensitive ecosystem from destruction. In the spirit of CHOP before them, new generations of Hamiltonians answered the call to become defenders of the valley, including finally, and a bit late to the cause, myself.

The Friends of Red Hill Valley (FORHV), the most prominent and intractable anti-expressway group to date, did extensive research on the expressway project's history and on the forces driving it. Not surprisingly, the main architects of the pro-expressway lobby consisted of wealthy developers and landowners. If the road was built, this small handful of business interests stood to make millions in construction contracts, and an even smaller handful of land speculators would reap a windfall of increased property values. Opposing this small corporate and wealthy clique were the majority of the city's inhabitants, all of the local environmentalists and conservationists, the federal environment ministry, numerous government wildlife and ecology specialists, and the Six Nations Confederacy.

The valley had archaeologically significant sites, including burials, and a strong Confederacy chief, Norm Jacobs, led a movement to prevent this loss of First Nations heritage. Six Nations member Larry Green took the fight to court by filing for an injunction against the expressway based on the 1701 Nanfan treaty.[8] At the height of the struggle the diverse group of defenders merged into one strong and determined community – The People of the Valley.

Those opposed to the expressway had an exhaustive bank of research and data backing up their position, but it soon became clear that the other side had a powerful ace up their sleeve – money, and the political influence it buys. Through campaign donations the developers were able to stack city council votes in their favour. Through advertising and influence they were able to saturate the local media with their message. Through high-priced lawyers they were able to successfully challenge a federal environmental assessment – overturning environmental law and exempting the project from an evaluative process it would surely have failed. At every point the efforts of the FORHV, the Six Nations, and their numerous allies were checked by money, corruption, and vested interest.

The thousands of Hamilton residents involved in the Red Hill struggle eventually realized that the battle to save an environmentally sensitive ecosystem was as much about economics, corporate influence, democracy, the justice system, and corporate media control as it was about ecological science, conservation, or even simple *reason*. In the end, despite a creative, inspiring, and courageous stand by the valley defenders, the expressway lobby won. Corporate interests and the politicians they controlled were able to divide the diverse coalition of protectors through threat and fear. Our great strengths – solidarity, scientific justification, broad community support – were broken through a combination of corrupt politics and coercive force.

When considering the Red Hill struggle in hindsight, it is clear that the citizens who attempted to stop the valley's destruction, like countless others who have attempted to protect green spaces, prevent conflicts, or end injustice, were completely outgunned and outspent by their adversaries. If we had understood more clearly the complex of political power and economic interest we faced in the Red Hill struggle, it's very likely the valley would be intact today. Instead, the defeat broke my heart, traumatized our community, and called into question every aspect of our industrial capitalist society. How could a project go forward that was so obviously destructive to a rare and sensitive ecosystem? How, in a community struggling with some of the worst air quality in North America, could forty thousand mature trees be destroyed to build a road designed to *increase* traffic? How could this happen when science, public interest, government environment ministries, and First Nations communities were all dead set against?

The People of the Valley were engaged in the same struggle faced by people in thousands of communities worldwide. The culture, language, and context may differ, but the essential conflict and stakes are remarkably similar. Modern civilization is defined by sweeping global processes like capitalism, colonialism, and industrialization, but each is grounded in space and time, in countless struggles by communities to protect their environment, their autonomy, and their dignity. If Red Hill is a microcosm of the processes driving industrial society itself, then what does the struggle say about the future of human civilization? What does it say about the challenges we face and how to overcome them? Most importantly, the next time such a conflict arises, *how can we save the valley*?

End Times

Since the battle for Red Hill Valley I've spent my share of time on the front lines of many different movements, and through each encounter with industrial civilization's power structures I've learned a little bit more about how the system works. It's been a heck of an education. Like many who've engaged in struggles for conservation, social justice, or human rights, I've more than once felt that the work we were doing was insignificant compared to the scope and intensity of damage being done. Coming face to face with our society's callous cruelty and destructiveness can take its toll, and it wasn't long into my activist work that I felt myself in a state of almost chronic anxiety. Was it possible that we were simply too late to change course? Were the deep dysfunctions of civilization too embedded in our nature to be altered?

There's no shortage of fuel to feed this pervasive fear, and as North Americans we've been living under the shadow of apocalyptic threats for decades. My generation grew up during the Cold War, when fears of nuclear Armageddon loomed constantly in the cultural background. I was in grade school in the early 1980s, and can still remember the drills we did, in which being nuclear-war prepared involved closing the classroom door, pulling the blinds, and crouching under our desks. That any of these things would matter in the event of a missile strike was highly dubious, and in hindsight it seems they mainly served to manage anxiety in the face of a threat so massive that it was difficult to comprehend.

From radio, television, and print public service announcements, the Cold War generation learned how long to stay inside to avoid the toxic fallout from a missile strike, and how long we might expect to languish under a "nuclear winter." We became used to the coloured bars and high-pitched tone of the Emergency Broadcast System as it regularly commandeered our televisions to finally announce, to our relief, "This is only a test." A 1983 made-for-television movie, *The Day After*, dramatized a bleak post-nuclear war existence. At the time it broke ratings' records, and reflected collective fears of "mutually assured destruction."[9] Albert Einstein captured the pessimistic mood when he remarked, "I know not with what weapons World War III will be fought, but World War IV will be fought with sticks and stones."[10]

After the Soviet Bloc collapsed and the Berlin wall fell, fears of nuclear war lessened significantly in North America. For a few years it seemed like apocalyptic paranoia might fully subside, until the 1999 Y2K scare had many thinking that malfunctioning computer clocks would cause airplanes to fall from the sky, reactors to melt down, and the global banking system to crash.[11] While some remained cynical, many others rushed to stock up on bottled water, canned goods, and duct tape. The complete non-event that was Y2K provided a comic denouement to the hysteria that preceded it; however, following the September 11, 2001, terror attacks, apocalypticism has only intensified. The anthrax letter incident, fears of a "dirty bomb" being detonated in major cities, and, in the United States, the colour-coding of fear through the Homeland Security Advisory System, succeeded in convincing much of the North American public that any day their fragile world might break apart.

Along with the danger of nuclear annihilation and terrorist attacks, recent decades have seen the emergence of other challenges sufficiently powerful to threaten civilization's collapse. Since the 1962 publication of Rachel Carson's ground-breaking *Silent Spring*, biologists, ecologists, geologists, and climatologists have been pointing to the unsustainable pressures industrial capitalism is placing on the biosphere. In her book, Carson details the mutagenic and carcinogenic effects of toxic chemicals, and is blunt about their dangers:

> The central problem of our age has therefore become the contamination of man's total environment with such substances of incredible potential for harm – substances that accumulate in the tissues of plants and animals and even penetrate the germ cells to shatter or alter the very material of heredity upon which the shape of the future depends.[12]

Carson's prescient warning about bioaccumulating toxins is now being echoed by a host of researchers in various fields. These scientists have pointed to other areas of acute crisis, including deforestation, mass species extinction, anthropogenic global warming, fossil fuel and fresh water depletion, and ocean acidification. From the landmark 1972 Club of Rome study *Limits to Growth*,[13] to the 2014 report of the Intergovernmental Panel on Climate Change (IPCC),[14] scientists have been sounding a clear and consistent alarm. In the past decade, this concern for individual ecological crises has turned increasingly toward fears of a complete ecological collapse. Derrick Jensen's anti-civilization testament, *Endgame*, became a bestseller in 2005.[15] In the same year, historian Jared Diamond's *Collapse* was read by hundreds of thousands.[16] Writers like James Lovelock,[17] George Monbiot,[18] and Bill McKibben[19] have also been sounding apocalyptic notes in their recent work.

While fears of ecological collapse have now entered mainstream discourse, the global economic crisis of 2008 has shown us that the world system of industrial capitalism is also vulnerable to *financial* collapse. With an impact comparable to the Great Depression, the credit crisis in the United States, followed a few years later by the bond crisis in Europe, revealed that a global banking system marked by corruption and high-risk speculation has the potential to bring multiple countries to the brink of economic ruin. The shock was so intense that, in an interview with the Wall Street Journal, far-from-radical economist Nouriel Roubini remarked: "Karl Marx had it right. At some point, Capitalism can destroy itself."[20] With the world's communities now linked in a single global market, crises can't be easily isolated, and a banking collapse in a single state can reverberate throughout the globe, presenting what complexity theorists call "systemic risk," in which a few falling dominoes end up bringing the whole structure down.[21]

In the past few years, scientific studies have surfaced that suggest modern civilization's collapse is not only possible, but even probable. In 2014, researchers Safa Motesharrei, Jorge Rivas, and Eugenia Kalnay published a study in *Ecological Economics* in which they argue that both ecological stress and increasing social inequality could independently lead to modern civilization's collapse. Their simple yet ingenious model HANDY – Human and Nature Dynamics – demonstrates that the societies most likely to collapse are those with a large division between rich and poor.[22] In June of 2015, UK insurance giant Lloyds released their *Food System Shock* report. The report follows current trends in population growth, climate change, food and water shortages, food prices, and energy availability. Models designed by Anglia Ruskin University's Global Resource Observatory show that a convergence of these trends could lead to widespread food riots, political turmoil, terrorism, and warfare as the global population reaches nine billion in 2050.[23] In 2015, Gerardo Ceballos and colleagues published a study showing that modern civilization is inducing a "sixth mass-extinction event." Their research shows that humanity's impact on the biosphere has led to a current rate of vertebrate extinction approximately one hundred times greater than that found in the fossil record.[24] In a survey of recent literature on societal collapse, biologists Paul and Anne Ehrlich note that scientific studies portending collapse are proposing nothing new:

> Virtually every past civilization has eventually undergone collapse, a loss of socio-political-economic complexity usually accompanied by a dramatic decline in population size . . . . But today, for the first time, humanity's global civilization – the worldwide, increasingly interconnected, highly technological society in which we are all to one degree or another, embedded – is threatened with collapse by an array of environmental problems.[25]

While there are plenty of scientific reasons to predict a collapse of industrial capitalist civilization, these fears have also taken hold in North American popular culture. Hollywood seems particularly fixated on apocalypse, a trend started by 2004's *The Day After Tomorrow*, which portrayed the destruction of human civilization by a new ice age.[26] In the thirteen years following this movie, dozens of films have sought to outdo each other in presenting the most epic and realistic representations of global destruction, caused variously by meteors, tornadoes, terrorists, seismic faults, tsunamis, volcanoes, invading aliens, ecological collapse, or giant monsters from the ocean depths. A particularly virulent form of the apocalyptic meme involves zombies. The notion of civilization collapsing through mass contamination and the onslaught of mindless, cannibalistic corpses has spawned an entire industry within literature, film, and television. Television series like *The Walking Dead*, books like *World War Z*,[27] and movies like *Zombieland* (2009) are capturing the imagination of North American youth, and spawning such collective phenomenon as annual zombie walks and even a Zombie Research Society.[28]

The cultural fascination with civilization collapse by fantastic means – whether an undead plague or alien invasion – can be read as an attempt to deal with the fear and anxiety that very real ecological and economic threats engender. In this sense apocalyptic film, literature, and television act as a kind of Freudian defence mechanism, a case of displacement in which fears of the world's end are projected onto imaginary scenarios made safe by their very impossibility. We see the world destroyed over and over again on the screen, and eventually, the unthinkable becomes normalized. Disaster films and zombie culture show no signs of abating, indicating just how much this fear pervades North American society, and the extent to which notions of crisis and collapse inform the current zeitgeist.

Fears of collapse are also highly dependent on what part of the world we live in and on our life experience. For many North Americans, the apocalypse we dread involves the kind of widespread institutional and infrastructural collapse that has not been experienced here for well over a century, with the American Civil War being the closest equivalent. In sharp contrast, for most of the world's peoples, experiences of crisis, catastrophe, and system failure have long been a regular feature of life. When considering challenges to human civilization as a whole, of equal importance to consider are seemingly endless wars in Africa and the Middle East, and the worldwide theft of land from Indigenous peoples for mining, forestry, and factory farming. Of dire concern are the billions of people who live daily in poverty and insecurity, the increasing income gap between the world's super rich and the rest, and the concentration of political and economic power into the hands of fewer and fewer massive corporations and mega tycoons. Add in fears about increasingly authoritarian governments in North America and the neocolonial exploitation of poor countries by wealthy and powerful states, and everywhere we look we can see signs that our social systems are breaking down.

The apocalyptic fear these multiple crises generate – the sense that situations in the world are spiralling out of control – is something I increasingly encounter in my daily interactions with people. In 2005 – some years ago – I attended a talk by Noam Chomsky, and it was here that this shift in popular discourse really hit home. Chomsky's arguments had taken on a new and urgent tone. Essentially, he was saying that we (meaning those in the industrialized, developed West) had a choice – either we could continue in our mad and ultimately futile ambition to dominate the world, or we could survive as a civilization, as creatures on a still habitable planet.[29] At the time I was struck by this apocalyptic overtone, something I'd never before detected in his writings or lectures. However, more than ten years on, Chomsky's tentative allusion to human society's collapse seems almost quaint. Today, prophesying the End Times isn't just the purview of eco-radicals or "Rapture Ready" religious cranks – the Apocalypse has gone fully mainstream.

Away with Them All!

Most of us can agree that human civilization is facing some very serious problems, and we also agree that solving these problems would be a good thing. However, we don't all agree on what change is required, or if this change is even possible.

Like most people, my understanding of the crisis we now face developed in stages. At each stage, as I was confronted with new information or a more comprehensive analysis, my thoughts about what was needed to solve our collective problems also evolved. At first it seemed that the central issue was simply one of governance – if we could just get the right people elected then they would make decisions in the interests of human rights and sustainability. Referencing Plato, this could be called the "philosopher-king" model of social change, in which appointing an enlightened leader (or leaders) is the most effective way to solve our societal ills. On the surface of it, this seems like a good idea, and one that is certainly reinforced by innumerable historical accounts in which Great Men single-handedly change entire societies, and also by innumerable Hollywood storylines in which The Hero (invariably male, invariably white) single-handedly overcomes overwhelming obstacles and changes entire societies.

Increasingly though, as my experience with politics and social movements grew and my analysis deepened, it became difficult to "suspend disbelief" (as they say in Hollywood) and continue buying into the philosopher-king myth. It doesn't take engaging too many political battles to see the futility of hoping for radical change within the conventional realm of electoral politics. Even in much-ballyhooed Western democracies, the tendency of politicians to disconnect from the wishes of regular folk (generally in keeping with the elected officials' own class interests), coupled with the conservative nature of state bureaucracies, make the prospects for purely electoral change limited at best. What the high school history texts suspiciously omit is that when Great Men of History *have* left their mark, more often than not it's been defending the privilege of the few over the many – launching predatory wars, colonizing new lands, clear cutting forests, and oppressing minority populations.

If politicians are incapable of leading the kind of radical change we need, I then reasoned that if enough *people* just knew what was going on and put pressure on politicians and business leaders, then we could succeed. The model here is that of mass social movements – of protests, boycotts, civil disobedience, and non-cooperation. These tactics had been successful in the past, and were integral aspects of victories won by the labour and civil rights movements in North America. However, it's also true that these mass-movement tactics have been largely neutralized in today's capitalist states. The fight to save Red Hill Valley brought this realization home to me, and demonstrated just how pervasive is the influence of wealth and corporate interest, and how powerful is their ability to buy politicians, mislead citizens, and thwart movements. Time and again I've witnessed the considerable barriers that stand in the way of broad-based movement-building in North America, and the several ways in which people in today's corporate-controlled states are taught to identify with an oppressive and destructive social order. Mass movements for reform were clearly effective in the past, but seem hard pressed to meet the new and pervasive challenges of today.

After twenty years of battling for change and puzzling over how it happens, I eventually came to an important realization: civilization's many problems can no longer (if they ever could) be solved by mere adjustments or reforms of our social, political, or economic ways of life. The forces driving the crisis are too intertwined and deeply ingrained to be dealt with by anything but a fundamental re-envisioning of society as a whole. Both enlightened leaders and mass movements can be useful motivators of change, but they are fatally limited if they fail to challenge the logic and functioning of the entire society.

Million person marches against the second US invasion of Iraq didn't stop a war, because the entire US political economy is based on militaristic expansion. Electing social democratic politicians won't prevent the collapse of sensitive ecosystems, because they continue to preside over a constant-growth consumer economy. Half measures won't avert the crisis of civilization, and only a complete overhaul – a full system re-boot – will suffice. Think of the rallying cry of the Cacerolazos, a vast movement of the poor, working class, and disenfranchised middle class that organized during the

Argentinean economic collapse of 1999. When the national economy unravelled under the collective weight of corruption, inequality, and failed neoliberal policies, the Cacerolazos didn't put their hope in electing different politicians. Instead, millions took to the streets in defiance of their leaders, challenging the very nature of neoliberal capitalism and chanting "Que se Vayan Todos!" – *Away with them all!*[30]

Understanding the Crisis

Realizing that the crisis of civilization was real and that drastic changes were needed was, for me, a process that took considerable time. For over twenty years I studied scientists, revolutionaries, and philosophers, and each new theory I encountered contributed to my understanding of our predicament and how it might be solved. This inquiry was guided by three objectives:

- To provide an analysis of the crisis that civilization currently faces
- To understand how the crisis developed
- To determine how we can avert the crisis and chart our course toward a sustainable and humane future

Tackling a subject as large as civilization's crisis presents several challenges. The first relates to the size of the topic of study, and the need for an analysis broad enough to enable a big-picture understanding, but also detailed enough to capture aspects of the crisis, like the Red Hill struggle, that are localized in space and time. A related challenge is how to create a model that moves beyond description, and that instead provides a detailed explanation of modern civilization's many dysfunctions. In this sense the goal is to provide a *radical* analysis, not in the popular (mis)understanding of being violent or confrontational, but in the spirit of the word's academic definition, which means "to get to the root of."

What became quickly apparent when researching various theories is that the variables each either includes or omits has a significant impact on the picture of society each produces. Many theories focus intently on one aspect of social dysfunction, whether economic, ideological, political, or ecological, and as a result, end up generating a model that misses key social dynamics, generates erroneous explanations for crisis, and prescribes ineffective strategies for change. In particular, an important tension exists between models that are systems-based, envisioning society as a complex and dynamic field of interacting variables, and those that come from a left critical tradition, which focus more narrowly on problems of political and economic power.

Systems theories

The great utility of systems theories is how they capture the kind of complex, dynamic interaction between institutions and individuals that defines the Red Hill struggle, and that in turn defines other manifestations of civilization's crisis. One of the most influential scholarly works on the collapse of civilizations is an example of this kind of analysis. In his 1988 book *The Collapse of Complex Societies*, anthropologist Joseph Tainter studies the collapse of several historical civilizations by analyzing the effects of ecological, political, economic, and demographic variables.[31] In 2005, Jared Diamond published *Collapse*, a bestselling update of Tainter's analysis that focuses on several ways in which societal decision making fails in the face of crisis.[32]

To Tainter, the main challenge that overwhelms a civilization's ability to adapt to existential threats is the distance between increasing social complexity and available energy. Tainter argues that civilizations tend to respond to threats by increasing their organizational complexity – adding levels of political hierarchy, expanding trade networks, and intensifying economic and agricultural production. These strategies provide temporary fixes to societal challenges, but at the same time they create new social infrastructure that increases the overall civilization's energy needs. Over time this process becomes a vicious cycle of increasing complexity and decreasing returns on energy. Ultimately, the expanded complexity makes civilization even more vulnerable to future threats, a process that eventually leads to collapse.

Tainter's theory of civilization collapse is informed by an in-depth study of the Roman Empire's rise and fall. The decline of ancient Rome is also the inspiration for another seminal study on civilization collapse published by political scientist Thomas Homer-Dixon in 2006. Homer-Dixon's impressive book, *The Upside of Down: Catastrophe, Creativity and the Renewal of Civilization*, deepens and updates the analysis of Tainter and incorporates contemporary research on complex adaptive systems. Homer-Dixon notes that complex systems adapt and respond to change, but that the process of adaptation often includes a four-stage cycle consisting of *growth, breakdown, reorganization*, and *renewal*. A key insight is that in the process of adaptation, the breakdown of some systems is actually useful, as they create within their demise the potential for "something new, unexpected, and potentially good." He calls this positive breakdown and subsequent renewal *catagenesis*, and argues that modern civilization, if it confronts its looming crisis effectively, can limit disruption to this more circumscribed and ultimately desirable form of "constrained breakdown."[33]

The systems-based models of Tainter, Diamond, and Homer-Dixon have several strengths. The first is that they see civilizations as "problem-solving organizations," as integrated social formations that must constantly adapt to changing circumstances. If societies are able to make correct decisions in the face of threats to their existence, then they are able to adapt, develop, and endure. If they are unable to solve these survival problems, then they fail. This perspective takes us away from over-simplified and unscientific explanations for collapse, like neo-Malthusian arguments that focus on population, or deterministic arguments that see human societies as helpless in the face of changing environmental conditions. It reminds us that civilizations are above all *cultures* – complex wholes consisting of values, beliefs, institutions, and practices. What makes us unique among all other animals on Earth is our use of collective cultures as a primary means of adaptation. Although the environment has a powerful impact on human communities, Tainter, Diamond, and Homer-Dixon argue that the adaptive mechanism of culture is capable of responding to nearly any environmental challenge. Because of this the ultimate locus of success or failure lies, not in any external challenge or threat, but within *culture* itself.

Given the adaptive power of culture, Diamond proposes that the most important question is whether, in the face of existential threat, a society's adaptive potential is either engaged or squandered. He argues that past civilizations have collapsed because societal decision making fails to anticipate and perceive crises, and because harmful cultural values and self-interested behaviour undermine possible solutions.[34] Homer-Dixon makes a similar argument, noting that societies generally prove shockingly bad at predicting the future, and that when faced with a crisis, they invariably underestimate it and attempt to address it with failed strategies and limited reforms. He argues that the challenge is for civilizations to cultivate a "prospective mind" in which institutions are prepared for change and instability, and in which they develop the "resilience" needed to endure periods of breakdown.[35]

But civilizations are complex systems, and as Tainter, Diamond, and Homer-Dixon acknowledge, their success or failure is also related to a complex interaction of forces. In applying Tainter's analysis to modern civilization, Homer-Dixon describes five "tectonic stresses" that are threatening collapse – population growth, energy scarcity, environmental degradation, climate change, and economic instability. These stresses are exacerbated by two "multipliers" – modern civilization's high degree of global connectivity, and the ability of "fanatics, insurgents, and criminal gangs" to obtain nuclear weapons and biological agents. To Homer-Dixon, it is the convergence of these factors that provides modern civilization with an unprecedented challenge:

> The stresses and multipliers are a lethal mixture that sharply boosts the risk of collapse of the political, social, and economic order in individual countries and globally – an outcome I call *synchronous failure*.[36]

Homer-Dixon's concept of synchronous failure is a crucial insight. History shows that it is rarely a single challenge that defeats a culture's adaptive capacity, rather it is the convergence in space and time of multiple and interlocking crises in several of a civilization's subsystems. Today's civilization faces just this kind of "negative synergy," and any attempt to change our trajectory from collapse to sustainability needs to understand this complex dynamic.

A final strength of systems-based models is their assertion that understanding the success or failure of civilizations involves taking a historical and even evolutionary approach. This final point is key, as it deals directly with the problem human cultures have with identifying negative cyclical patterns and predicting potential catastrophes. If we focus only on recent historical events, certain developments can seem novel and unprecedented when in fact they are simply recent manifestations of ancient patterns. An example would be attributing current issues of ecosystemic degradation or man-made climate change to the recent phenomenon of industrial capitalism. While capitalism and industrialization are undoubtedly destructive of our planet's ecology, they are far from the first social processes to be so. When an evolutionary view is taken, human societies are shown to have destroyed their ecological base numerous times in the past. This realization should then prompt us to search for more fundamental system dynamics beneath the phenomenon of collapse, as did Tainter, with his powerful insight into the contradiction of increasing complexity versus available energy. An evolutionary perspective is crucial for us to understand the nature of the crisis that civilization faces, its genesis, and its potential for positive transformation.

Where Tainter, Diamond, and Homer-Dixon show the weakness of systems theories is in their weighting of various societal factors, and their failure to adequately account for political, economic, and social constraints to decision making. Under-emphasizing the impact on decision making of inequalities in political and economic power leads systems theorists to assign too much weight to certain variables and not enough to others. This can lead to erroneous conclusions, as when Diamond resorts to a population pressure argument to help explain the Rwandan "genocide," as opposed to the well-documented historical influence of Belgian, French, and US imperialism. Diamond uses Rwanda's civil war as an example of a catastrophic event challenging the viability of an entire society, and in this sense he is correct. However, in failing to understand the impact that foreign powers have on African politics, the cause of the catastrophe is misattributed, and a powerful determining force is left unconsidered.[37] Homer-Dixon makes a similar error when attributing ancient Rome's collapse to a growing population and to Tainter's energy versus complexity contradiction (as Romans ran out of food to support their urban population and armies):

> The empire's loss of internal order, coherence, and complexity was, in significant part, a thermodynamic crisis. The empire tipped into irreversible decline precisely because it couldn't feed its energy hunger.[38]

While population pressure and energy scarcity clearly had an influence on Roman civilization's crisis, Homer-Dixon seems to dismiss the equally important impact of Rome's political culture. He describes a toxic mix of endless imperial expansion, civil war, and aggrandizing emperors, yet misses the effect that this political system would have on determining societal priorities and making critical decisions in the face of mounting food shortages.

A related weakness present in Diamond's and Tainter's work is the tendency to attribute a false unity to societies and civilizations. Systems theories tend to be *functionalist* in nature, in that they see societies as complex systems comprising parts that are integrated and interdependent. Each part has a function, and each contributes to the workability and distinct identity of the whole. This is actually an important insight, and reflects that social institutions *do* have a logic of interaction greater than their individual parts. An example of this is that institutions as diverse as corporations, universities, hospitals, and municipalities each have a distinct culture, and can be distinguished from similar institutions on this basis. Where the idea of systemic integration becomes a problem is when it is stretched too far and begins to conceal important sources of heterogeneity and contradiction within integrated systems. This problem can be seen when systems theorists conceive of societies as unitary "decision-making organizations," and downplay the significant differentials in decision-making power that exist between various actors and institutions.

This functionalist fallacy occurs in much popular thought about societies and civilizations, and is exemplified in statements as common and seemingly uncontroversial as "in 2003 the United States invaded Iraq." In response to this assertion, it is important to interrogate the implied totality of "United States." Who or what do we mean when we reference the country in this way? Do we mean the American *people*, or do we mean the *state*? Do we mean the percentage of the American public who supported an invasion, or do we mean those political "hawks" and members of the military-industrial complex who actually orchestrated and perpetrated the invasion? What do we make of the significant number of American citizens who opposed the invasion, and who even protested vehemently against it? In such cases, discernment is key, and understanding the differentials in interests and decision-making power between an average working-class American and Dick Cheney, or between the town council of Gary, Indiana, and the board of directors of the Carlisle Group, is crucial if we're to understand how events like the Iraq invasion actually occur.

The left critical tradition

In these moments, the left critical tradition provides a necessary corrective to systems theorists by highlighting the ways in which inequalities in social power are constituted, whether based on socioeconomic class, gender, race, religion, or other categories. This includes neocolonial analyses concerning the influence of powerful, militaristic states like the United States, China, Russia, Britain, France, and Canada, as they pursue their economic interests in other countries.

Of course, the left critical tradition has its weaknesses as well, and many stem from an overly narrow focus on specific power relationships. Marxists tend to see every social dysfunction through the lens of class conflict, even when other factors – cultural, religious, technological, ecological, demographic – play a powerful role. Feminists tend to see social dysfunction primarily through the lens of gender socialization and patriarchy, while critical-race theorists focus on the impact of prejudice, racism, and privilege. These various perspectives are necessary to understand industrial capitalist civilization's crisis, and their contribution to this research is invaluable. However, their myopic tendencies can also oversimplify social reality, and risk producing the same kind of erroneous conclusions that uncritical systems theories can. Throughout history women have embodied a variety of political identities ranging from Emma Goldman to Margaret Thatcher. Similarly, black American men can occupy a range of ideological and socioeconomic positions ranging from Barack Obama to Fred Hampton. Finally, none of Marxism, feminism, or critical-race theory are equipped to understand the societal challenges posed by ecosystem collapse. No one analytical lens is sufficient to encompass this diversity, and ultimately the combination of systems and left critical perspectives provides the best chance of understanding our predicament and of proposing workable solutions.

Apart from the question of what variables are included or excluded from analysis, the way in which inequalities in political and economic power are factored into analysis leads to important differences in how civilization's crisis is understood, and in how it might be changed. In this regard I've found that thinkers can be divided into two broadly defined groups – reformers and radicals. A goal of my research has been to critically evaluate these perspectives, and to determine how they variously aid or hinder a scientific explanation of civilization's crisis.

Reformist thinkers are those for whom the challenges facing civilization are reducible to simple aberrations or unintended consequences of an essentially sound society. These writers can be described as adhering to a "few bad apples and a few malfunctioning parts" viewpoint, and they tend to feel that reforms of the existing system are all that is needed. Reformist writers often have an insightful analysis concerning a narrow spectrum of our global crisis, and even some solid ideas for action that could be undertaken to produce a slightly more democratic and humane, and slightly less destructive civilization. Authors like Joseph Tainter, Jared Diamond, David Suzuki, Bill McKibben, Lester Brown, George Monbiot, Thomas Homer-Dixon, and Al Gore all fit into this reformist category. While I respect each one as an individual thinker and activist, I find their respective writings weak concerning the actual workings of political and economic power, and concerning the kinds of action that will achieve the goal of a sane, humane, and sustainable planet. While each is often strong on individual descriptions of the crisis civilization is facing, these writers don't give me much hope for actually *solving* it.

In contrast to the many reformist thinkers contributing to the modern debate on civilization, several radical theories present a deeper analysis of power and a much more militant approach to social change. From traditional left political philosophy, both Marxism and anarchism provide invaluable insights into how power works in the modern world, and how it might be decisively transformed (they would likely say *overthrown*). These philosophical currents provide an important corrective to moderate and reformist thinkers, and yet they suffer from significant weaknesses themselves.

With Marxism, the insights of class conflict, a materialist approach to history and social development, and the utopian vision of a classless, cooperative society free from domination are all invaluable tools for radical change. At the same time though, much Marxist theory and practice suffers from the philosophical fallacies of *essentialism* and *teleology*. Essentialism is a logical fallacy in which a complex, historically contingent, and socially constructed reality is instead presented as unitary, unchanging, and based in nature.[39] Marxists often fall prey to an essentialist view of social classes, in which bourgeoisie and proletariat are seen to embody fundamental forces of history. Teleology is a fallacy that sees a given historical or social process as *inevitable*, and involves aspects of circular reasoning. Teleology appears in fundamentalist Christianity, in which the apocalypse is seen as inevitable because *it has been foretold*. As a result, all events in the present are seen as confirming a predetermined outcome. In some schools of Marxist thought, teleology emerges in the belief that the progression from capitalism to socialism is inevitable, and that it reflects the unfolding of historical laws.[40] Both fallacies tend to greatly oversimplify social processes, and thus to conceal their concrete and complex reality.

As well, Marxist politics, although radically transformative, contains seeds of authoritarianism within it. Centralization of political control into a vanguard party and the goal of seizing total state power are the shadow aspects of Marxist politics.[41] I argue that centralized power in the form of oligarchy (rule of the many by the few) is *the* defining characteristic of civilization's fatal dysfunction and imminent collapse. Many Marxists fail to account for the corrupting power of oligarchy, yet it is this very critique that their radical cousins, the anarchists, make central to their theory and practice.

Anarchism is arguably the most misunderstood political philosophy. This isn't particularly surprising, as anarchists are acutely focused on the problems of authoritarianism and oligarchy (tendencies that are liable to dominate in mainstream political practice – whether left, right or centre). Although there are many variants of anarchist thought and practice, in general they see the ills of human civilization deriving from class domination as exercised through concentrated state power. In this regard anarchism presents a foundational truth about our crisis.

However, anarchism has its theoretical weaknesses as well, and needs to be approached with a critical eye. It shares with Marxism an essentialist view of social class, while also presenting a totalizing and over-simplified view of the modern state as wholly despotic and impervious to positive reform. Because anarchists conceive of the state as essentially violent and oppressive, most espouse an approach to social change known as *insurrectionism* – the violent overthrow of the existing social order. Insurrectionists believe that substantial social change can *only* come from violent revolution, and they tend to dismiss other, non-revolutionary forms of social change as minimally effective or even counter-productive.[42] Not all anarchists are insurrectionists; however, a tendency to prefer spontaneous, direct action over gradual, organized movement *is* largely defining of anarchist philosophy and practice. This is particularly true of contemporary North American anarchism, which tends to focus on an individualistic "lifestyle" approach to politics.

Anarchist philosophy is also important due to the creative variations it has spawned since the writings of early theorists like Pierre-Joseph Proudhon, Mikhail Bakunin, and Peter Kropotkin. In particular, perspectives known variously as *green anarchy* or *anarcho-primitivism* have presented a very radical (some might say nihilistic) challenge to the mainstream reformist environmental movement. According to theorists in these traditions, human civilization is inherently oppressive and unsustainable and, instead of being modified or reformed, should be destroyed entirely. As anarcho-primitivism has been associated with some authors who reject the label, I will instead use the broader term *anti-civilization* when discussing thinkers in this tradition.

To many North Americans the idea that human civilization is completely irredeemable and should be destroyed still seems like a shockingly controversial perspective. However, the idea is gaining traction among a growing number of people, and particularly among radical youth. The reality today is that anti-civilization authors are writing bestsellers, attracting large audiences, and profoundly influencing young environmental activists. One author in particular, Derrick Jensen, has had a significant impact on the environmental movement, and his two-volume bestseller *Endgame* is widely quoted. In *Endgame* Jensen makes an emotionally urgent argument for civilization's terminal decadence, and invites his readers to take action to hasten its inevitable collapse. Throughout the book he repeatedly advocates blowing up dams, hydro and cell phone towers, and other civil infrastructure – a far cry from reduce, re-use, recycle! Jensen argues, beyond an imminent yet vaguely defined eco-apocalypse, that human societies could be sustainable at a stone-age level of technology.[43]

Contemporary anti-civilization thought emerged in the 1990s through the work of writers like John Zerzan[44] and Daniel Quinn,[45] but in Jensen these ideas have filtered into the mainstream of environmentalist discourse. There is much of value in Jensen's work, and he clearly captures the deep pathology of industrial capitalist society and the direct and structural violence – against humans and the natural world – on which it rests. I would also argue that anti-civilization activists are the group that takes most seriously the implications of *ecological overshoot* (using resources at a rate greater than they are replenished), *peak oil* (the fact that world oil reserves are running out), and climate change. In contrast with reformist environmentalists, anti-civilization authors are deadly clear when spelling out ecological limits and the likely consequences of ignoring them.

And yet, most of us balk at the argument that industrial civilization is *all* nightmare, *all* destruction, and presents nothing worth saving. In this sense, anti-civilization activists fall into a similar philosophical trap as the reformist authors mentioned earlier. Both groups have near diametrically opposed views of human society, but what unites their perspectives is a monolithic view of civilization – as either *inherently* good or *inherently* bad. Reformist environmentalists tend to view civilization as essentially good, just and defensible. In their writings they seldom entertain foundational critiques concerning the systems of governance, economy, or socialization on which society rests. Because they take the entire system to be essentially good, they are able to focus instead on fixing or tweaking its minor dysfunctions and advocating reformism as their model for change. The anti-civilization group, in contrast, tends to view our society as monolithically bad – as inherently violent, oppressive, and unsustainable. Because of this perspective, they see any reform, change, or even transformation as impossible. "If it can't be changed," they argue, "better to destroy it all and have done with it."

Combining analytic models

The more I contemplate the ideas of civilization being either monolithically good or monolithically bad, the more problems appear in either perspective. For starters, Zerzan, Jensen, and friends would have us believe that countless aspects of modern civilization that we experience as intuitively good, just, or desirable simply . . . well . . . *aren't*. For example, as a Canadian citizen, there are many things I detest about my country's social structure, and especially about the Canadian state's internal colonization of Native people and promotion of Western imperialism abroad.[46] However, I *am* very glad to have publicly funded healthcare and reasonable access to a quality education system. I'm glad that there are laws protecting civil rights and preventing discrimination based on age, ethnicity, gender, or sexual identity. When referencing industrial civilization more broadly, I'm appreciative of accumulated scientific knowledge concerning ecology, renewable energy, health, and human development. I find invaluable the open communication and knowledge-exchange medium of the internet, the creative productivity provided by computers, and the countless manifestations of art, music, theatre, cinema, architecture, philosophy, and spirituality that have been generated throughout the history of various civilizations. If civilization has been completely and irredeemably bad, then how do we account for the profound beauty and humanity that exist alongside the undeniable presence of violence, domination, and environmental devastation?

Understanding both the destructive and life-sustaining aspects of human civilization requires a level of analytic complexity that many theorists lack. The systems-based model I use throughout the book seeks to address this deficit. In the tradition of radical analysts, this includes a full and unflinching accounting of the dynamics of inhumanity and ecological destruction. However, my analysis also includes those pro-social, ecologically sustainable patterns of interaction that have always existed – at times in open defiance and opposition, at times in uneasy balance – with structures of oppression.

Ultimately, my model seeks to combine the holistic understanding and explanatory depth of systems theory with a radical analysis of political and economic power informed by the left critical tradition. The model I use focuses on four subsystems within the totality of industrial capitalist civilization. These subsystems relate to key aspects of society – economic, political, sociocultural, and ecological. This is a macro-systems model in that it encompasses dynamics and processes that define entire countries (in particular Canada, the United States, and the Eurozone members), and that also has transnational effects. However, the model can also reveal how particular patterns of interaction in the four subsystems contribute to events localized in space and time. This micro-level interaction is illustrated by the Red Hill Valley struggle, in which ecological sustainability, vested economic interest, political corruption, and cultural assumptions all factor into the stakes of the conflict (protecting a sensitive ecosystem from highway development), and its outcome (the victory of vested political and economic interests and destruction of the valley).

A similar project has recently been undertaken by UK political scientist Nafeez Ahmed in his 2010 book *A User's Guide to the Crisis of Civilization: And How to Save It*. Building on Tainter and Homer-Dixon, Ahmed details six crisis points: 1) climate change, 2) energy scarcity, 3) food insecurity, 4) economic instability, 5) international terrorism, and 6) the militarization of Western domestic and foreign policy. Although he repeats many of the "tectonic stresses" mentioned by Homer-Dixon, Ahmed grounds his analysis firmly within a Marxian critique of global capitalism and its tendency toward economic and political instability and ecological destruction. Ahmed identifies ten key structural problems related to industrial capitalism's contradictions, and in the end presents a model with considerably more analytic power than that of Homer-Dixon.[47]

Ahmed's excellent work goes a long way toward addressing the main failing of systems models of civilization collapse – their underdeveloped understanding of political and economic power. I refer to the arguments in *A User's Guide* later in this book, building on Ahmed's skillful linking of environmental and socioeconomic crises. However, my analysis differs in that I focus more intently on the problem of political oligarchy and on the ancient history of this societal form. Just as taking an evolutionary view helped Joseph Tainter highlight the essential contradiction between increasing complexity and available energy, my analysis reveals an equally powerful contradiction. When viewed through an evolutionary lens, industrial capitalism is just the latest manifestation of a toxic social formation that emerged thousands of years ago at the dawn of complex civilizations. Oligarchic governance locks societies into a cycle of overshoot and collapse, a *Death System* that repeatedly leads to human misery and ecological devastation. I argue that unless we understand this ancient cycle, and the equally ancient counter-power that opposes it, we have little chance of transforming our civilization into a humane and sustainable form.

Origins

If modern civilization has aspects that are clearly destructive of human life and ecosystems, but also aspects that are sustaining of life and of human potential, then the model we use to analyze our predicament needs to account for this dual nature. Tainter's and Diamond's systems approaches fail to address this dichotomy, instead presenting a misleading equivalency of forces. In contrast, left theorists do recognize civilization's duality, yet tend to explain it as the result of historically recent movements that fought against despotic rule and expanded the concept of democracy.[48] These movements led first to anti-monarchist revolutions in Europe in the seventeenth and eighteenth centuries, then to worldwide feminist struggle and socialist and anti-colonial revolutions in the nineteenth and twentieth centuries, and finally to civil rights and global justice movements that swept through democratic states in the twentieth and twenty-first centuries. Because of the partial success of these "democratic revolutions," modern civilization contains both constraint and freedom, both justice and inequality.

While the past three centuries of democratic struggles have had an undeniable impact on today's civilization, the conflict that drives them – between elite control and popular governance – is actually far older. In this sense, understanding civilization's current predicament necessitates looking further back into human history and even into prehistory. When we trace the evolution of human societies from their earliest, most technologically simple forms to their modern, highly complex forms, a compelling story emerges. This story speaks to our innate capacities for democratic association. However, it also speaks to our susceptibility to social structures based on dominance, exploitation, and environmental destruction. Exploring this evolutionary trajectory can teach us much about how the crisis we face emerged, and how it might be successfully transformed.

An evolutionary understanding of civilization's crisis integrates research from cultural anthropology, archaeology, and even primatology. These fields give us a glimpse into how small-scale, egalitarian societies function in remarkably democratic and ecologically sustainable ways. Human beings lived in these kinds of societies for over 180,000 years, implying our innate capacity for, and impulse toward, democratic and cooperative forms of living.

Considering our innate capacities brings us into the realm of human nature, a discursive terrain that most critical intellectuals shy away from. This reticence is understandable given the long history of biological racism and sexism, in which arguments about the innate inferiority of women in relation to men, and other ethnicities in relation to Europeans, have justified systems of domination. In addition to oppressive political uses of biology, discussions of human nature also risk lapsing into naturalistic fallacy, in which subjective interpretations of social phenomena are presented as objective, essential, and unchangeable. Despite the real dangers inherent in discourses of human nature, I argue that we have more to gain than to lose in engaging them. In the first place, as our current civilization faces threats to its very survival, it makes sense to explore those characteristics – both biological and cultural – that enabled early human communities to not only survive, but to thrive in nearly every ecological niche they encountered. There are important lessons that industrial societies can take from the ability of small-scale societies to exist for thousands of years within ecological limits.

Beyond living sustainably, exploring our origins can also help us address the social and political aspects of our crisis. It is understandable that political philosophers throughout the ages – from Plato, to the social contract theorists, to Marx – have sought to define humanity in relation to other species. To all of these thinkers it makes logical sense to ask who human beings are before they can consider their ultimate goal – the ideal human community. Based on their conception of human nature, thinkers argue that the ideal society involves either authoritarian rule by an aristocratic elite (in the case of Plato, Hobbes, Augustine, and many modern neo-conservatives), or else the democratic association of free individuals (in the case of Rousseau, Bakunin, Kropotkin, and Marx). The debate over human nature, and by extension the best form of society, continues to this day.

The Life System and the Death System

Because people's understanding of human nature (whether scientifically accurate or not) is so important, I argue that critical scholars need to re-examine the biological bases of behaviour. Particularly, we need to contend with new research from anthropology, evolutionary biology, and primatology that takes a non-deterministic approach to biology, that acknowledges the incredible power of culture and socialization, and that actually refutes widespread, pessimistic conceptions of human beings as inherently selfish, aggressive, and violent. Our evolved bio-cultural capacity constitutes what I call the *Life System* – a form of social organization that balances humans' autonomy and sociality, that enables the fulfillment of individual and collective potential, and that holds human community in ecological symbiosis with non-human nature. Studies of human origins show that we are literally *built* for democracy, and that forms of authoritarian social control are both unnecessary, and also profoundly distorting of our natural creativity, empathy, and sociality.

While our first communities were egalitarian, research into human evolution also helps us understand how early democratic societies could fall prey to relations of hierarchy and dominance caused by increasing social complexity. At the dawn of agriculture and sedentary living, our distant ancestors confronted challenges related to population growth, resource scarcity, and greater susceptibility to climatic variation. In certain communities, these pressures led to cycles of increasing social scale and complexity, and also to conflict and warfare. As a result, a small number of societies became oligarchic in character, with an elite few able to exert power over the democratic human community. These first oligarchic societies gave birth to what I call the *Death System* – a form of social organization based on dominance, exploitation, warfare, and environmental destruction. The social and ecological contradictions inherent in the Death System lead ultimately to civilization collapse – a phenomenon that has occurred several times in human history, and that threatens us once again.

In chapter 7, I explore the question of human origins, and consider the lessons it can teach us about today's crisis. I argue that, despite our considerable advances, modern states are still captive to the logic of the oligarchic Death System. The challenge facing those who would solve civilization's crisis is to determine how to effectively resist and dismantle this system of destruction, and how to vitalize and expand the more ancient, and still potent Life System. In this twin process lies the path to radically transforming society, and to changing the trajectory of human evolution from collapse to sustainability.

Possible Worlds

Perhaps the biggest challenge to anti-civilization notions of an inevitable collapse, reformist notions of the need for only minor adjustments, and insurrectionist beliefs that change will come only through violent revolution, is the proliferation of recent theories showcasing other compelling possibilities for thought and action. Between nihilism and reformism there lies a fertile space in which visionaries and practical utopians have been working on the forms of a new society and on the tools to create it. These inspired thinkers and movements show us a viable way forward.

Where the anti-civilization crowd sees no possibility for a sustainable civilization that incorporates appropriate technology and those positive aspects of modernity that we'd like to preserve (the Internet!), the philosophy of *social ecology* presents cogent arguments and practical solutions suggesting otherwise. This broad field of thought and practice began with the writings of Murray Bookchin – a complicated thinker who expressed an innovative view of humanity's relation to the natural world he called *dialectical naturalism*. Bookchin's philosophy grounds human ethics in the organic unfolding of natural evolution – the tendency toward greater complexity, and the mutuality and diversity found in thriving ecosystems.[49] Similar to another important theoretical innovation, *deep ecology*, dialectical naturalism shifts our normal, anthropocentric worldview toward one in which human beings are embedded deeply within ecosystems.[50] No longer does *man* dominate and use nature for *his* own ends, but instead humanity exists in mutually beneficial symbiosis with all life.

The critique that social ecology and deep ecology present of our current situation is profound, with both traditions arguing for a fundamental upending of our relationship to the environment, and both also highlighting the link between industrial capitalism's domination of nature and man's domination of both men *and* women. *Eco-feminism* takes this important critique a step further, and questions the entire patriarchal edifice upon which our high-tech, competitive, ecocidal, and homicidal system rests.[51] Each of these theories has important differences and makes specific contributions, but the salient thing to stress at this point is that they all present creative and viable possibilities for a sustainable and equitable human civilization. Without recourse to the spectre of inevitable collapse, the romanticization of stone-age life, or a naive denial of ecological limits, these philosophies provide real, livable models. Eco-communities, local economies, bioregionalism, permaculture, and renewable energy are all examples, and there are many more that I will discuss later on in the book, where I describe modern manifestations of the Life System – the creative, pro-social, and ecologically sustainable application of science, art, and community. The good news is that these potentials are very real and very present right here, right now in our own communities. A philosophy and practice of *Radical Transformation* focuses on identifying and amplifying these elements of the Life System.

However, this book wouldn't be breaking any new ground if my goal was simply to point out that viable theories and models for a sustainable civilization exist. For people involved in the radical environmental movement, such ideas have long been understood, and countless innovative experiments in real sustainability provide ample evidence of their practicability. Instead, I want to focus on how we undergo the difficult process of moving from where we are, in the *world of the real*, toward a world in which the sustainable, democratic, and communal dynamics of the Life System are ascendant. For anti-civilization activists this is a moot point, as destruction and collapse are assured. Because of this, they advocate a process of helping destroy civilization more rapidly. For the reformers, the goal appears much more easily attained, as we can simply modify existing processes and structures (through elections, improved city bylaws, and so on) to meet our objectives. However, for radical transformation to occur, the task is considerably more difficult. If we want a truly sustainable and equitable human civilization, then we have no choice but to directly confront the nexus of control that drives our current system of ecological destruction and human misery. We have to *take power back*, and this, as they say, is a whole other kettle of fish.

Power and hegemony

The question of power – how it functions and how it might be challenged, overthrown, and transformed – is thus by necessity one of the central concerns of this book. If we're not okay with collapsing and we're not naive enough to assume that some new elected official will save us, then we're faced with the daunting task of actually taking on the powers that be. This is really the great insight provided by revolutionary theorists of the left, who long ago identified the direct cause of class inequality and social misery. The problem, according to levellers, diggers, chartists, Jacobins, communists, and anarchists alike, is that a small minority of wealthy individuals benefit immensely from the current set-up, and create a social system in which they maintain a near total monopoly on decision-making power. This describes a system of class-based political oligarchy, and its most extreme historical variants are the absolutist monarchy (for example, France under Louis XIII) or the totalitarian state (for example, Stalinist Russia, Fascist Italy, or Nazi Germany).

The reasons oligarchy is the most intractable feature of human civilization's destructive and oppressive aspect is something I discuss at length, but particularly in chapter 6. This discussion is heavily informed by the revolutionary theories of radical left thinkers and movements, but not without significant critique and modification. While I argue that the *intent* of early revolutionary movements is generally correct – to overthrow oligarchic control and establish a democratic and inclusive social and political order – their analysis of power is no longer adequate to describe today's industrial capitalist societies. If you're up against the total and despotic reign of a Louis XVI, then storming the Bastille is a likely strategy. However, can we envision storming Parliament Hill in Ottawa, or the White House in Washington, DC? It's likely that contemplating such an action would make many of us smile wistfully, but would people actually get behind it? If they did, would it likely succeed?

The history and dynamics of revolutionary movements and revolutionary situations is a fascinating subject, and important to understand. However, it would also occupy one or more books in itself. Although I do go into more detail discussing revolution and insurrectionism later in the book, for now I'd simply like to point out that a successful revolution in Canada, the United States, or for that matter any similar country in the global North is likely off the table for the foreseeable future. Given this, we then have a dilemma. For if radical transformation is the only thing that will avert the looming crisis of civilization, and radical transformation involves taking back power – directly confronting and overthrowing the oligarchic interests that control society – then we need another way to think about social change.

Luckily, just as social ecologists, deep ecologists, and eco-feminists have been thinking about new and innovative ways to live sustainably and humanely, modern revolutionary theorists have been thinking about new ways of understanding and transforming power. One of the most important thinkers in this regard is Italian Marxist Antonio Gramsci. His writing about modern democratic states has birthed a fertile intellectual tradition. Gramsci lived and died in Italy at the dawn of the twentieth century, but his thought has been advanced by contemporary radical theorists like Cornel West, Stuart Hall, Ernesto Laclau, and Chantal Mouffe, and continues to inform the work of many scholars in media and cultural studies.

A key aspect of Gramsci's writing addresses the way power is constituted and exercised in modern states. In such societies, he argues, the ruling elite shows "moral and intellectual leadership,"[52] and enjoys a critical degree of legitimacy in the eyes of the ruled. He calls this form of power *hegemony*, and theorizes that it is fundamentally different from the forms of power that radicals had struggled against throughout Europe's anti-monarchist revolutions.

Gramsci's thought is more complicated than this thumbnail sketch, and in later chapters, I explore it in greater detail. The essential brilliance of hegemony as a concept is that it describes the kind of mediated, negotiated, and culturally based form of political power prevalent in countries like Canada, the United States, Japan, Australia, and the Eurozone members. Beyond even this, it helps us understand an entire continuum of configurations of state power – from the most authoritarian to the most seemingly democratic. Hegemony is able to explain, for instance, why the Bastille could be stormed by French revolutionaries in 1789, or why the Winter Palace could be taken by members of the Petrograd Soviet in 1917. Hegemony is equally able to explain why, should we try to enact a similar uprising in downtown Manhattan today (say, against the Federal Reserve Bank), we wouldn't stand a chance.

Gramsci's writing on hegemony, and its successful challenge through a process of *counter-hegemony*, informs my thinking about social change, and of the way radical transformation can occur in societies like Canada and the United States that seem, on the surface, to be effectively managed by political and corporate elites. It also reflects civilization's dual character, and the intertwining of Death System and Life System in historical and present day societies.

Understanding the complex of control mechanisms serving to keep the forces of destruction moving forward and to keep the populace quiescent is critical. From there we can design effective counter-movements and engage in struggles capable of taking back power. From all of my research and direct experience in social movements, I believe such a goal is achievable, and in the final chapter, "Toward the Life System," I discuss how a movement of movements could take on the oligarchs, and *win*.

A movement of movements

There have been many successful social movements in recent history, whether we speak of women and minorities marching for equal rights or of workers who beat back capital to form unions and win the social concessions of the welfare state. What made these movements successful? And what made them ultimately fail in radically transforming society? Answering these questions is especially important given the current state of progressive communities and progressive movements in North America. On one hand there is a growing nihilism and apocalypticism among North American radicals – the sense that change is impossible and society doomed. On the other hand there are reformers clinging to an essentially defeatist political program in which they try to ameliorate the worst excesses of runaway destructive forces, all the while lurching toward collapse. In the middle, committed radicals, visionaries, and hardworking organizers struggle to do the actual work needed to change course, all while fighting the corrosive gravity of either pole.

Can we understand the cause of this fracturing? Can we envision and enact a political program that can unite people's deepest-held aspirations and fundamentally change society? Beneath the fault lines of post-modern identity politics and old-left sectarianism, there continues to lie a vast common ground of interests defined by direct democracy, economic equality, human and citizenship rights, and the need for a clean, viable, sustainable environment. In fact, this ground is shared by the great majority of people worldwide – those 80 per cent who exist outside of the controlling interests and oligarchs. This is the unifying base for a movement for radical transformation to build on, and this necessitates creating a new language for thinking and speaking about transformative politics, and a new set of practices for realizing them.

The need for such a movement has never been more pressing, nor the time more propitious. Signs of looming system failure are everywhere – whether the fragility of the global economy, inevitable shortages of food, oil, and fresh water, or advancing climate change. Any one of these challenges should be enough to spur us to immediate action, and each also contains within itself the very preconditions required to shift the sociopolitical context and enhance movement effectiveness. The heat is getting turned up, but paradoxically, so are the conditions for our success.

As fossil fuel reserves dwindle, economies will necessarily localize to offset increasing transportation costs. The far-flung global production and supply networks used by multinational corporations to defeat social movements in the global North will become increasingly frail, and the resulting economic relocalization will also relocalize struggles for justice. Another effect of dwindling energy resources will be the reduced ability of the world's military powers to project force around the globe. Without this capability, the artificially created inequity in the global economic system will begin to crumble, and countries long held under thumb by the G8 and permanent security council members will revert once more to local political processes. Under these conditions, movements for progressive change have a much better chance of success, and there is every likelihood that conditions will change in their favour. Signs of this are already apparent in the Arab Spring, the leftward turn in Latin America, the global Occupy Movement, resistance to austerity in Eurozone countries, the North American Black Lives Matter movement, the political campaigns of Bernie Sanders in the United States and Jeremy Corbyn in England, and Canada's Idle No More and Quebec student movements.

Despite the emergence of more favourable terms of struggle for North American movements, we are a long way off from having the kind of vision, strategy, and organization needed to take full advantage. The Occupy Movement is a compelling example of this gap between structural hardship, spontaneous popular revolt and the coordinated power needed to create fundamental change. In chapter 8, "Toward the Life System," I discuss the process of movement-building in North America within a radically transformative context. I argue that movements need to engage in four key tasks: solidarity-building, resistance, education, and alternatives-building. Solidarity-building involves doing the hard work of creating a "movement of movements" – a bloc of political and identity groups that shares a common vision and will commit to coordinated (but still autonomous) action. Resistance describes jamming, de-legitimating, monkey-wrenching, and opposing the forces of destruction as they manifest in given spaces and times. Education deals with individual and collective consciousness, and helps people to understand the world around them to and develop their capacity to change it. Finally, alternatives-building necessitates creating the communities, institutions, and systems of governance that will enable us to transition through human civilization's time of crisis. They are the transitional forms linking the present to a utopian, but practically attainable future society.

The Coming Storm

A mistake many activists make, myself included, is that we're often great at telling those around us what's wrong with the world, what's wrong with the way we're living, and what we're *against*. What we're not so good at, is talking about what we're *for*. The truth is that it's hard for all of us to listen to a consistently negative message, and harder still to believe in a better world without first seeing it described in concrete terms. Because of this, it's not surprising that many of us remain captive to the logic of our current dysfunctional reality and lack the inspiration and *know how* to move beyond it.

It also doesn't help that the cultural voices competing with humane and sustainable alternatives are strident and ever-present. Corporate media replay an endless loop of materialistic and individualistic fantasy – utopia as a gilded shopping mall stocked with wealth, celebrity, and ever-expanding consumption. Elites present fear, violence, and economic ruin as constant threats should we deviate from our prescribed life-paths – work hard, embrace debt, don't question. Unfortunately, even progressive movements seeking to counter the dominant culture's mad exhortations often resort to fear and threat in their language. Can people truly be blamed for their apathy when the manipulations of elites (terrorism! job loss!) blur into the doomsaying of movements (collapse! conspiracy!), with all combining to short-circuit and overwhelm?

To live in today's industrial society is to continually endure this psychic assault, under which even the most radical and visionary of us can become short-sighted, doubtful, and confused. We may start believing that mere survival should be our goal, that only world leaders can solve our problems, that civilization is doomed to collapse, or that human nature resigns us to eternal strife. We may easily forget the larger visions bequeathed to us from earlier centuries' movements – of a world without classes, poverty, and warfare; of a society based on the respect and celebration of both masculine and feminine; of a civilization based on ecological symbiosis with the earth. We may forget the inspiring legacy of research passed down by enlightened thinkers throughout history. We may forget, and in forgetting, lose sight of where and what we could be.

For thousands of years humankind has struggled with the fateful historical move we took toward what I term the Death System – the oligarchic cycle of dominance and destruction that now moves us toward collapse. Today this system has never been more potent in its ecocidal and anti-human effect, and yet it has also never been more vulnerable, nor confronted with such fundamental and multiplying contradictions. These challenges come not only from steadily contracting ecological and social limits, but also from the cumulative movement and development of civilization's ancient counter-power – the Life System. We have thousands of years of resistance, enlightenment, human ingenuity, and human compassion to draw on. We can learn from our past and from insights gained through science, struggle, and social movement. We can create a new future.

Today's best scientific minds are sending us a clear warning. There's a storm coming, and a reckoning unlike any humanity has faced. If we're to weather it, we need to start, right here, right now, to take responsibility for our current predicament, and to work committedly toward our future emancipation. Far more than just a valley, this time there's a world to save. *Radical Transformation* is only one perspective, one story of who we are and of how we might live freely, compassionately, and sustainably on this earth. The true test will be to make the story live through words and deeds of your own. Future generations will look to us and our actions during modern civilization's time of crisis. What accounting will we give?

Part I
The Crisis of Civilization

1
Collapse

> And when he had opened the fourth seal, I heard the voice of the fourth beast say, Come and see. And I looked, and behold a pale horse: and his name that sat on him was Death, and Hell followed with him. And power was given unto them over the fourth part of the earth, to kill with sword, and with hunger, and with death, and with the beasts of the earth.
> — Revelation 6:7–8

Diagnosis

In the biblical Apocalypse of John, also known as the Book of Revelation, one of the more evocative passages describes the emergence of four horsemen as each of the first four seals of the book of the Apocalypse are opened. These horsemen – the first riding a white horse, the second a red one, third a black, and fourth a pale green – were originally thought to represent conquest, war, famine, and death, although some later interpretations gave the first horseman the title of pestilence. The riders were believed to bring forth global tribulations that heralded the end of the world, and prefigured natural cataclysms to be unleashed when the sixth seal was breached.

Like all religious texts, the Bible is fascinating when read from a socio-historic perspective, revealing aspects of the time and culture in which the various passages were recorded, compiled, and revised. The Book of Revelation deals with the end of days, a story common to many religious and mythic traditions. That most traditions have a story of the end of the world is interesting to begin with, and suggests that their authors had direct or historical knowledge of the collapse of prior civilizations, that such knowledge existed in the broader cultural memory, or that their current civilization experienced threats sufficient to evoke fears of its end.

The other interesting aspect of the Revelation passages, in particular, is that the authors and later medieval interpreters also had a good sense of what forces could or likely would lead to humankind's final destruction. Given the list of pestilence, war, famine, and death, the horsemen were astutely named. The authorship of Revelation is attributed to John of Patmos, a citizen of the Roman Empire writing between AD 68 and 95.[1] If the time of authorship is accurate, then John would have had much experience with threat of conquest and war, as the expanding empire battled continually with neighbouring states. In addition, Rome had recently experienced civil war in 69 AD (the year of the four emperors), plagues and devastating fires, all with disastrous impacts on the empire's citizens.[2]

Today's civilization faces similarly grave challenges to those faced by the authors of biblical texts, and it's more than a little depressing that some of the forces threatening destruction haven't changed over the past two thousand years. War and conquest are still powerful determining factors, and famine in the form of water and food shortages is also a mounting concern. However, other challenges facing modern civilization are substantially different, including anthropogenic (human caused) climate change and an increasingly unstable global economy.

In this chapter I present an analysis of civilization's crisis, and particularly of the key factors that make our situation today so intractable – our present day "four horsemen." In the introduction I mention several examples of modern civilization's dysfunction – from the kind of destructive development that devastated the Red Hill Valley in Hamilton, to the militaristic expansion of the American empire. There are numerous other examples of social, ecological, and economic dysfunction that could be cited, and listing them would be enough for many to conclude that the entire system is in crisis.

However, there are also many people who would argue that such situations are relatively isolated events amidst a generally functional whole. These are the people who would also argue that the problems we face aren't critical, and that reform of our existing society is all that's needed. While I may disagree with this perspective, it does present an important challenge to the notion of terminal crisis and impending collapse. I've been talking about a crisis for a while now, and it's time to put some proof behind the assertion. Just *what is it* about our current situation that can't be isolated or addressed through reform? How is our modern predicament different from other societal challenges we've faced, and overcome, in the past?

In answering these questions, I'll need to move beyond a simple listing of the multiple crises we face both socially and ecologically and to provide evidence to support three key premises. The first premise is that the crisis of modern civilization can't be geographically isolated, and instead presents a global problem. The second premise is that the crisis is dire, having reached a terminal phase that leads, if the current trajectory holds, toward system collapse. The third premise is that the crisis is not amenable to reform, and instead presents a problem that necessitates radical change. To present and support these premises, I'll outline an analytic model of civilization, and offer some concrete examples of its critical, macro-level dysfunction.

It makes sense to begin with some definitions and a bit of context for my analysis. The first point of clarification is actually long overdue, and concerns just what I'm referring to when I say "civilization." Clarity here is important for two reasons – first because there is considerable debate among scholars concerning a definitive definition of civilization, and second because the definition chosen has far-reaching implications for understanding civilization's structure and characteristics, and for thinking about how it can change.

In his anti-civilization manifesto, *Endgame*, Derrick Jensen makes an important point about commonly used definitions of the word civilization. In dictionary definitions of the term, the first interpretation given is usually evaluative in nature.[3] Some examples include,

> "A relatively advanced stage of social, political and cultural development."[4]
>
> "An advanced state of human society, in which a high level of culture, science, industry, and government has been reached."[5]

Even the built-in dictionary on my computer suffers from the same evaluative bias, defining civilization as, "the stage of human development and social organization that is considered most advanced: *they equated the railroad with progress and civilization.*"

Present in these definitions, and in most other standard English dictionary listings, are terms like "advanced," "high," and "progress" – evaluative and comparative language asserting that civilization is the best or most evolved form of human social organization. Jensen understandably balks at these evaluative terms, arguing that in the first place they are unsuitable as the basis of a scientific definition, and second, that they are thoroughly biased, or what a cultural anthropologist would call *ethnocentric*. Ethnocentrism refers to the tendency for members of a given culture or society to assume that their way of life is the most natural, most developed or "best" (both morally and rationally). Ethnocentric bias is found in all cultures, but social scientists see it for the subjective fallacy that it is. Clearly, the creators of the term "civilization" invested their own bias into its definition – presenting their society and culture as the apogee of human development.

Jensen argues that the first important step to critically evaluating modern civilization is to understand, and then to jettison, this ethnocentric bias. I'm in complete agreement with this sentiment, and doubly so when considering the word's origin in the cultural/historical context of mid-eighteenth century France. In his 1954 essay "Civilization: Contribution to the History of the Word," linguist Emile Benveniste traces first use of the word civilization to a 1757 treatise by Victor de Riquetti, the Marquis de Mirabeau. In this treatise, civilization represented the pinnacle of human progress as embodied in the monarchial, French, and Christian state.[6] From its genesis then, the definition of civilization has reflected the legitimating ideology of European empire and colonialism, expressed in French society of the day as the *mission civilatrice* – the inherent superiority of white European culture, and the responsibility to impose this culture (through war and conquest) on "barbaric" or "uncivilized" societies.[7]

Beyond simply rejecting the notion of civilization as a more advanced form of society, tracing the roots of the term also helps us understand how both colonial European civilization and modern industrial civilization are intimately linked to processes of war and empire-building. From the experience of the world's Indigenous peoples or of colonized populations in India, Africa, Asia, and the Middle East, modern civilization's normative associations would likely be far more negative than salutary. To these peoples, "advanced" might more appropriately be replaced with "oppressive" or "destructive."

A final issue with considering civilization more "advanced" than less complex societies concerns the criteria we use for comparison. For instance, many contemporary writers would point to industrial civilization's technological marvels (nanotechnology, heart transplants, nuclear reactors) as examples of its advanced character in relation to, for example, the subsistence culture of the Inuit. This is fine, but by different criteria the tables are easily turned. To an ecologist, for instance, a society with impressive technology that is heading for imminent resource depletion and collapse is woefully maladapted compared to a technologically simple society that has existed sustainably on its land base for thousands of years. In such a case, "advanced" means very little, and the only criteria worth using for comparison are if a society is more or less adapted to its biome and more or less able to adapt to environmental change.

Thus, defining civilization as a characteristic associated with societies that are morally and rationally superior to "non-civilized" societies is unscientific and untenable. But we must still contend with the differences in more scholarly and critical definitions of the term. An early and still-influential approach to defining civilization is presented by Australian archaeologist V. Gordon Childe.

In his book *Man Makes Himself* (1936), Childe presents a list of characteristics and structural features that a society needs to have to be considered a civilization. These include cities, specialized division of labour, agricultural food production and payment of surplus food to rulers, monumental art and architecture, state structures including religion and bureaucracy, importation of resources, metallurgy, writing, standards of measurement, and economic complexity (the interdependence of different types of labour and social classes).[8]

Childe's list of characteristics of civilization is compiled from common features of the earliest states that emerged in Mesopotamia around 5,500 BP (years before present) and in Mesoamerica around 2,500 BP. Certain items of his list have become the focus of subsequent anthropologists who took a less descriptive and more structural/developmental approach to civilizations. These more recent definitions by scholars like Elman Service (1962),[9] William Sanders and Barbara Price (1968),[10] and Eric Wolf (1982)[11] stress the importance of cities, state political structures, class inequality, social complexity and interdependence, cultural interaction, writing, mathematics and practical science, and extensive agriculture. While different theorists focus on different aspects of civilization, there are several points of overlap among these definitions. To simplify things, I've accounted for the overlap and further reduced the list of defining characteristics and structural features to three categories: social scale and complexity, agricultural economy, and social stratification. These categories and their associated characteristics are listed in table 1.1.

Characteristics of Civilization

Category	Characteristics
Social Scale and Complexity	Cities, state-level political organization, importation of resources, bureaucracy, writing, mathematics & practical science, metallurgy, large population
Agricultural Economy	Extensive agricultural production, complex irrigation, surplus food supports rulers & non-workers
Social Stratification	Oligarchic political structure, hierarchical division of labour, monumental architecture, class stratification

It's helpful to have a clear definition of civilization for two reasons: First, defining civilization as a society with massive social scale and complexity that is sustained by extensive agriculture and exhibits extreme social stratification helps us separate it out from various other forms of human social organization, both historical and contemporary. This is necessary because, as numerous anthropologists and popular authors like Daniel Quinn, Murray Bookchin, and Derrick Jensen have pointed out, the cultures of Indigenous peoples worldwide present qualitatively different forms of human society and often *radically* different forms of relationship between human beings and nature. When I talk about the crisis of modern civilization, I'm not talking about the subsistence economy of the Innu people of Nunavut, or the hunter-gatherer lifestyle of Africa's 'Kung San bushmen. These other cultures actually possess many of the characteristics of a sustainable and directly democratic society, and lumping them into the global web of industrial civilization would be misleading and grossly unfair.

To distinguish my usage of "civilization" in this book from other sustainable human cultures that still survive, adding the prefixes *industrial* and *capitalist* is necessary. As such, I am referring to a particular form of civilization that emerged during the eighteenth and nineteenth centuries in Europe and then spread to every part of the globe via processes of warfare, colonialism, trade, migration, and electronic communications. This form of civilization is based on industrial mass production and industrial agriculture, both made possible through heavy exploitation of fossil fuels. It is true that most variants of this mode of civilization also possess market-based, consumer economies; however, more centralized, state-controlled political economies do exist, with current examples including China, Cuba, and North Korea.

The second benefit of defining civilization is that it causes us to realize that no one characteristic or structure is either necessary or sufficient, and that civilizations, by definition, are complex systems of several interacting variables. Appreciating the complex nature of civilization helps us to identify which specific variables are involved (such as, extensive agriculture, state-level political organization, writing), and then to analyze them both individually and in relation to other variables. In turn this leads us away from a definition that is *totalizing,* that manufactures from disparate elements a unity or essential character that may not be scientifically or practically valid. Totalizing definitions can be either positive, such as the common notion of civilization as "advanced" or "high-level" culture, or negative, such as the definition posed by Derrick Jensen and other anti-civilization authors, in which civilization is taken to be totally unsustainable, immoral, and irredeemable.

An example of a totalizing definition of civilization can be found in *Endgame,* where Jensen defines civilization as any form of social organization that involves cities. He then defines cities as sedentary communities large enough to require the importation of food from the surrounding countryside.

Jensen argues that this defining characteristic – the need for cities to import food – means that civilization can never be sustainable. Cities need food and raw materials from the surrounding countryside, and this requires oppressing the inhabitants of this vital hinterland and denuding its resources. This process is replicated in every city in every country and leads to increasing conflict, misery, and ecological devastation. As every country in the world today consists largely of people living in cities, Jensen thus declares civilization *in toto* (global, industrial, capitalist) to be unsustainable.[12]

The issue with Jensen's definition is that it is overly simplistic and, when tested empirically, easily refuted. First, there are historical examples of cities that did not exhibit all of the necessary elements of civilization as most academics define it, and certainly not as we experience it today. During the Natufian period in the Middle East (approximately 11,000 BP), year-round villages had arisen that were sustained by foraging, not by extensive agriculture.[13] Later Mesopotamian cities in the "formative period" (7,000 to 5,500 BP) were sustained by surrounding agricultural areas, but lacked the other critical aspects of civilization, including states and writing, which later developed.[14] These other aspects of civilization emerged through intensifying cycles of population growth, agricultural expansion, conflict, warfare, and the consolidation of victorious cities into imperial states. In such cases, Jensen's definition is shown to be at once too narrow, in that it focuses on only one component of civilization, and too broad, in that it blurs important distinctions between early cities and later state-based societies.

A second problem with Jensen's civilization = cities definition is that there are recent examples of cities that have shown how urban environments can deal successfully with the essential problem of procuring food, energy, and other resources. In Havana, Cuba, 90 per cent of the fresh produce consumed by residents is grown within the city itself.[15] The Danish island of Samso produces 100 per cent of its electricity through wind power and generates a considerable excess which it exports to the rest of the country. Samso is on track to be a fossil-fuel free community by 2030.[16] Projects worldwide advancing energy efficient building construction, urban agriculture, renewable energy production, and sustainable city design are directly challenging the idea that cities *have* to be ecologically unsustainable.

Of course, Jensen's indictment of modern cities being inherently unsustainable also has countless corroborating examples. Massive metropolises worldwide *are* totally unsustainable. An example is Toronto, Canada, a city of 2.6 million that exports its garbage, imports its food from all over the world, imports its fuel, and would be completely crippled if any of these extra-local relationships were severed. There are many other examples, and in reality, unsustainable cities are today overwhelmingly the norm. Despite this, given the knowledge that some cities *can* be sustainable, the problem isn't really cities per se, but certain *kinds* of cities – cities that are based on unsustainable principles and practices. This is an important caveat that then carries over into considerations of civilization as a whole.

The issue isn't really that civilizations as an entire category are *essentially* unsustainable, rather that certain *kinds* of civilizations are, based on the particular confluence of social, political, economic, and ecological factors on which they rest. This distinction may seem like hair-splitting, but the implications are great. If cities and civilizations *can* be sustainable, then the possibility exists for our civilization to be so as well. Given this allowance, the important task then becomes to identify those aspects of our civilization that are keeping us from sustainability and to figure out how to change them.

Analyzing Civilization: A Systems Perspective

Perhaps the strongest criticism of evaluative definitions of civilization – as representing the "highest" or "most developed" form of social organization – is how these definitions contribute little to understanding the phenomenon defined in a scientific manner. Knowing that industrial capitalist civilization is "the best" form of society gives us about as much information as knowing that it's "the worst" – which is very little. Scarcely better are more analytic but still overly narrow definitions like Jensen's "civilization is any culture based on cities" version.

To advance our understanding of industrial capitalist civilization, and in particular to address its looming crisis, we need to ask several basic, but important questions. What are its characteristics? How does it function? What effects does it have? How did it develop and how might it change? Simplistic definitions won't provide the necessary answers, but more sophisticated systems-based models can be helpful in this task. When contemplating the entirety of global, industrial, capitalist, civilization, a systems approach lets us appreciate the overall complexity of the topic, but also allows us to analyze key elements, interactions, and patterns. In turn, this makes it possible to focus in on those dynamics that are destructive and dysfunctional, and to analytically separate them from other dynamics that are healing, generative, and transformative.

However, because the different elements and dynamics of a system are in relationship with each other, it's not possible to just change one component and as a result reliably change the whole. Such an assumption is more indicative of a mechanistic approach, where systems are perceived as linear and predictable, and their constituent elements interchangeable. The phenomena studied by modern systems theorists don't play by these rules, and the reason for this is *feedback* – the exchange of information by mutually interacting elements within a system.

Altering one dynamic within a system introduces change, but it's really the feedback processes involved that determine whether the change will be significant in fundamentally altering the system's dynamic, or else be countered as other forces push the system back to a stable state (equilibrium). In systems, the information that one element sends to another is called a *feedback signal*, and the impact this signal has on the behaviour of both elements is known as a *feedback loop*.[17]

Systems thinking is closely associated with conceptual modelling. Scientists use models to describe various processes in the natural world, and they can be very useful. However, the detail of a given model is extremely important. Complex systems theory forces us to pay special attention to the question "What's *not* included in our model?" In simple systems, like a home thermostat, the models are also simple, and predicting the effect of feedback loops can seem easy enough. However, when a system comprises a multitude of interacting elements and feedback loops, such as an entire ecosystem, a human brain, or a human civilization, its *complexity* makes it very difficult to predict the effects of altering any one dynamic. Further difficulty arises when studying living systems, which by their very nature adapt over time in relation to changing environmental conditions.

If we were to characterize industrial capitalist society in the language of systems theory, it would be a complex adaptive system (CAS) distinguished by a large number of interacting agents (humans) and complex feedback loops.[18] Stated somewhat differently, civilization can be thought of as a macrosystem comprising innumerable subsystems, comprising in turn the complex interactions of billions of human and non-human agents.

An analogy that's long been useful in describing societies as systems is that of civilization as a gigantic organism, with functionally integrated parts operating at several different levels of organization. In the human body, at the subcellular level interaction between molecules and organelles enables cellular function. At the cellular level, different kinds of cells in systemic interaction perform various functions, such as glial cells that create structure within the brain, or neurons that allow the transmission of electrochemical signals. At the next level, dynamic interaction of the organ systems provides the necessary functions to sustain the entire human body – respiration, circulation, digestion, waste disposal. Finally, at the body level of organization, humans interact with other humans and their environment to provide the basic necessities of life – food, shelter, water, and social interaction.

Thus, one human being is in reality a complex system comprising numerous nested subsystems, all of which are in mutual interaction with each other. This nesting of subsystems always brings to my mind the image of a Russian doll which, when opened, reveals smaller and smaller dolls within. Mutual interaction refers to the fact that changes in one element, relationship, or level of a system has impacts on others, and vice versa. For example, changes in the state of systems at microscopic and cellular levels can have a profound effect on greater systemic levels – as can be seen whenever a flu virus exceeds the body's immune defences and causes the congestion and nausea associated with sickness. Similarly, changes in the state of greater systemic levels can profoundly influence microscopic system dynamics, as demonstrated by behaviours such as smoking or excessive alcohol consumption. Health epidemiology shows us that such changes in macrosystem dynamics (lifestyle choices) have serious impacts on cellular and organ function in the heart, lungs, and liver.

Like a human body, civilization can be viewed as a collection of nested subsystems at international, national, regional, municipal, institutional, and individual levels of organization. Like an organism, changes in the dynamics of interaction between agents and institutions at each of these levels can have effects that radiate throughout same-level systems and also through systems at different levels. For instance, a community group might form around the issue of cosmetic pesticide use in their neighbourhood. This group could content itself with educating neighbours about the harm caused by pesticides and discouraging local use. However, they could also successfully petition municipal council to pass a bylaw banning the cosmetic use of pesticides city-wide. From there the group might create a formal organization, reach out to other communities and other municipalities and begin spreading the pesticide ban. Eventually, such a movement might lead to a national ban, and even pressure for international action.[19]

Conversely, changes in the dynamics of interaction of macro-level social systems can also have effects that ripple out through the network of same-order systems and down through the levels of nested subsystems and interacting agents. An example of this would be the decision by a government to go to war. In today's capitalist states, a small group within the institution of government generally makes the decision to go to war. In nominally "democratic" states this decision is supposed to be debated and voted on in parliament, but increasingly military action is taken without such recourse. In the United States, for example, the Constitution states that only Congress has the right to declare war, a right they have formally exercised five times in the nation's history, the last time being World War II.[20] Since World War II, presidents have been able to launch military adventures without congressional approval, thus making the circle of those responsible for such an impactful decision much smaller. In over one hundred cases of a presidentially mandated use of military force, it has largely been the executive, along with the corporate influences they represent, who have determined when war will be waged.[21]

And what happens when this small group of people declares war? Based on innumerable historical examples, several powerful feedback processes are unleashed and the entire society begins to change. The budget and size of the military swells, recruitment increases and often conscripted service occurs, economic activity turns toward producing munitions, civil rights are truncated (often through new war-time legislation), and state propaganda and corporate media begin a steady campaign of jingoism designed to win "hearts and minds." Conscription and casualties have a profound impact on military families, and patterns of employment can change significantly. Finally, the actual effects of military assault can wreak profound societal changes, including displaced populations, economic hardship, mass death, starvation, and destruction of civil infrastructure. War may be the ultimate example of systemic connectivity's potentially catastrophic consequences.

Figure 1.1. Civilization system

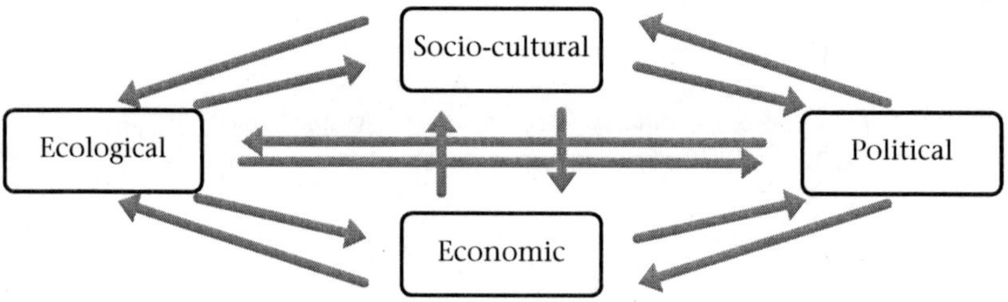

For my purposes, a systems approach is useful in that it helps to organize a complex topic with several different aspects into a coherent and intelligible whole. My goal is to make the workings of industrial capitalist civilization clear and comprehensible without resorting to over-simplification, or conversely without getting overly technical. The model I use looks at four key patterns of interaction within civilization as a whole – sociocultural, economic, ecological, and political (see figure 1.1). Each of these patterns of interaction in turn impacts on several nested subsystems of relationships among institutions (organizations), relationships among individual agents (human actors), and relationships among institutions and agents. Each pattern of interaction can be viewed as a lens that enables us to focus on certain aspects of the entire system, while still realizing that functionally the patterns are deeply integrated. In fact, it's the high level of systemic integration that contributes to industrial capitalist civilization's deep state of crisis.

I stated at the outset that my goal in this book is to support three premises. These are that the crisis of civilization is global, is dire, and is only resolvable through radical change. Evidence for these premises can be found when looking at the entire system through any one of the analytic lenses I've mentioned – sociocultural, economic, ecological, or political. When the lenses are combined, a total picture of the crisis emerges and modern civilization's "four horsemen" – the forces moving it toward collapse – become clear.

2
Dissociation

> The number on the price tag has very little to do with the costs involved in making Stuff. Sure, some of the direct costs like labour and material are included in the price, but those are dwarfed by externalized, hidden costs like the pollution of drinking water, health impacts on workers and host communities, even changes in the global climate. Who pays for these things?
> — Annie Leonard, *The Story of Stuff* [1]

As Jared Diamond notes in his book *Collapse: How Societies Choose to Fail or Succeed*, at points throughout history various civilizations have faced critical challenges to their viability, and in many cases have succumbed to them and collapsed entirely. Civilizations based on Easter Island and Pitcairn Island and the ancient Maya are all examples.[2] To this list one could also add ancient Mycenaean and Mesopotamian civilizations.[3] In each case, archaeologists have debated the particular constellation of factors that overwhelmed these past societies and caused their ruin. These factors include climate change, warfare, disease, food shortage, and human-caused ecological destruction.

Industrial capitalist civilization has its own particular challenges based on a specific interaction of sociocultural, economic, political, and ecological variables. In the sociocultural and economic realms, these challenges can be characterized in terms of *dissociation, complexity,* and *stratification.* In the ecological realm the challenge is *overshoot*, and in the political realm it is *oligarchy*. These factors constitute the five horsemen of the "modern day apocalypse," and in this chapter and the following four I'll examine them in detail.

Each of the five horsemen relates to an important aspect of complex systems – the existence of limits. Returning to the analogy of the human body, biomedical science tells us about the physical limits within which human life is possible. We know that if the human body experiences sustained temperatures above 60 degrees Celsius, it can lead to fatal hyperthermia. Similarly, if body temperature falls below 21 degrees Celsius, fatal hypothermia results.[4]

These temperature extremes represent limits that the system has to operate within to remain viable, in this case for a human being to remain alive. Similarly, human civilization has limits to its continued viability, expressed through the challenges under discussion here.

Physical limits to survival are incredibly important for any civilization to be viable. However, there's also a danger of focusing solely on survival as the measure of limits. Human societies aren't simply energy-capturing and reproductive systems. They are also *moral*, and an equally important question to then address is what kind of society do we want? What is the most fair, ethical, and supportive of human growth and potential? In the coming chapters I'll describe the challenges posed by both physical and moral limits and explain how their complex interaction presents modern civilization with a crisis unlike any it has faced before.

Dissociation

For many North Americans today, thinking about industrial civilization's collapse involves a profound level of abstraction. How can something that seemingly runs so predictably and *unconsciously* be on the verge of catastrophe? This sense of taken for granted stability is particularly true for wealthy and middle-class families, but also for many working-class families and the poor. Those experiencing more economic hardship may very well perceive a crisis in the sociocultural and economic realms, from job loss and insufficient social supports, but the imminent ecological crisis and the negative effects of government foreign policies often remain shrouded. Essentially, in industrial capitalist societies we are *dissociated* from critical feedback concerning the impact of our actions on the world around us. Dissociation occurs via processes of *spatial displacement, temporal displacement*, and *empathic displacement*. The perceptual disconnect resulting from these three processes is the first challenge threatening our social system with collapse.

Space

Walking down the aisle in a grocery store in my home town of Hamilton, I'm given a small factoid or two hinting at the origins of the products lining the shelves – a sign saying "USA" or "Ontario Grown," a sticker that says "Organic." However, we generally have little sense of exactly where the food comes from, how it is grown, what resources are used to transport it, and if the farming methods are sustainable. Many of our groceries and much of our restaurant food is heavily packaged and processed, originating from multiple locations across the globe. This is a simple illustration, familiar to most of us living in North America and in industrialized countries worldwide, of the *spatial displacement* between our day-to day lives and their ecological and extraterritorial impacts.

A similar problem occurs when we dispose of the massive amount of daily waste produced in a constant-growth consumer economy. Garbage goes into bags and is picked up at the curbside. Recycling goes into separate bags and is also picked up. Wastewater gets flushed down sinks and toilets. Old cars get brought to a wrecking yard, and household waste that doesn't sell at garage sales gets hauled off to transfer stations. In terms of our vehicles, the by-products of combustion simply blast from exhaust pipes and dissipate into the sky. The experience of most people in industrial societies is that our waste simply *disappears*.

Equally mysterious are those resources absolutely essential to our physical survival and our ability to function in a modern society. Water comes from our tap, and few people think beyond this to consider what kind of water-treatment facility it has passed through, or even further to which natural reservoir it was originally drawn from. Electricity is the same. We plug in appliances and flip breakers and magically our modern conveniences spark to life – computers, air conditioners, fridges, and stoves. We rarely consider where the electricity was generated – how far away, by what means? Was it produced by a coal-fired plant or nuclear reactor? Was it produced by a massive hydroelectric dam? The same goes when we turn on gas appliances or fill up our vehicles. Where does the gas and oil come from? What are the environmental impacts of its production and combustion?

The origin of products we use on a regular basis is also obscured behind a shroud of ignorance. Where are our ipods manufactured? What rare minerals are necessary for their function and where are they mined? What happens to them after they break or become functionally obsolete? Where and how are the steel and plastic in our automobiles produced? Where is our clothing made and under what conditions? What pollutants are released in the industrial processes that make our paper, carpets, office chairs, and cell-phones? To the vast majority of people in industrialized countries these questions are seldom asked, and if they are, then answers are almost nowhere to be found.

The shroud of ignorance extends beyond our sense of ecological impacts and toward the experience of people from different status groups, and our impact on people in different parts of the world. In the first case, it's true that even in the wealthiest industrialized nations, such as Canada or the United States, there are vast differences between people based on socioeconomic status, ethnicity, and gender.[5] In either country millions of people live in poverty and visible minorities are over-represented among prison populations and among the poor. For instance in Canada, the status of First Nations individuals and communities is, on average, much lower than that of non-Natives, exhibiting lower income, education, and life expectancy and higher rates of child poverty, suicide, incarceration, diabetes, and infectious disease.[6] To non-Natives, these conditions are largely invisible due to the isolation of First Nations people on reservations or in poor, inner-city neighbourhoods. The same holds for other marginal communities – whether the poor, prison inmates, the homeless, or the mentally ill. They all exist, in growing number, yet our society is structured such that the majority of people don't actually *see* them.

An even greater deficit exists concerning our sense of how patterns of domestic production and consumption and our government's foreign policy affect people in other parts of the world. In the West we have become rabid consumers of products made extremely cheaply in Asian countries. Our clothing, electronic goods, and household items are now almost exclusively imported, yet we know next to nothing about the conditions under which these products are made. How much money do the workers receive for their labour? Are they unionized? What are the health and safety conditions at their workplace? Unless we are privy to information prospected by a handful of non-profit labour monitoring organizations, we have no answer to these questions.

These many examples are the results of what I call *spatial displacement* – the removal of our ability to directly comprehend the results of our actions due to their unfolding "off stage," so to speak. As capitalism and industrialization harnessed cheap fossil fuel energy and produced global trade and supply networks, and as deleterious effects of production and consumption were relegated to shadowy hinterlands, citizens in the most industrialized countries steadily lost their ability to make moral and rational decisions concerning their own behaviour and the behaviour of political and economic elites.

And so, the first great challenge of human civilization that we need to confront is this: In certain regions of the globe, among certain communities, we have an almost total rupture of the individual from natural environmental feedback mechanisms. We are also, as citizens of industrialized states, largely isolated from understanding our impact on marginal communities and on citizens of other countries.

The only feedback mechanism that many of us do experience is that of the price and availability of the products and services that we consume. It is a central fiction of the "free market" that commodity prices are supposed to accurately reflect all of the information necessary for individuals to make rational decisions regarding their consumption. If the price of a commodity is too high, we can reduce our consumption, look for substitute products, or allocate more of our scarce monetary resources toward acquiring that product. We have *choice*, according to the classical economic paradigm that industrial capitalism rests on, and this is sufficient to regulate our economies, our societies, and our environment.[7]

A closer look at how this supposedly free market functions is instructive. For starters, we can ask how accurately the pricing of commodities and resources actually reflects such considerations as cost of production and cost of environmental resources. Who determines the cost of clean water used in industrial processes, of raw materials mined from the earth, and of the human labour used to procure resources, assemble products, and distribute them? Does pricing accurately reflect such considerations as energy efficiency, raw materials efficiency, product durability and re-usability, ethical labour practices, and ethical resource procurement practices? Even a cursory view of the evidence reveals the almost complete failure of the market system to account for these important aspects of production and consumption.[8] Even more seriously, other writers have pointed out that the capitalist market system completely omits the interests of subsequent generations and the risk or cost of complete systemic collapse. If anything, in our economic system the most competitive and desirable price is likely to be associated with the most ecologically destructive and unethical production practices. Far from being a reliable source of systemic feedback on which to base decisions, the commodity pricing of the free market actually acts as one of the most potent forces obscuring and distorting this feedback.[9]

Time

Another way in which dissociation occurs in modern civilization is through the phenomenon of *temporal displacement* – the fact that we are socialized into a culture that is only intelligible within drastically shortened time scales, or what can be considered *corporate time*. Such a scale roughly encompasses from one business quarter to five years. As can be adduced by its name, the dominance of corporate time within industrial civilization is directly related to the dominant position of capitalism and corporations in all areas of social life. Capitalism's economic life-blood consists of private property rents, investment, and profit accumulation, all of which are reckoned over short durations. Homeowners negotiate five-year terms for mortgages; debentures mature over two, three, or five years; corporate business plans consider five-year projections to be long-term planning; and international economic relations are tied to yearly cycles of trade summits.

Corporate time influences the decision-making process of every citizen in industrialized countries, but is particularly evident in the world of business and finance. In these economic subsystems, decisions are generally made based on quarterly profitability, while global financial markets now function under a form of temporal *hyper-compression*, as fortunes are lost or won based on fluctuations in currency and commodity pricing measured in fractions of a second. A cultural correlate of this hyper-compression can be seen in the continuous development of faster and more efficient technology for information, communication, and entertainment purposes. Social geographer David Harvey writes about this phenomenon in *The Condition of Postmodernity: An Inquiry into the Origins of Cultural Change*. Harvey theorizes that the demands of capitalist globalization for new markets and accelerated profitability spur development of technologies such as the telephone, internet, and cell phone.[10]

Harvey argues that this acceleration of time stems from a fundamental contradiction in capitalist economics. Starting from Marx, Harvey argues that capitalism suffers from two recurring and related crises: *over-accumulation* and *over-production*. Over-accumulation refers to wealth in capitalist economies concentrating over time in increasingly fewer hands, leading to insufficient purchasing power among workers, decreased consumer demand, and declining rates of profit. In essence, if working people can't afford to purchase the products that drive the industrial economy, then the entire system stalls. Over-production describes the tendency of competition among capitalists to continually expand productive capacity to maximize profit. This causes the rate of production to outstrip the rate of consumption, leading to lower prices and, again, reduced profits for producers. In response to these crises and the tendency of rates of profit to fall over time, capitalists have needed to continually restructure the economy to raise profitability. In the past they have used several strategies to accomplish this goal, including introducing new technologies and production efficiencies, reducing labour costs, opening new markets, changing state regulations, and accelerating the rate of the turnover of capital.

The first strategy, technological innovation in production, is designed to reduce the costs of production, expand productive capacity, and increase profitability. Historical examples include Henry Ford's automotive assembly line, in which the process of production was re-organized and rationalized to maximize efficiency, and also the mechanization of production, in which machines and later computers and robots are used to both augment and replace human labour. Apart from increased efficiency, capitalists have traditionally controlled costs through suppressing the wages of workers. This is apparent in the long history of capitalist attempts to crush the trade union movement and its demands for fair wages and other concessions (like health and safety and environmental protections) that increase the costs of production.

A central capitalist strategy for overcoming crises of over-production has been to continually seek new markets for products. This is the driving force behind globalization, which in its first incarnation saw highly productive capitalist economies in North America and Europe force less powerful economies to purchase their productive surplus. Due to the "off-shoring" of production in these original manufacturing centres, the character of globalized production has now shifted, with emerging economies in China, India, and South America exporting surplus production to Western countries.

In addition to rationalizing production and finding new markets for their products, capitalists have also forced changes to government regulations. These changes include weakening the legislation that protects workers and the environment, de-regulating and privatizing economic sectors that provide public goods (like education, health, and policing), and supporting economic imperialism. This final strategy involves using economic and military power to secure foreign resources (especially oil!), and to extort political and economic changes in foreign governments that are beneficial to the interests of producers in powerful countries.

The last strategy for overcoming the tendency of profit to fall over time involves increasing the rate of turnover of capital. This sees capitalists constantly increasing the speed at which commodities are transported and at which investment capital and profit flows. Improvements in communication and transportation are also needed to overcome the greater time involved in globalized production and consumption. In the end, Harvey argues that this need to speed up economic activity results in another contradiction, in which economic activity needs to be simultaneously fixed in space and time through infrastructure (roads, telephone lines, banking systems), and yet also needs to be continuously destroyed and re-built to increase speed and efficiency. Harvey describes this as capitalism's need to "annihilate space and time" to expand and increase profitability.[11]

The greatest effect of the resulting hyper-compressed corporate time scale is our civilization's difficulty in shifting perception to time scales of longer duration. As a result, we become dissociated from critical systemic feedback that only registers over longer durations, and we fail to consider long-term consequences of our actions. When we are able to shift our time scale to *socio-*

logical time (the past or future one hundred years of human society), to *historical time* (the past or future one thousand years of human society), or even greater to *evolutionary time* (the past or future one hundred thousand years of human society), then our decisions about the rationality of any given belief or action also change greatly.

Concrete examples of the tension created between a hyper-compressed corporate time scale and the longer-term implications of action can be found all around us. We see it in decisions that individuals make to take on excess debt when interest rates are low and asset prices (for homes, stocks, etc.) are sharply rising. During the North American housing bubble of 2007, hundreds of thousands of home buyers took on large levels of debt to purchase houses that they hoped would continue increasing in value at rates that were historically, and unsustainably, high. When the housing bubble burst, over-leveraged buyers were unable to sustain their purchases and foreclosed en masse – one of the triggers of the global financial crisis.[12]

The same tension also plays out continually in decisions made by corporations and governments concerning environmental impacts that destroy long-term resource viability in favour of short-term profitability. Examples include clear-cut logging, industrial fishing, and industrial water use (for bottling, industrial production processes, and hydroelectric projects). When looked at as a whole, industrial capitalism itself perches precariously on this tension, with economies based on constant short-term growth and increasing demand for finite and steadily dwindling energy sources.[13] To the extent that modern civilization's compressed perception of time permeates decisions made at all levels, in all societies, it can be likened to the man in the cautionary tale who, having leapt from a high-rise building, can be heard to remark "So far, so good!" while plummeting past every floor.

Like spatial displacement, temporal displacement cuts us off from critical feedback about the effects of our actions as individuals, and the effects of decisions made by institutions and elites, including corporations and government. This condition then leads to behaviour that is demonstrably irrational, even insane, when considered at different time scales. There is no surprise that industrial capitalist civilization has often seemed insane to those other cultures who have encountered it (usually violently, usually through conquest). In North America, a startling contrast is provided by the culture of the Haudenosaunee, the Six Nations Confederacy. The Haudenosaunee originally lived in the northeastern United States, but today live primarily in New York state, Quebec, and Ontario. A founding principle of the Constitution that binds the six Iroquois nations together is the idea that decisions made today need to consider the effect on community seven generations from the present.[14]

If we consider an average of twenty-five years for a generational cycle, the Haudenosaunee Constitution thus entreats decision makers to consider the effects of their actions on those living an incredible 175 years from now. This would seem like a radical notion to most non-Native North Americans, existing as we do in our severely truncated, four-month to five-year timeframes. The view of the Haudenosaunee is much closer to what I call sociological or historical time and, if actually applied, would lead to dramatically different decisions concerning economic production and consumption, political organization, social structure, and food production. It would be hard to see a civilization adhering to the law of seven generations deciding to build infrastructure dependent on non-renewable resources, or to sustain levels of social inequality that lead repeatedly to economic stagnation, social instability, and rebellion.

Of course, I'm not arguing that it's always better to exist, conceptually, in greater and greater time scales. For instance, if we attempt to evaluate our life decisions based on our conception of evolutionary time, we are likely to make several personally disastrous choices. (What will it matter one hundred thousand years from now if I show up to work today or not?) Similarly, it doesn't make much sense to make decisions solely on what is happening in other parts of the world. (A Spanish trade union is being unfairly treated in contract negotiations. I live in North America and I'm not unionized, but I'm going to stop work in solidarity until the situation is rectified.) Instead, it's important first to have an awareness of what other time scales and geographical realities say about our current circumstances, choices, and decisions. Second, it's important to integrate these different perspectives into our actions in the present.

Empathy

What helps us strike the appropriate balance between different time scales is an understanding of how broader temporal and geographic contexts either impact on or are impacted by our immediate life experience. For example, after the terrorist attacks of 9/11, the US government quickly began preparing to invade Afghanistan and Iraq, ostensibly in pursuit of Osama Bin Laden and his shadowy Al Qaeda network. At the time I was involved in a peace organization that mobilized against the planned invasions. Our group regularly went to public spaces to talk with people about the march to war in the Middle East and its potentially disastrous consequences. Talking with Canadians about the looming US invasions was particularly difficult, as many people I spoke with either sided with the Bush government's propaganda line concerning terrorist threats and weapons of mass destruction, or else they felt the entire situation didn't concern them directly.

At the time, peace activists struggled to deconstruct the media messages being sent from the American political and corporate elite, but also to combat Canadians' false sense of being insulated from the effects of a US war. To the Canadian citizens who asked "Why should I care if the United States invades Afghanistan and Iraq?" we replied, "Because Canada is likely to get pulled into the conflict, both countries' citizens will then become targets for political terrorism, and we will see a steady militarization of Canadian society with serious governmental budget and spending priority impacts. This could then negatively affect our employment, our quality of life, the civil liberties we take for granted, and so on." It's cold comfort that the situations we warned about all eventually came to pass, but the difficulty of convincing people in downtown Hamilton of our connection to US foreign policy really stuck with me. Why is it so hard for us to make these connections?

Since my days in the peace movement I've come to appreciate that we have difficulty understanding causal connections because we tend to think of time in terms of our own life span, and of geographical context as our own community and locale. These "natural" limits to our sense of space and time present their own major challenge toward understanding the entirety of industrial capitalism's global impact. However, our culture's predilection for dissociation extends further into our sense of ethics and of our own individual consciousness. If we are unable to discern the effects of our actions on people from distant countries, then how can we be in ethical relationship with them? In this sense, our globalized economy presents a paradox. On one hand it has created an unprecedented linkage of disparate communities through economic and information flows. We can look up detailed facts about other peoples instantly on the internet. We can hear about events in other countries via any number of global news services. In this sense global capitalism's ability to accelerate the rate of communication over greater and greater distances, what Anthony Giddens terms "time-space distanciation," has created a more integrated world.[15] This is the "global village" hypothesized by McLuhan, in which new communications media make the world seem smaller.[16]

However, at the same time, the form of connection and the way in which it is understood remain highly stylized and contextually shallow. Today's North Americans may know of famine sweeping East Africa, but without an understanding of why the famine is occurring (economic destabilization, government corruption, and paramilitary infighting funded by foreign powers), the surface knowledge can lead to a lack of empathy for the famine victims. Similar to the dissociation middle-class North Americans have in relation to the Indigenous poor, the plight of those who are less fortunate is all too easily understood to be "their own fault." This contradiction is the third aspect of dissociation we experience in industrial capitalist civilization, what I call *empathic displacement*.

Placing our interaction with human beings separated from us through space and time into a coherent ethical framework depends on the quality of knowledge we have concerning these other persons. In this sense, the problems of spatial and temporal displacement present a highly distorted view of other lives. We can think of this in terms of Marshall McLuhan's "global village" misinterpreted as Celebration, the Disney Corporation designed and controlled town in Florida. In Celebration, as of the 2010 census, 7,427 people lived in a low-density urban environment designed to resemble a fictitious "small town USA." The population was 91 per cent white and had a per household median income of $80,693. In contrast, the 2010 median household income in Florida was $47,309 and the ethnic mix only 75 per cent white.[17]

For many North Americans and Europeans, their sense of the global village is more like Celebration, Florida, than like its more representative environs. As we are cut off from accurate information and experience concerning the lives of the world's billions of poor and oppressed, these masses either remain invisible, or else exist as caricatures (images of starving children used by NGOs for fundraising purposes), or as de-humanized statistics. There is little empathic connection to the world's estimated 15 million refugees,[18] to the hundreds of civilians killed by US drone strikes,[19] or to marginalized populations worldwide. A more accurate conception of the global village is provided by the 100 People project, in which global demographics are simplified and expressed through a population of 100. Based on this data, far from Celebration, Florida, today's representative global village is 70 per cent non-white and has a 48 per cent poverty rate. Only 7 per cent of its members have a college degree, only 22 per cent own computers, and half are unable to freely express their spiritual or political views for fear of arrest, violence or death.[20]

Perhaps the most telling example of the effects of spatial, temporal, and empathic displacement can be seen in the decision-making and accounting processes that govern modern corporations. Corporations are mandated by law to maximize profit for their shareholders, and this creates an incentive to increase revenues and decrease business costs. Some of the ways in which corporations minimize costs are to lower wages, lower input costs, and increase efficiencies. However, another common strategy is to avoid paying for certain inputs or by-products of production entirely. Aspects of a corporation's business activities that have an impact on or present a cost to society but for which the corporation is not required to pay are known as *externalities*. These externalized costs include such things as the negative ecological impacts of industrial pollution, the use of fresh water for industrial processes, the social impact of poor employment practices (such as sweatshops), and the impact of collective societal investments, such as the military power needed to secure foreign oil resources for US corporations.[21]

The results of modern corporations' externalizing tendencies are apparent everywhere in North America, if we know to look for them. We drink Coca Cola without realizing its contribution to critical water shortages in India, or the murder of union activists in Colombia.[22] We drink coffee without wondering about the low wages paid to growers in developing countries.[23] We spend endless hours on iphones without seeing the sweatshop conditions that Chinese workers endure to produce them.[24] We drink bottled water without thinking about the landfills the containers will end up in.[25] Beneath an illusory veil spun from spatial, temporal, and empathic displacement, industrial capitalism's corporate agents preside over a deeply dysfunctional and increasingly precarious system of exploitation and environmental destruction.

3

Complexity

> Man's efforts, even at their mightiest, were tiny compared to the size of the planet – the Roman Empire meant nothing to the Arctic or the Amazon. But now, the way of life of one part of the world in one half-century is altering every inch and every hour of the globe.
>
> — Bill McKibben, *The End of Nature*[1]

We in modern civilization are cut off from the impacts of our actions on other people and on the natural world. This is the first aspect of the looming global crisis. Dissociation means that key information and understanding is not available to the majority of the world's people, such that even those who *want* to make rational and ethical choices find it incredibly difficult to do so. This critical lack of systemic feedback is enough to doom any one society to failure, and yet what's different today is that one particular form of human civilization – industrial capitalism – has spread over the entire globe and integrated every country in every region into a single economic system. If the issue was just that one country, say, the United States alone, was under threat of collapse due to its specific socioeconomic context, then we couldn't speak of a crisis of human civilization as a whole. However, the root of catastrophe is found directly in the globalized forms of industrial capitalism itself, not in any one country's specific cultural practices.

In the past, when civilizations have faced collapse, the catastrophic consequences were generally limited because the civilizations themselves were geographically limited. Jared Diamond gives several excellent examples of this phenomenon in *Collapse*, and in particular his account of Easter Island. He presents an in-depth exploration of the evidence pointing to Easter's collapse due to human-made environmental destruction:

> The parallels between Easter Island and the whole modern world are chillingly obvious. Thanks to globalization, international trade, jet planes and the internet, all countries on Earth today share resources and affect

each other, just as did Easter's dozen clans. Polynesian Easter Island was as isolated in the Pacific Ocean as the Earth is today in space. When the Easter Islanders got into difficulties, there was nowhere to which they could flee, nor to which they could turn for help; nor shall we modern Earthlings have recourse elsewhere if our troubles increase. Those are the reasons why people see the collapse of Easter Island society as a metaphor, a worst-case scenario, for what may lie ahead of us in our own future.[2]

Diamond argues that Easter Island's isolation contributed to its fragility – its vulnerability to collapse. However, Easter's isolation also meant that the crisis on the island was largely geographically contained, and couldn't ripple outward to impact other civilizations. This couldn't be further from today's industrial capitalist civilization, the global scale of which means that its multiple and compounding crises have become the *world's* crises, with no safe space for our escape.

Of course, the simple fact that industrial capitalist civilization has come to dominate societies worldwide is not, in and of itself, a harbinger of global collapse. What makes civilization's lack of systemic feedback and massive scale so dangerous is the cultural, political, and economic practices it rests on. Done in isolation, many of these practices would be destructive, but not catastrophic. However, when the same practices are scaled up, done in increasing frequency over an expanding area, they present a serious challenge to the entire system's viability.

Related to the problem of *scale* is the issue of *complexity* – the proliferation of interactions and feedback processes that occur as any system grows in size. The rise of a system's level of complexity means that it becomes increasingly difficult to predict the effects of a given change in the system's dynamics. In the case of a social system, this can mean the difficulty of determining the impact of a certain action, decision, or policy. In the case of ecological systems, this could mean the unintended consequences of resource extraction and production methods, or the introduction of foreign species into a given environment.

Global Economic Meltdowns

Examples of the problems of scale and complexity abound. In the case of economics, the buildup and collapse of asset bubbles is a classic case of unintended consequences that emerge when individual behaviours are drastically scaled up. The infamous "dot-com" bubble in North America saw valuations of internet start-up companies rise steeply from 1997 through early 2000. Buzz surrounding the economic potential of the internet caused several different behaviours to compound. First off, entrepreneurs began starting up internet companies in greater number, and increasingly without the sound business plans, management skill, and capitalization necessary for success. Second, investors began pouring money into the sector and over-valuing the new start-ups. Finally, as the surge of investment caught on, stock market traders began buying up all available tech sector stocks, further inflating their prices. At its height, investment in the burgeoning internet sector amounted to $1.3 trillion, or 8 per cent of the entire US stock market.[3]

It wasn't long before the substandard performance of many new tech sector companies began to be felt, as over-valued and unprofitable companies burned through their start-up capital and then declared bankruptcy. In 2001, the bubble burst, and the NASDAQ stock exchange lost $5 trillion in value.[4] In addition to the market losses, thousands of jobs were lost as large tech sector companies like Nortel and WorldCom either downsized or declared bankruptcy. In the case of WorldCom, massive accounting fraud was also implicated in their financial collapse.[5]

The collapse of the dot-com bubble was a serious blow to the North American economy, but paled in comparison to the housing bubble that came immediately after. By 2002, housing prices in the United States and in several other countries were rising sharply. Low interest rates and rising house prices encouraged families to take on increasing levels of debt, and mortgage brokers began offering "subprime" mortgages that had extremely low interest rates and that were offered to clients who had no discernible means of making payments. In the United States, mortgages were backed by Fannie Mae and Freddie Mac – federally constituted organizations designed to increase investment in the housing market by taking mortgages and turning them into securities that could then be sold to investors on the stock market. These mortgage-backed securities were seen as safe investments, and spurred the demand of investors looking for a high rate of return in relation to sluggish Treasury bond markets.[6]

In addition, rising property values encouraged speculators to enter the housing market aggressively. "Flipping" houses became a lucrative investment strategy as property values were increasing at rates of 15 to 20 per cent per year at the height of the bubble. Between 1997 and 2006, the price of the typical American house increased by 132 per cent.[7] During the same period, the national median home price ranged from 3.1 to 3.4 times median household income. This ratio rose to 4.0 in 2004, and 4.6 in 2006.[8] Buyers were taking on record levels of debt to finance their purchases, and existing homeowners were encouraged by lenders to remortgage properties and cash in on their increased value.

The first strain on the bubble occurred as subprime mortgages reverted to higher interest rates and tens of thousands of families were unable to make payments. Foreclosures began compounding, and banks were unable to cover their losses due to being heavily leveraged and loaded with bad mortgage investments. Insurance companies, hedge funds, and large investment firms were also heavily invested in unsound mortgage-backed securities and credit default swaps, and thus when the mortgages began to unravel, financial institutions countrywide and internationally were thrown into crisis. More so than the earlier tech sector crash, the housing market crash rippled out through world financial markets, causing the 2008 Global Financial Crash – the closest that the international capitalist system has come to collapse since the Great Depression.[9]

Of course, we are all now familiar with the widespread economic fallout from the 2008 financial crisis. As overly indebted families defaulted on mortgage payments and banks scrambled to cover their losses, global credit began to freeze up. This put pressure on other economic sectors that experienced capital crunches, business failures, and layoffs. In several countries banking systems were only saved by massive infusions of public money – the infamous "bailouts" that in the United States amounted to the $700 billion government Troubled Asset Relief Program (TARP), $6.4 trillion in Federal Reserve funding, and another $1.4 trillion in government economic stimulus spending.[10]

In all, the US government bailout of its financial sector represents the largest single transfer of wealth ever from the working and middle classes to the wealthiest Americans. Financial institutions that received bailout money turned around and paid record levels of compensation to their executive officers. In 2009, Merrill Lynch paid out $3.6 billion in bonuses after being bailed out, while CEO Stan O'Neal received a $159 million[11] severance package after the company failed. In addition, the financial crisis further increased inequality, as the percentage of wealth owned by the richest 1 per cent of Americans climbed from 34.6 per cent in 2007 to 35.4 per cent in 2010.[12]

The financial crisis nearly caused a collapse in the global banking system that only drastic intervention by governments prevented. What's interesting to note however, is that the crisis was not an aberration that occurred despite the best intentions of players in the global financial markets. Instead, the conditions for the crisis were actively created by elites in the US economy who lobbied to deregulate financial markets to allow for easier investment in increasingly riskier securities. These strategies were pursued by thousands of individuals and corporations driven by the core capitalist tenet of profit maximization. In essence, these people were acting rationally and playing by the "rules" of the global capitalist economy, yet the impact of their aggregate behaviour created fluctuations sufficient to crash the very financial system on which their wealth creation depended. Most of the players who drove the asset bubbles and created the legislative environment in which they could grow were intelligent people, many with advanced degrees in business and economics. Despite this, when their actions were scaled up and complexly linked with broader economic processes, the result was catastrophic.

Another interesting point about the global financial crisis of 2008 is the debate it has re-energized about capitalism's inherent contradictions and vulnerabilities to crisis. In the aftermath of the banking meltdown, most right-wing economists focus attention on essentially technocratic explanations. They cite key changes in legislation, such as repealing the 1933 Glass-Steagall Act in the United States, the statute that separated the activities of investment and commercial banks and protected against fraud and conflicts of interest between the two. Other reasons given include Fannie and Freddie's backing of securities from unsustainable subprime mortgages, or the low interest rates that encouraged homebuyers to become over-leveraged. All of these factors did play into the crisis, but another group of economists take a broader view, and contextualize the financial collapse in terms of more fundamental contradictions present within capitalism itself.

To Marxian theorists like Walden Bello and Robert Brenner, the financial crash was caused by the same recurring crisis discussed earlier, in the context of temporal displacement and capitalism's need to continually speed up the turnover of investment capital. As in chapter 2, this crisis can be variously described as one of *over-accumulation* or *over-production*. Over-accumulation refers to the accumulation of profit, and arises over time when wealth concentrates increasingly in the hands of a small economic elite. When this happens, there is insufficient wealth among consumers to drive economic demand. As a result, sales decline, the rate of profit falls, production facilities close, and resulting unemployment then serves to exacerbate the situation.[13]

The other recurring crisis is the crisis of over-production, in which excess productive capacity leads to a reduction in the rate of profit. This tendency of competition to reduce prices and reduce profit margin can be traced back to Adam Smith, who espoused it as one of the benefits of free market competition. However, history has shown that the capitalist class is not content to see profits decline, and instead is driven to increase profitability at all costs. For this reason, when profits decline in one economic sector due to over-production (excess competition) or other factors such as increased production costs (for instance from higher wages and environmental standards), investors will move their money to other sectors where gains can be maximized. The search for areas of high investment return is what leads to economic bubbles, and in North America what has been called "bubblenomics" has become increasingly dominant.

According to Walden Bello, the roots of the 2008 crisis reach back to the period from World War II to the mid-1970s, the Golden Age of North American capitalism. During this time governments pursued Keynesian policies that stabilized effective demand through promoting high wages and social security. These policies were won by what historians have termed the "post-war compromise" between capital and labour. Trade unions were able to win legal acceptance and concessions from government and factory owners in exchange for workplace peace. In the mid-1970s this period of growth and stability was challenged by an increase in oil prices caused by the OPEC (Organization of the Petroleum Exporting Countries) crisis and also by increased competition from Europe and growing second-world economies like India, China, and Brazil. As a result of these factors, investment in the goods economy, including resource extraction, manufacturing, and transportation, showed decreasing rates of profit.[14]

In response to the crisis in profitability, the North American capitalist class pursued four different strategies. The first was globalization, the aggressive expansion of trade and commerce into foreign markets. The second was neoliberal restructuring, a set of government policies designed to suppress wages, deregulate protected markets, and privatize public services. The third strategy was financialization, in which bankers created new forms of investment vehicles – securities and derivatives – that would provide higher rates of return than investment in the real economy – the production of goods through raw materials, labour, and technology. A fourth strategy included taking on increasing levels of both consumer debt and debt incurred by banks and investment companies.[15]

The strategies designed to rescue North American capitalists from declining rates of profit worked for some time, and served to keep economic growth relatively stable throughout the 1980s, 90s, and most of the 2000s, until the wheels came off in 2008. In each case, the strategies were enacted as rational responses to a deeper structural contradiction, and in each case they proved of limited, short-term utility while ultimately ending up exacerbating the crisis. According to Marxist economists, the lack of enduring success in stabilizing capitalist economies is due to the essential contradiction between increasing productive capacity and decreasing profitability. With capitalism's global reach, the entire world system now rests on this precarious ground, facing a future of multiple and intensifying crises. These cycles of leveraging and deleveraging also tend to concentrate capital and economic control into the hands of fewer and larger corporate players.

Global Climate Change

Another important example of the challenge presented by modern civilization's scale and complexity is the phenomenon of global climate change. In this instance, the challenge is ecological, and results from the compounding effects of human economic activity on the planetary climate – an incredibly complex system that determines temperature and precipitation, and in turn impacts water levels, the frequency and intensity of storms, drought, desertification, wildlife ranges, and food production. Climatology is a relatively new science and still struggles with the ability to accurately predict changes in such a complex system; however, today's reputable climate scientists are unanimous concerning the reality of global warming and its relation to human activity.[16]

Human impact on climatic temperature comes from the twin processes of greenhouse gas production, predominantly from burning fossil fuels, and deforestation. As more carbon dioxide is released into the air from combustion of oil, coal, and natural gas, the blanket of solar radiation insulating gas that surrounds the earth thickens, trapping heat within the atmosphere. Cutting down trees exacerbates the warming, as forests act as natural carbon dioxide filters. According to the Intergovernmental Panel on Climate Change (IPCC), the international group of climate scientists convened in 1988 by the United Nations, the projected increase in average global temperature will have massive and wide-ranging effects on populations worldwide. In their 2007 report, the IPCC noted that with warming above 2.5 degrees Celsius, we risk metres of sea level rise and the threatened extinction of 20 to 30 per cent of the earth's species. The resulting flooding would displace millions of people and radically reconfigure patterns of habitation worldwide.[17]

The reality of global climate change has been slow to dawn on the scientific community, and even slower to dawn on the rest of us. As the science of climatology is formidably complex, and as temperature fluctuates naturally both from year to year and in much longer cycles, linking the observable increase in temperature over the past one hundred years to human activity has been a challenge. The idea that our localized and normalized patterns of economy and lifestyle – factory production, logging, driving cars, and running air conditioners – could have such catastrophic cumulative effects, has been hard for many of us to realize. Only through major publicity initiatives, such as Al Gore's documentary *An Inconvenient Truth*, and awareness-raising campaigns from environmental organizations, like Greenpeace, 350.org, and the David Suzuki Foundation, has climate change begun to register with us and to influence our behaviour.

The problems with the scale and complexity of industrial capitalist civilization, highlighted by the financial meltdown of 2008 and global warming, concern what is known as "systemic risk" in the language of systems analysts. Systemic risk refers to the probability that a set of actions will not just negatively affect the dynamics of a given system – whether economic or climatic – but that the actions will lead to the collapse of the system itself. For example, the day traders making millions selling junk mortgage-backed securities were risking personal financial loss, and invariably balanced this risk against the seemingly greater promise of significant financial gain. However, what they weren't considering was the impact their behaviour might have on the viability of the entire securities market, stock market, or global banking system. Such systemic risks are hard to calculate, and the implications of complex, compounding behaviours are extremely difficult to predict.[18]

Systemic risk is associated with another aspect of complex systems known as *tipping points*. A tipping point is a point in any process of change at which the process begins increasing dramatically. An example from global warming is the effect that increasing temperature has on melting ice, what scientists refer to as the *ice-albedo effect*. As the global temperature rises, increasing amounts of land and sea ice melt. This process can proceed at a stable and linear rate, with x increases in temperature equalling y amounts of melted ice. However, because open water absorbs more heat from sunlight than does reflective ice, once a critical mass of ice melts, the process of warming begins to accelerate considerably due to the extra warmth being absorbed. This extra warming then melts ice even more quickly, which in turn further increases sunlight absorption by open water. This accelerating cycle is what systems theorists call a *positive feedback loop*, in which a system process that seemed predictable and stable starts to "run away." The problem is, it can be devilishly difficult to predict where tipping points might lie in a complex system, when they might be reached, and what the results will be.[19]

Another way of thinking about systemic risk is presented by Homer-Dixon in *The Upside of Down*. He describes the work of ecologist Crawford Holling, who for decades has studied cycles of forest ecosystem growth, collapse, and regeneration. Taking his insights from forest systems, Holling envisions the entire biosphere as a collection of nested complex systems at different levels, which he calls a *panarchy*. An example of nested systems would be the ecosystems in specific biomes, say the eastern deciduous forest zone in North America, or the Arctic ice shield, being contained within the global climate system. Nested systems affect each other, as changes in the ecology of specific biomes can affect the larger global climate system, and vice versa. According to Holling, each system within the panarchy is undergoing its own cycle of growth, collapse, reorganization, and rebirth. When these cycles are staggered (that is, not all facing a crisis at once), then the entire panarchy can be remarkably durable, and collapses limited to certain systemic levels can be precursors to future revitalization. However, Holling notes that if the cycles were synchronized, and multiple systems at different levels were to be in crisis at the same time, that the entire panarchy risks "deep collapse," described as "a collapse that cascades across adaptive cycles – a kind of pancaking implosion of the entire system as higher-level adaptive cycles collapse, which causes progressive collapse at lower levels."[20]

Holling's concept of "deep collapse" speaks to the dangers faced by modern civilization. Like a panarchy facing synchronous crises, industrial capitalist civilization comprises numerous, complexly integrated social and ecological subsystems, the majority of which are in terminal states of dysfunction and susceptible to harmful feedback loops, tipping points, and systemic risk. This toxic stew of massive scale, complexity, and dysfunction prevents a quick fix of such pressing issues as financial instability and climate change, but also of threats to ecosystem viability and social stability. Even with good information and correct intentions, it's difficult to know how to act.

4
Stratification

> To be sure, labour produces marvels for the wealthy but it produces deprivation for the worker. It produces palaces, but hovels for the worker. It produces beauty, but mutilation for the worker. It displaces labour through machines, but it throws some workers back into barbarous labour and turns others into machines. — Karl Marx[1]

The third challenge facing civilization's survival involves its economic and social aspects equally, and concerns the impact that industrial capitalism is having on populations worldwide. Until now my discussion of the crisis has focused on systemic limits imposed by imperfect information, scale, and complexity. All of these are important aspects of civilization's dysfunction, but they don't speak directly to the effects this dysfunction has on human lives, and especially on the most vulnerable of peoples – the poor, the Indigenous, women, and children. When looking at civilization's human impact, we see a crisis of massive proportion, with fully half of the earth's citizens living lives of hardship and desperation. Inequality and conflict are the twin agents of this human misery, and both are permanent, structural features of modern civilization.

Social stratification is a term used by social scientists to describe the reality of inequality that exists within every nation on Earth. This inequality has been a defining feature of all human civilizations, although the degree of inequality, poverty, and oppression has varied considerably among different civilizations and different time periods.[2] Under industrial capitalism, inequalities in wealth and power between rich and poor, men and women, and dominant and marginal ethnic groups have been perpetuated, institutionalized, and in many cases intensified in relation to earlier forms of civilization.

The impact of inequality that is structural (built into the very social, political, and economic fabric) and often extreme (including a large gap between rich and poor and significant numbers struggling to make ends meet) can be seen worldwide. Many of the world's poor live in developing countries with low levels of industrialization. This leads to a stark disparity in life experience depending on the country where one is born. A child born in Japan can expect to live to an age of eighty-three years, while a child born in Sierra Leone can expect to live an average of forty-five years. Similarly, nearly two in ten children born in Sierra Leone will not survive past the age of five years, while only two in one thousand Icelandic children will fail to survive past childhood.[3]

Despite the marked difference in poverty between wealthy and developing countries, even in heavily industrialized countries poverty is widespread and persistent. In 2013, approximately 15 per cent of Americans were found to be poor,[4] and in 2010, 15 per cent of Canadians were considered low income (the Canadian government's equivalent of "poverty," defined as those who earn less than half the median income).[5] Despite a public commitment by the government to end child poverty by 2000, as of 2012, approximately one in five Canadian children were still living in a low-income family.[6] In the United States, the wealthiest country in the world, a shocking one in four children live in poverty.[7] A 2014 study of poverty in the UK revealed that 33 per cent of families were unable to provide three or more "basic necessities of life," such as adequate food, clothing, or shelter.[8] That these poverty levels are found in three of the wealthiest countries in the world is particularly telling.

A 2016 report released by Oxfam reveals the extent to which social stratification defines political and economic relations worldwide. According to the study, in 2015 just 62 people had the same wealth as 3.6 billion people – fully half of humanity. The wealth of these 62 individuals had risen by 45 per cent since 2010.[9] In a 2015 report, Oxfam reports that in 2014 the richest 1 per cent of the global population possessed 48 per cent of global wealth. Of the remaining 52 per cent of wealth, 94.5 per cent of it was owned by the richest 20 per cent of people, while the remaining 80 per cent of the world's people shared the 5.5 per cent of wealth that remained. The gap between the world's richest and the rest is growing steadily, and is projected to increase. In 2010 the richest 80 people in the world had a net worth of $1.3 trillion, while by 2014 that number increased to $1.9 trillion. Over the same time period, the net wealth of the poorest half of humanity decreased. The acceleration of global inequality is also clear. In 2010, 388 billionaires had wealth equal to the bottom half of humanity, while in 2015, it took only the top 62 people to match the poorest half.[10]

Social researchers tell us that inequality and poverty are also associated with gender, nationality, ethnicity, and membership in a racialized minority group. The 2015 Oxfam study notes that of 1,645 people listed as billionaires by Forbes, 90 per cent of them are men and 30 per cent are from the United States.[11] The 2010 US census shows that poverty rates for visible minorities are much higher than for white Americans. For black Americans, 27.4 per cent were poor; for Hispanic Americans, it was 26.6 per cent; and for whites, only 9.9 per cent. The racialized nature of inequality in the United States is particularly apparent when considering child poverty. In 2010, 38.2 per cent of black children were poor, compared to 12.4 per cent of white children.[12] Women are also more susceptible to low income, with 24.1 per cent of women living in poverty in the United States in 2010, compared with 21.7 per cent of men.[13]

In Canada, as in many other countries, Indigenous peoples experience poverty and other forms of social hardship at much greater levels than non-aboriginals. The 2014 data show that Indigenous peoples are almost twice as likely to be poor than non-Indigenous, with a low-income rate of 25.3 per cent.[14] The rate is even higher for aboriginal children, more than half of whom live in poverty.[15] Indigenous peoples in Canada are also four times more likely than non-Indigenous peoples to live in substandard housing and three times more likely to experience food insecurity. These stark differences in socioeconomic status translate directly into differences in health, with Indigenous peoples in both Canada and Australia living an average of twenty years less than non-Indigenous peoples.

The extensive poverty found in North America is alarming. Equally so is the even greater number of citizens existing just above national poverty lines and living from paycheque to paycheque. In a 2014 national poll conducted by the Canadian Payroll Association, 51 per cent of respondents said that they would be in dire economic circumstances if their paycheque was delayed even one week.[16] In Canada, the ranks of the economically insecure have been growing significantly over the past thirty years, as incomes for the lowest 40 per cent of earners decline.[17] To make up for this shortfall, families are relying on two incomes and record levels of household debt. In Canada today, debt levels are at an all-time high of 160 per cent of income.[18] This means that Canadians are $1.60 in debt for every dollar they earn. A similar situation prevails in the United States, with the added risk of catastrophic debt introduced by healthcare costs – still the single most common cause for bankruptcy. A 2013 Associated Press article notes that an astonishing four out of five American adults had experienced "joblessness, near-poverty, or reliance on welfare" at some point in their lives.[19]

What is easily missed in the simple listing of statistics is the lived experience of poverty – the daily struggle to survive, constant stress, ill health, political marginalization, and increased rates of violence, addiction, abuse, and incarceration. The world's poor are shut out from the opportunities and privileges enjoyed by the world's middle-class and wealthy citizens, and many poor families become trapped in a generational cycle that is almost impossible to escape.

The downtown Hamilton neighbourhood I've lived in since 1998 is statistically one of the poorest in Canada.[20] Hamilton was once an industrial powerhouse in the 1950s, 60s, and 70s. When capitalists began globalizing production by moving factories to countries with lower wages and weaker labour and environmental laws, Hamilton's high-paying manufacturing jobs started vanishing. After twenty years of this, the city became an economic dead zone. Working families lost their homes, levels of social assistance climbed, and working-class neighbourhoods became blighted with poverty, abandoned buildings, and drugs.

In my years as a student, artist, and activist, I experienced Hamilton's depressed economy directly, and also saw it written in the lives lived around me. As an undergraduate student in the recession-wracked early 1990s, good jobs were almost impossible to find, money was always tight, and making rent was a monthly challenge. Phone calls were avoided – we could never tell if it was the landlord calling, the utility companies, or a collection agent. The food we ate was cheap and poor quality – packaged noodles and tuna, spaghetti, pizza slices, whatever would fill us up for the least amount. Clothes were bought second hand, not to be trendy, but because $5 was all we could afford for a shirt or pair of jeans.

To middle and upper class Canadians, the poor are often invisible, or at best form an unsightly, undifferentiated mass that haunts the hollowed-out city cores that the well-off avoid at all cost. When I lived in poverty, I felt this invisibility acutely. I noticed how, based on the clothes I wore, people would not make eye contact, would cross the street when they saw me coming, or would sneer disapprovingly. As a young man I was especially aware of how attractive and well-dressed young women would studiously ignore my presence. I felt directly the shame, insecurity, and anger that comes from being treated as worthless, or worse, as a threat.

When I was invisible, the other invisibles became easy to see. They are the "downtown people," people I still see every day – families dressed in cheap or shabby clothes, pushing buggies stuffed with dollar store purchases, eating fast food, or lined up at food banks. Some overweight, some gaunt, many smoke, all look older than their years. They are the tough and wiry men of indeterminate age who ride second-hand bicycles to and from work every day – rain, shine, or snow. They are the underage girls dressed in too tight clothes who stare brazenly, defiantly at passing men. They are the young mothers pushing strollers onto the bus, looking harried and hollow-eyed, refusing to meet the disapproving stares cast at them. They are the young tough guys swaggering through the core with awkward, loping gaits, pants falling down in the best imitation of prison fashion, ball caps skewed, muscle shirts revealing cheap tattoos. In Hamilton most of these young men are white, although they do their best to emulate the inner-city black aesthetic popularized by gangsta rap. They are the people stopped repeatedly by police, told to leave by security guards, followed by store attendants, and socially isolated by a hundred small acts of disapproval and moral censure directed at them by more privileged classes.

The poor I see each day in Hamilton can be found in every North American town. They are a stark reminder of the stratification caused by industrial capitalism, and yet our society perpetuates a myth as to how the millions living in poverty end up in their predicament. They are lazy, or they make poor life choices. They are unwilling to "delay gratification" like the successful middle and upper classes – the "winners" of capitalism's winner-take-all game. Of course, the myth is utter nonsense, and only serves to hide the simple fact that modern economies are designed to create and perpetuate a precarious underclass. Structural unemployment wipes out thousands of decent jobs every year – throwing hardworking people into poverty and crisis through no fault of their own. Children growing up in poverty struggle to surmount massive economic and cultural barriers that middle and upper class children can scarcely imagine. Instead of realizing the structural violence that causes poverty, those unlucky enough to fall into its grip are instead either vilified or ignored.

As debilitating as the experience of poverty in Hamilton is, in many other countries the situation is far worse, with millions living in what researchers call *extreme poverty*, as opposed to the *relative poverty* experienced by struggling families in wealthy countries. Extreme poverty means living on less than US $1.25 per day, and describes the plight of over 1.2 billion souls.[21] At this level of destitution, mere survival is a challenge. People struggle to find food, children die early from disease and malnutrition, and families live in barely habitable accommodations situated in overcrowded slums. In a 2012 report, the United Nations Food and Agriculture Organization (FAO) revealed that one in eight of the world's people are undernourished, with food insecurity steadily increasing in developing countries since 2004.[22] Exacerbating this food insecurity are world food prices, which according to the UN Food Agency reached a peak in 2011. Close to half the world's children experience poverty that leads to serious material deprivation, and over 400 million of them experience extreme poverty.[23]

In countries across the globe, persistent poverty, growing income inequality, and a struggling working class lead to misery, stress, lost productivity, soaring healthcare costs, social unrest, and economic instability. After the brief period of the post-war compromise in the industrialized North, the effects of runaway capital accumulation and neoliberal assaults on social infrastructure are being felt. Today's youth are being told that they will be the first generation in a century to expect less than their parents, signalling the end of industrial capitalism's promise of perpetual and escalating wealth creation and distribution. The shock of this economic reality is newly felt by working people in wealthy nations, but in other parts of the world, it is nothing new.

For millions of the world's people, the crisis I've been describing has been unfolding for hundreds of years – in the case of modern civilization, reaching back to the 1500s, the early days of mercantile capitalism. At this time, the states and proto-states of Europe were embroiled in constant warfare, as empires struggled for territory locally, and raced to secure colonial fiefdoms worldwide. Exploration and trade delegations from Holland, England, France, Spain, and Portugal sailed to Africa, Asia, and the New World, at various times trading with, killing, conquering, and enslaving the populations they encountered.

In his 1997 book *Guns, Germs and Steel*, Jared Diamond uses the Spanish conquest of Peru to illustrate the broader pattern of imperial encounters between Europeans and other civilizations. He describes in detail the audacity with which Francisco Pizarro, leading 168 Spanish conquistadores, manages to capture the Incan king Atahualpa, and then to extort the largest ransom in history – enough gold to fill a room twenty-two feet long by seventeen feet wide to a height of eight feet. Diamond comments on the factors that contributed to the European colonial conquests:

> Pizarro's capture of Atahualpa illustrates the set of proximate factors that resulted in European's colonizing the New World instead of Native Americans' colonizing Europe. Immediate reasons for Pizarro's success included military technology based on guns, steel weapons and horses; infectious diseases endemic in Eurasia; European maritime technology; the centralized political organization of European states; and writing.[24]

With the advantages gained from superior military technology and infectious disease, European colonizers were responsible for the death of up to 95 per cent of the New World's Indigenous inhabitants – a holocaust unprecedented in history.[25] The prime beneficiaries of this mass extermination were the nobles, monarchs, and wealthy merchants who commanded the early imperial expeditions and later managed lucrative trade and slave routes from colonies to imperial centres. Examples of the massive profits extracted from overseas colonies can be seen in records of the world's first corporations – the British East India Company, incorporated in 1600, and the Dutch East India Company, incorporated two years later. Early expeditions under the flag of both corporations routinely produced rates of profit from 100 to 400 per cent. The Dutch East India Company was so successful in its pillage that it paid 18 per cent yearly dividends to its stockholders for over two hundred years.[26] Timber, silk, furs, opium, and precious metals from Asia and South America built the fortunes of Europe.

The same processes played out in Africa, where colonial oppression and exploitation of Indigenous peoples were equally brutal. The Belgian colonial occupation of the Congo is particularly instructive, and shows again how stark the difference can be between the experience of colonizer and colonized. At the 1884 Conference of Berlin, Otto von Bismarck invited the fourteen powers of Europe to decide how the African continent would be divided up for colonial exploitation. Belgian monarch King Leopold II was able to secure personal control over two million kilometres of Central Africa, which he called the Congo Free State. Leopold immediately set to work establishing rubber plantations in his new protectorate, presiding over one of the most atrocious and exploitative regimes in world history.[27]

Adam Hochschild's 1998 book *King Leopold's Ghost* describes how in just twenty-three years of occupation, Leopold's regime killed over ten million Congolese and maimed countless others. One of the ways in which Belgian managers of the rubber plantations would discipline their enslaved labourers was to chop their hands off for failing to meet quotas. The atrocities of the Free State were so abhorrent that they became inspiration for Joseph Conrad's famous novel *Heart of Darkness*, and King Leopold was excoriated by contemporary writers, like Mark Twain, who wrote a scathing 1905 pamphlet entitled *King Leopold's Soliloquy*.[28] A 1901 *New York Times* article describes testimony by Edgar Canisius, an American observer of the Free State:

> Canisius, who accompanied Major Lothaire, commander of the Belgian troops in the Congo, on his earlier expedition in search of rubber, says 900 natives were killed in six weeks by that expedition, while a smaller expedition, commanded by a Belgian Lieutenant, killed 300 natives in three weeks.

> The district is practically under martial law, on the strength of which such endless barbarities are committed that the natives are absolutely terror-stricken. Canisius further declares that the so-called punitive expeditions are in reality rubber-squeezing raids, conducted in such an iniquitous manner that the natives are in a constant state of revolt.
>
> While the conditions are somewhat improved in the territories worked by the concession companies, the lot of the natives in the State Domain, Canisius declares, is far worse than before the advent of the whites. The natives are practically forced to work rubber at the muzzles of rifles, receiving 2 cents a pound for what is sold for 75 cents at Antwerp. Thousands of natives have fled to the bush and live like wild animals. Along the jungle paths bodies of those who have died of starvation are frequently seen.[29]

The history of the colonial era, from 1500 to the mid-twentieth century, tells a similar tale in a hundred different times and places. As early mercantilism evolved into industrial capitalism, its spread to all corners of the globe brought a similar record of atrocity, displacement, and conquest. For the untold millions who died in the process of its expansion, the experience of modern civilization was of a crisis so profound that it meant the end of the world as they knew it. Entire peoples ceased to exist, like the Taíno people of the Caribbean, the Beothuk of eastern Canada, the Yuki of California, or the Tasmanian aborigines.[30] For those who managed to survive the onslaught, languages, culture, and lands were lost, and generations were consigned to poverty and marginality.

The unfortunate truth is that the atrocities caused by colonial expansion, warfare, and exploitation have not been safely relegated to the past, but exist right now worldwide, and continue to lead to untold misery. The NATO-led neocolonial occupations of Iraq and Afghanistan have led to hundreds of thousands of deaths, with economic sanctions against Iraq from 1991 to 1998 alone being responsible for just under one million deaths, almost half of them children.[31] The Palestinians in the occupied West Bank and Gaza strip continue to exist under a brutal Israeli military occupation. The occupation has a devastating impact on civilians not simply in terms of death and disability caused by Israeli tanks, air strikes, and unmanned drones, but also in terms of economic hardship, with over one third of the population living in poverty and close to one quarter unemployed.[32] In Israel's 2008 invasion of Gaza alone (Operation Cast Lead), over 1,400 Palestinians were killed and 5,000 wounded.[33]

Other communities currently facing acute threats to their survival include

Indigenous peoples worldwide. Logging, mining, agribusiness, and dam-building have led to massive displacement of the Indigenous in North, Central, and South America, and this trend continues unabated. Canadian mining companies are particularly implicated in this attack on First Nations cultures, with companies like GoldCorp and Barrick Gold helping to rig elections and undermine resistance to highly controversial mines. In a disturbing echo of Peru's colonial history, in 2008, McGill professor Daviken Stuenicki estimated that 40 per cent of local conflicts in the country were due to mining, overwhelmingly by Canadian corporations.[34] In Peru, Guatemala, Ecuador, and Colombia leaders of mine resistance movements are regularly killed by government or paramilitary forces.[35]

A small portion of the world's privileged people, largely in North America, have yet to experience the horrors of war, oppression, land theft, and culture loss that have been and continue to be a constant part of many people's lives. Because of this it is difficult for the privileged to realize that industrial capitalist civilization was created through massive human suffering, and depends on it today for its very survival. Consumer economies in the most industrialized countries depend on poor and oppressed workers in newly industrialized countries. New corporate agricultural and resource extraction projects rely on the continual disenfranchisement and genocide of First Nations people and peasant farmers. Unfair trade relationships rely on the massive use of military force worldwide, resulting in hundreds of thousands of deaths and injuries.

Modern civilization's extreme stratification doesn't just present us with the moral outrage of countless human lives lost through violence or relegated to poverty and despair. It also poses a direct threat to social structures and institutions at all levels through political instability, terrorism, and warfare. Increasingly, social inequality is being factored into models of civilization collapse, such as the HANDY study mentioned in the introduction, in which computer generated civilization models show societies high in social inequality to be much more prone to collapse.[36] Both Nafeez Ahmed and Homer-Dixon note the huge impact that inequality has on the global system, as capitalism continually displaces labour through technological innovation and as rich individuals, corporations, and countries use their power to exploit wealth from the poor and from developing nations.[37] Homer-Dixon calls economic instability and wealth disparity the fifth *tectonic stress* threatening civilization with collapse:

> [Economic instability and wealth disparity] can devastate lives and sometimes even wreck whole economies. They can also generate resentment, frustration, and anger around the world that could, under the

right conditions, tear apart countries – both rich and poor – and shred the fragile institutions and moral consensus that underpin our global society.[38]

The capacity for human destruction exhibited by industrial capitalism is why I, like several other authors, have considered this to be its essential and defining characteristic. In "Overshoot," the next chapter, I will deal with the other aspect of our civilization's destructive character – its impact on the biosphere. Like the human tragedy experienced every day by billions of people, an equal tragedy plays out in the form of despoiled and denuded ecosystems, species extinction, and resource depletion.

5
Overshoot

> The difference in effects between the anthropocentric and ecocentric worldviews is incalculable. At present, we human beings – while considering ourselves the most intelligent species on the planet – are engaged in the most unintelligent enterprise imaginable: the destruction of our own natural life-support system.
> — Richard Heinberg[1]

Easter Island society collapsed due to several environmental variables, according to Jared Diamond's analysis, which made the island particularly vulnerable to ecosystemic degradation. Out of the dozens of successfully colonized and relatively sustainable Polynesian island societies, Easter had some of the lowest rainfall, coolest temperatures, and furthest distances from surrounding islands. These aspects made Easter more environmentally fragile than surrounding societies, and help explain how activities common to all of the Polynesian islands, like logging and hunting, ended up causing so much damage to Easter's ecosystem. Low rainfall and cool temperatures meant that trees regrew much more slowly than on other islands, and Easter's isolation meant that in time of crisis help couldn't be solicited from neighbours.[2]

Diamond is careful to point out these existing environmental variables to stave off facile explanations arguing that Easter Islanders were simply aberrant offshoots of Polynesian society, or that they were particularly wasteful. On the contrary, research shows that Easter Islanders were participating in many of the same cultural, political, and ritual practices engaged by other island peoples. Despite this important caveat, the fact remains that Easter's society did collapse through human-made environmental degradation. By not understanding the natural limits in which their island ecosystem operated, and by not modifying their behaviour when faced with these limits, their society sank into acute environmental crisis. In ecological terms, Easter Islanders were in a state of *overshoot*, in which a population exceeds the carrying capacity of its environment. In the case of overshoot, the result is a population crash, generally involving a mass die-off as the population is reduced to a level that is once more sustainable within current ecological carrying capacities.[3]

The idea of ecological overshoot was first introduced by American sociologist William Catton Jr. in his 1980 book *Overshoot: The Ecological Basis of Revolutionary Change*. In *Overshoot* Catton argues that industrial civilization had already exceeded its ecological limits due to a combination of population growth and an increase in the energy intensiveness of modern lifestyles. In the vein of Thomas Malthus's famous analysis of population growth in Tasmania, Catton simply did the math – too many people using too much energy would eventually exhaust finite resources. At the time his message was considered radical, not because Catton maintained that industrial societies were *headed* for ecological overshoot, but because he said *we were already there*. He argued the need for far-reaching changes to avoid a serious population crash.[4]

The importance of Catton's work is in elucidating powerful limits on human civilization – the same limits that constrained Easter Islanders and led to their society's collapse. We live on a finite planet, with finite natural resources and energy. To exist sustainably within such an environment, societies need to manage their behaviour to live within natural limits. Failure to do so means overshoot, societal collapse, and population crash – the fourth major component to civilization's global crisis, and the fourth horseman of the modern day apocalypse.

Catton's concept of ecological overshoot follows directly from the preceding horseman, stratification. There is only one Earth, and the global economic system is as destructive of ecological carrying capacity as it is of human populations. Because of this, it is completely unsustainable.

Our Unnatural Selves

The violence that industrial civilization visits on the biosphere is deeply embedded in culture, and in our understanding of humanity's relation to non-human nature. In North America and other heavily industrialized countries, humans tend to view themselves as separate from the natural world. We consider ourselves morally superior to non-human life, and view the non-sentient biosphere as a collection of devitalized, commodified "resources," whose only value lies in their utility. These notions are a marked change from early human foraging and agricultural societies, in which the natural world was seen as sacred and humans as intimately embedded in a network of reciprocal ecological relationships. As human civilizations changed into more complex forms and technology was used to exert human will over nature, the forces of science, industrialism, and capitalism forever altered our sense of the biosphere. From something that was literally a part of us, nature became something external and alien. Today, our disconnected environmental worldview, variously described as *anthropocentric* (human-centred), or mechanistic, presents another key to civilization's crisis.

An early example of anthropocentric conceptions of nature can be found in the Christian Bible, where in Genesis (King James, 1:26–30) God gives Adam and Eve dominion over the creatures of the earth:

> And God said, Let us make man in our image, after our likeness: and let them have dominion over the fish of the sea, and over the fowl of the air, and over the cattle, and over all the earth, and over every creeping thing that creepeth upon the earth.
>
> So God created man in his own image, in the image of God created he him; male and female created he them.
>
> And God blessed them, and God said unto them, Be fruitful, and multiply, and replenish the earth, and subdue it: and have dominion over the fish of the sea, and over the fowl of the air, and over every living thing that moveth upon the earth.[5]

These passages have long been interpreted as justification for a hierarchical relationship between humanity and the natural world. In Genesis, God goes on to specifically say that the plants and animals exist for Adam and Eve as food, or objectified "resources," that can be used to sustain the growth and spread of their children. There are other, similar passages in the Bible that reaffirm humanity's dominance of nature; however there are also several passages that expound the beauty and goodness of nature and its status as an expression of God's will. These other statements seem to argue for an inherent value and sacredness in nature, and the organization of medieval European society reflected this more *ecocentric* perspective. The medieval Church's conception of nature was based largely on Aristotelian philosophy, combined with Christian scripture. In the Aristotelian tradition, nature was viewed as a dynamic whole, with each species having its own *telos*, or divine function and purpose. It is from this time period (twelfth through fifteenth century) that the concept of Natural Law comes – the principle that nature is a lawful expression of God's will, and to go against nature is to violate this will, in effect to sin. The idea of nature as an expression of the good and the sacred is still found today in commonly held notions of "natural" and "unnatural."[6]

Where Western conceptions of the natural world shift decisively to the first interpretation present in Genesis (as resources to serve humankind) is at the birth of the natural sciences – in the work of René Descartes, Francis Bacon,

Galileo, Newton, Leibniz, and subsequent philosophers and scientists. In the late sixteenth and early seventeenth centuries, Cartesian rationalism and Baconian empiricism began stripping away the sacred from nature, and replacing it with a mechanistic view of inert matter obeying deterministic laws. With a goal of removing Church barriers to scientific exploration, the natural world was devitalized and reconceptualized as a thing to be dissected, conquered, and used by humanity for its own purposes. Ecofeminist historian Carolyn Merchant writes about this shift from holism and organicism to mechanism in her classic 1981 book *The Death of Nature*.[7]

As Merchant describes, Bacon, Descartes, and later champions of empirical and rational science present living organisms as machines, indicating that they can be dissected into their constituent elements and studied. In Merchant's text, this new physical sciences approach is linked with ideas concerning the torture of witches and subjugation of midwives and other wisewomen. In several passages where Bacon is describing his new experimental method of induction, he refers to nature as a woman to be harassed, interrogated, and forced to reveal her secrets. In a passage from the 1605 *Advancement of Learning*, he writes that science can only happen when nature is "put in constraint, moulded, and made as it were new by art and the hand of man." He continues, "For you have but to follow and as it were hound nature in her wanderings, and you will be able, when you like, to lead and drive her afterward to the same place again." In this same passage, Bacon compares the interrogation of nature to the interrogation of witches by the inquisition, an allusion that leads subsequent scientists such as Leibniz to refer to Bacon's method (experimental science) as "putting nature on the rack," or "torturing her to reveal her secrets."[8]

In *Technics and Civilization*, Lewis Mumford also describes the transition that occurred from a religious approach to the natural world in the early middle ages to one focused on magic and active attempts to intervene in natural processes on humanity's behalf. Eventually, Mumford argues, the birth of science leads to an atomistic, mechanistic view of the natural world:

> By his consistent metaphysical principles and his factual method of research, the physical scientist denuded the world of natural and organic objects and turned his back upon real experience: he substituted for the body and blood of reality a skeleton of effective abstractions which he could manipulate with appropriate wires and pulleys. What was left was the bare, depopulated world of matter and motion: a wasteland.[9]

Mumford argues that this devitalization of nature was necessary for the material world to be later filled with scientific invention and technology. Science was made possible, but at the expense of humankind "renouncing a large part of his (sic) humanity."

Of course, it is important to remember that the early fathers of the Enlightenment were rebelling against centuries of stifling control over knowledge by Church and monarch. This was arguably a noble goal; however in doing so, science, while liberated from dogma, is also loosed from a cultural framework that gave the natural world moral standing. This doesn't mean that all subsequent Enlightenment scientists placed nature "on the rack," but it does enable such practices to proliferate, as scientific inquiry comes increasingly to serve the interests of political and economic elites.

The other major social forces emerging during the scientific revolution are capitalism and industrialism. Both of these movements have world-altering effects, and both further erode a sense of the natural world as a sacred whole. Built on early mercantilist trading and colonial pillage, natural commodities like sugar, cotton, tea, and lumber become powerful vehicles for profit making and capital accumulation. In addition, mechanized production and resource extraction drastically increase the rate at which the offerings of the earth can be exploited, commodified, and consumed. From this increasing pace of extraction, production, and consumption, the great forests of Europe are destroyed, and explorers and early corporations are forced outward into the undiscovered world, searching for more land, more resources, and more wealth.[10]

The commodification of "natural resources" under capitalism is a key development in humans' evolving relationship with nature. As fish, cropland, forests, minerals, and water become things to be bought, sold, traded, and hoarded, they also become less and less things of inherent value. The value of nature is found only in its commodity form, and is fixed with a price in the marketplace. In this way, nature becomes a means to the end of wealth accumulation and power for the capitalist elite, and a source of employment and livelihood for workers. Just as capitalism alienates workers from their labour through job de-skilling, it also alienates both bourgeoisie and proletariat from nature itself.[11]

Industrialization brings numerous changes to our relationship with the natural world and among the biggest influences is industrial agriculture. With mechanized farming at massive scales, fewer farms produce more food, and fewer people live on and work the land. Employment opportunities move increasingly to cities, and urban populations begin to swell, further increasing the divide between city dwellers and the natural environments that support them. In societies dominated increasingly by mega cities and technology, even wild nature becomes something to be commodified in the form of lawns, parks, and nature preserves. The suburb becomes the symbol of this new relationship to the natural world, as families who can afford it stake out small, neatly ordered patches of "faux nature" on which to live. Suburbs provide the aesthetic comfort of manicured lawns and landscaped gardens – hidden from the industrial city core, but just a short drive away from supermarkets, shopping centres, and entertainment complexes.[12]

The result of industrial capitalism's triumph in the West is seen today in a deep division between most of its citizens and the natural world. In relation to the tangible solidity of the urban technological landscape, to many, wild nature seems distant and abstract. It has value for many as a vacation destination, but not as an integral part of what it means to be human, to be one species among many in a fragile ecosystem. For this reason, critical natural systems, like Hamilton's Red Hill Valley, are destroyed to make way for infrastructure projects. Land speculators, developers, builders, and politicians pursuing individual economic interest are able to sell the project by speaking to human convenience. You will arrive ten minutes earlier to work each day! You will have construction jobs! You will have more development, more business, more prosperity!

As nature has long been "hounded" and "constrained," chopped into convenient pieces for sale and exploitation, what can the loss of one more piece matter?

Points of Crisis

Industrial culture, with its devitalized and mechanistic conception of nature, has had a devastating impact. The research of countless scientists details the ecological deficit that human civilization is now experiencing, and shows how the sum total of all of the earth's ecosystems – the biosphere – is being critically degraded. Climate change is one result of this degradation, already discussed in the context of systemic complexity. But that's only one part of the picture. The ecological crisis can also be seen in *energy depletion, natural resource depletion, habitat destruction and wildlife loss,* and the legacy of *toxic contamination.*

Energy depletion

Issues surrounding global energy can fit into two basic categories:

1. *Consumption:* the level of energy needed to maintain the lifestyles of a given society, for example, to produce and distribute goods through the

economy, to grow food, maintain shelter, engage in recreation and provide necessary services
2. *Source:* the kinds of energy exploited to meet societal needs, in particular, its availability, and its renewability or finite nature

We have known for some years now that the consumer lifestyle associated with industrial capitalist societies is extremely energy intensive. Not too long ago, this was seen by theorists of social evolution to be a hallmark of advanced civilization. Writing in 1959, prominent anthropologist Leslie White theorized that human cultures evolve in a *unilineal* or *synchronic* fashion.[13] This echoed the work of earlier theorists such as Herbert Spencer, who argued that human cultures can be ranked on a single scale of evolutionary achievement – from least to most advanced. Spencer used complexity as the criterion for ranking cultures, while White argued that a society's ability to capture and utilize energy expressed its greater evolutionary advancement.[14] From this perspective, industrial capitalism's massive use of fossil fuels and development of nuclear power are hallmarks of its advanced character, and separate it from less-developed societies that continue to rely on animal power or muscle power to drive their economies.

White's theory that an energy intensive economy is more evolved than an energy efficient economy also dovetailed with dominant theories of the time in political science and economics. After World War II, American academics like economist Walt Rostow and political scientist David Apter promoted a theory of unilineal political and economic evolution that saw the industrial, free market US society as a template for all other countries to follow.[15] Known today as modernization theory, its proponents believed that becoming more like industrial capitalist democracies should be the overarching goal of the countries of Asia and Africa, and that this process would lead to greater freedom and prosperity.

In practice, modernization theory provided thin intellectual cover to the US government's neocolonial involvement in Asia, Africa, and Latin America. The growth of critical development studies in anthropology and other disciplines began poking holes in the idea of unilineal and beneficent modernization, as they detailed how exploitative "development" projects serve Western corporate interest above local needs.[16] The burgeoning fields of ecology and environmental studies similarly challenged White's ideas concerning energy intensiveness and social evolution. As the ecological impacts of rampant industrialism became documented, and energy scarcity hit North America in the late 1970s, consumer capitalism's excessive energy use began to be seen as a serious problem.[17]

In the past ten years there's been some important work done on understanding the energy and resource demands made by a modern consumer lifestyle. One of the most useful concepts is the ecological footprint, developed by Canadian ecologist William Rees and Swiss engineer Mathis Wackernagel. In 1996 they published an influential book titled *Our Ecological Footprint: Reducing Human Impact on the Earth*. Rees and Wackernagel developed a formula to calculate the amount of resources used in different activities, and then to relate these calculations to the overall ecological carrying capacity of the planet. The formula provides an impact "footprint" for each individual based on their lifestyle, and measures it in global hectares of productive land (gha).[18]

According to Rees and Wackernagel's calculations, given a global population of six billion people, in 2007 the available per person productive land is 1.8 gha. When combining the calculated footprints of various countries, human civilization is collectively overshooting global carrying capacity by 0.9 hectares per person. Put in other terms, to sustain the current global population at current average energy and resource consumption levels, we need 1.5 earths. This knowledge is disconcerting enough, and gives evidence supporting Catton's claim that human civilization is already in a state of ecological overshoot. However, the footprint calculation is particularly instructive in highlighting how energy intensive lifestyles associated with consumer capitalism far outstrip the impact of the "animal and muscle powered" economies of less industrialized countries. For instance, the average footprint of a person living in the United States is 8 gha, or more than four times the available per person amount of 1.8 gha. In contrast, the average footprint in India is 0.91 gha, 11 per cent of the US person's footprint. Most industrialized countries have footprints above the sustainability level, making it clear that global overshoot is today largely because of excessive consumption and energy use by the world's wealthiest.[19]

Per country, per capita energy use is another indicator of how ecological impact varies substantially between wealthy and poor nations. In data collected by the World Bank in 2011, the largest energy consumers map reliably onto the largest footprints. European, North American, Middle Eastern, and far northern countries have the highest rates of energy use, with Canadians using the equivalent of 7,333 kilograms of oil per person, per year, Icelanders using 17,964 kilograms per person, and Americans using 7,032. In contrast, Bangladeshis use 205 kilograms, and Nepalese use 383. By these measures, the average Canadian uses an incredible 35 times as much energy as the average Bangladeshi. This is a massive difference, and only partly explained by the colder Canadian climate. The bulk of the discrepancy is due to Canada's high levels of automobile use, air conditioning, fossil-fuel based industrial agriculture, and other industrial processes.[20]

So, to recap, researchers today have determined both that human civilization is using energy and other productive resources at unsustainable levels, and also that energy and resource use varies drastically from country to country, based on such variables as climate, affluence, and degree of industrialization. By any measure the world's wealthiest countries are also its biggest energy users, highlighting the sharp inequity that characterizes global ecological exploitation. Inequity also emerges when considering the location of strategic energy resources worldwide. In particular, the fossil fuels that sustain the global industrial capitalist economy are not evenly distributed geographically, nor are they renewable.

In his 2003 book *The Party's Over: Oil, War and the Fate of Industrial Societies*, journalist and professor Richard Heinberg describes the looming problem of oil scarcity and its potential impacts on industrial societies. *Peak oil* is the term used to describe the point in an oil production process where the rate at which oil can be pumped reaches its maximum and then begins to decline. The concept of an oil production peak was first proposed by American geologist M. King Hubbert in 1969. Through studying the production curves of individual oil wells, Hubbert observed that a new oilfield would at first see exponential growth in production as extraction facilities expand. This growth would continue until it would reach a peak, after which point it would steadily decline. This research led to creation of the Hubbert curve, with which Hubbert was able to correctly predict the peak of US oil production in 1970. Hubbert went on to predict a peak in global oil production in the year 2000, based on available data concerning current global reserves and projected oilfield discoveries.[21]

There is considerable debate among researchers as to whether Hubbert's prediction for global production peak was accurate, or whether reduced oil consumption due to energy efficiency and economic recessions, or reduced production from events such as the 1970s OPEC oil embargo, have stretched the peak out to 2015 or beyond. Despite this, non-oil industry scientists studying peak oil are unanimous in their belief that peak production has either happened or is coming soon, with the general consensus being a date between 2010 and 2020.[22]

Recent discoveries of extensive shale oil and gas deposits in the United States have also complicated the debate about when global oil production will peak. While some oil industry sources have trumpeted the "end of peak oil" as technological innovations make shale gas and tar sands extraction possible, more sober researchers have noted that these new sources are much more costly and energy intensive to exploit, and are still subject to the law of diminishing returns that governs any finite resource. In a 2014 article, Michael Klare, author of *The Race for What's Left: The Global Scramble for the World's Last Resources* evaluated the arguments of peak oil deniers and declared: "Peak Oil is Dead! Long Live Peak Oil!" Klare notes that the recent spike in "unconventional oil" production simply delays the problem of oil depletion, and is a far cry from solving it. Eventually, the ability of new technology to extract dwindling pockets of fossil fuels will succumb to the increased costs of extraction.[23]

There is also debate surrounding the extent to which alternative sources can make up the energy shortfall that will occur with declining oil production. There are still massive coal reserves in several countries, as well as natural gas deposits. In addition, nuclear power and renewables like solar and wind have been touted as possible replacements. When evaluating alternatives to oil, coal and natural gas suffer from higher extraction, processing, and storage expense. Natural gas is also subject to the same peak in production as oil; and coal, while more plentiful, is extremely environmentally destructive to burn.[24] In terms of renewable energy sources, while they are likely sufficient to provide much of the world's current energy needs, they produce nowhere near the same *net energy* as fossil fuels, and cannot sustain continued industrial growth.[25]

Net energy is a concept used by geologists and fuel researchers to compare the amount of energy delivered by a primary energy source to the total energy expended in finding, extracting, processing, delivering, and converting the energy into an end-usable form. An equation called energy return on investment (EROI) represents a ratio of the energy extracted or delivered by a process to the energy used directly and indirectly in the process itself. For example, an EROI of 1:1 means that to produce one joule of energy from a process requires the expense of one joule of energy. In this example the process would lead to no net energy gain, and as a result there would be no societal benefit (as there would be no additional energy available for growing food, building shelter, or transporting people and goods).

EROI research has been steadily refined since the early 2000s, and the ratio has become a useful tool to compare the relative effectiveness and efficiency of various energy capture and production processes. According to Heinberg in his 2009 report, *Searching for a Miracle*, the "easy oil" that has fuelled our industrial economy for the past one hundred years has an EROI of approximately 100:1 in the largest Middle Eastern oilfields, and 19:1 on global average. Coal has an EROI of approximately 50:1, and natural gas, 10:1. In contrast, solar power has an EROI of from 3.75:1 to 10:1, and wind power has an average EROI of 18:1. So-called "unconventional" oil sources like tar sands bitumen and oil shale (released by "fracking," or pumping water into underground oil and gas reservoirs to release the fuel) have approximate EROIs of between 5.2:1 and 5.8:1 and 1.5:1 to 4:1, respectively.[26]

As the comparable EROI ratios clearly illustrate, the light crude oil that fuelled the global industrial revolution has a net energy return much larger than that of comparable alternative energy sources. And oil has the added advantage of being an energy carrier. As a stable liquid it is easily transportable, whereas other forms of energy must be converted into electricity or hydrogen before they can be widely used. Although some points about the EROI formula are debated among scientists, there is general agreement on two important points.

First, that the EROI of fossil fuel production has been steadily declining. Easily accessible oil, coal, and natural gas has already been extracted, and we are relying more heavily on harder to get at sources (such as deep sea oil deposits and the deep coal veins accessed by environmentally destructive "mountain-top removal" processes).[27]

The second point of agreement among net energy researchers is that the alternative energy sources available to us will not be able to keep up with current energy demands, let alone deal with the increasing energy needs caused by future population growth and economic expansion. Fossil fuels today account for approximately 85 per cent of global energy usage, and as these highly efficient fuel sources decline, huge gaps will occur between supply and demand. As Heinberg notes,

> There is little likelihood that either conventional fossil fuels or alternative energy sources can reliably be counted on to provide the amount and quality of energy that will be needed to sustain economic growth – or even current levels of economic activity – during the remainder of the current century.[28]

The energy crunch resulting from the gap in declining fossil fuels and the ability of renewables to take their place will have profound impacts on industrial societies. In his book *The Empathic Civilization*, economist and peak oil researcher Jeremy Rifkin describes the stakes entailed in the end of easy oil:

> The rising cost of fossil fuel energy and the increasing deterioration of the Earth's climate and ecology are the driving factors that will condition and constrain all of the economic and political decisions we make in the course of the next half-century. The economic question every country and industry needs to ask is how to grow a sustainable global economy in the sunset decades of an energy regime whose rising externalities and deficiencies are beginning to outweigh what were once its vast potential benefits.[29]

The looming energy crisis itself will irrevocably change industrial civilization in ways that are difficult to comprehend at present. Although it is hard to exactly predict, possible scenarios include severe economic contraction, acute social unrest, intensified warfare over dwindling fossil fuel deposits, and the collapse of globalized transportation and food production systems. In effect, the result may be a catastrophic reorganization of societies worldwide, with untold impacts on human life.

Natural resource depletion

As dismal as the future looks through the lens of ecological footprints and energy use, the picture gets bleaker still when considering the other effects of ecological overshoot. Long before global warming or peak oil deal their devastating blows to industrial capitalist society, multiple and intensifying crises will confront us in the decline of every natural system we depend on for our survival.

In a 2015 paper published in *Science*, an international team of eighteen researchers measure the state of nine key subsystems that contribute to the overall health of the biosphere, or what they call the "Earth system." Lead author Will Steffen from Australian National University and the Stockholm Resilience Centre argues that crises in multiple subsystems could lead to destabilization of the Earth system within decades.[30] The paper identifies four "planetary boundaries," or thresholds for ecological crisis, that have already been exceeded – the rate of extinction, levels of atmospheric carbon, the rate of deforestation, and the flow of phosphorous and nitrogen (primarily through fertilizers) into the oceans. Other critical boundaries being threatened include freshwater resources, ocean acidification, toxic pollution, and modified organisms.[31]

Apart from the depletion of fossil fuel energy, the most critical resource shortage facing civilization is the growing scarcity of fresh water. Of the Earth's water, 97 per cent is saltwater and most of the remaining 3 per cent is frozen in glaciers or found so deep underground that it is unavailable for human use. The 1 per cent that is left constitutes usable fresh water, of which human beings need approximately thirteen gallons per person, per day: 10 per cent for drinking, 40 per cent for cleaning, 30 per cent for bathing, and 20 per cent for cooking. Globally, 70 per cent of fresh water is used for agriculture, 22 per cent for industry, and the remaining 8 per cent for household use.[32]

Population pressure has put a severe strain on freshwater resources, and major rivers worldwide have been depleted to dangerously low levels, while underground aquifers, immensely important for irrigation in several countries, are also dropping precipitously. Severe droughts from 2003 to 2009 in Australia and in parts of India have sent warning signals to ecologists that we may be witnessing the onset of *peak water*, a similar condition to peak oil.

In their book *The World's Water 2008–2009*, Peter Gleick and Meena Palaniappan use the concept of peak water to argue that most of the earth's fresh water in rivers, lakes, and aquifers acts as a non-renewable resource, as it is depleted at much higher than replacement rates. Current projections suggest that by 2025, 1.8 billion people will be facing *absolute water scarcity*, in which they struggle to obtain sufficient fresh water to survive. In addition, two thirds of the earth's population will experience *water stress*, in which water resources must be carefully rationed, and water reserves become acutely vulnerable to cyclical periods of low rainfall.[33]

A 2016 study by Dutch researchers at the University of Twente Water Centre suggest that Gleick and Palaniappan's predictions are actually conservative. Authors Mesfin Mekonnen and Arjen Hoekstra estimate that approximately 4 billion people experience severe water scarcity right now, with half of those affected living in India and China.[34] A 2015 World Bank study highlights the particular vulnerability of urban centres to future water shortages, predicting that cities worldwide could witness a two thirds reduction in available fresh water by 2050.[35]

Today's ecologists are also using the concept of *peak soil* to highlight the worldwide disappearance of arable land and degradation of topsoil.[36] The issue of peak soil speaks to the impact of agriculture on natural systems, a problem that human communities have faced since the dawn of what anthropologists call *extensive cultivation*, as distinguished from the *intensive cultivation* practised in many pre-industrial cultures by individual household gardeners. There are several historical examples in which extensive cultivation, and its attendant impacts of deforestation, over-planting, over-irrigation, soil erosion, and over-grazing, has led to the collapse of food production, ecosystem integrity, and even entire civilizations. In his book *The Collapse of Complex Societies*, Joseph Tainter notes that agricultural exhaustion, caused by both over-production and climatic changes, is implicated in the collapse of ancient Mesoamerican, Roman, and Mesopotamian civilizations.[37] Since agriculture began approximately ten thousand years ago, about five billion acres of arable land have been rendered infertile due to topsoil erosion.[38]

The depletion of soil has accelerated rapidly with the advent of a monocrop, industrial system of agriculture that began in Western countries in the 1940s, and spread worldwide during the 1960s.[39] The intensification of agriculture using fertilizers, pesticides, new seed varietals, and technology-intensive cultivation was deemed a "Green Revolution" in 1968 by US International Development administrator William Gaud.[40] At first the revolution saw an impressive increase in crop yields per acre; however, in a few decades production increases stalled as soil exhaustion, pesticide resistance, and water shortages offset earlier gains.[41] The ecological impacts of industrial agriculture have been severe; in the past forty years alone, one third of the earth's arable land has become unproductive due to erosion. The approximately eleven billion acres of viable crop and grazing land remaining suffer from varying degrees of degradation, with most exhibiting a 30 to 60 per cent loss of carbon, the critical element that enables plant growth.[42] Across the globe, fertile soils are being destroyed faster than they can be replenished.[43] As a result, in a relatively short timeframe landscapes undergo drastic changes. Environmental journalist Stephen Leahy describes such a catastrophic change in Iceland:

> Eleven hundred years ago, the first Icelandic settlers came to a cold island mostly covered by forests and lush meadows, and blessed with deep volcanic soils. In a pattern repeated around the world, settlers cleared the forests and put too many animals on the meadows, until 96 percent of the forest was gone and half the grassland destroyed. By the 1800s, Iceland had become Europe's largest desert; the people starved, and the once prosperous country became one of the world's poorest.[44]

The kind of deforestation that devastated Iceland is now widespread. According to a 2010 report by the Food and Agriculture Organization (FAO), the world's forests continue to decline at alarming rates. In 2005, forest covered 3.69 billion hectares, or approximately 30 per cent of global land area. Between 1990 and 2005, there was a net reduction in forest of 72.9 million hectares.[45] Despite a slight drop in the rate of deforestation between 2005 and 2010, by the FAO's calculations, forest is still vanishing at a rate of 5.5 million hectares per year.[46] The depletion of forest is more acute in Africa and South America, and is associated everywhere with clearing land for agricultural food production (both commercial and subsistence), livestock grazing, and logging.

Of the earth's remaining forests, 44 per cent are located in the tropics, the areas experiencing the highest rate of deforestation.[47]

Habitat destruction and wildlife loss

With a loss of forest comes a critical depletion of wildlife habitat and a resulting decline in biodiversity. Biodiversity includes the number and health of different kinds of ecosystems (ecosystem biodiversity) and also the diversity and population health of various species within a given ecosystem (species biodiversity). Both forms are crucial for supporting the vast array of life on Earth, including those plant and animal species that are essential for human survival. The assault on biodiversity brought on by industrial capitalism's global spread is massive, leading to the extinction and threatened extinction of numerous species and the degradation of nearly every planetary ecosystem.

A 2005 *Millennium Ecosystem Report* produced by the World Resources Institute finds that 60 per cent of the earth's ecosystems are being degraded through unsustainable use. The report also suggests that ecosystem degradation is leading to dangerous tipping points:

> There is *established but incomplete* evidence that changes being made in ecosystems are increasing the likelihood of nonlinear changes in ecosystems (including accelerating, abrupt, and potentially irreversible changes) that have important consequences for human well-being. Examples of such changes include disease emergence, abrupt alterations in water quality, the creation of "dead zones" in coastal waters, the collapse of fisheries, and shifts in regional climate.[48]

Although a broad spectrum of Earth's ecosystems are under stress, some are under acute stress and in danger of complete collapse. According to the International Union for the Conservation of Nature (IUCN), 20 per cent of the earth's coral reefs, incredibly important centres of ocean biodiversity, have already been destroyed. Coral reefs provide habitat for approximately 25 per cent of ocean fish, and one formation can contain as many as 750 separate species. Of the world's remaining reefs, 24 per cent are at immediate risk of collapse, while another 26 per cent are likely to collapse in the near future. In all, if present rates of destruction continue, 70 per cent of coral reef ecosystems will be destroyed by 2050, representing a deadly and irreversible blow to ocean habitat.[49]

Along with over-fishing, one of the greatest threats to coral reef ecosystems is *ocean acidification*, the process through which carbon dioxide produced by burning fossil fuels is absorbed by oceans and turned into carbonic acid. This acid then impairs the ability of sea life to form shells, and also leads to reproductive disruptions in fish.[50] Over the past two centuries, scientists estimate that ocean ph levels have risen by 30 per cent.[51] Alarmingly, recent studies show that the rate of increase is now much greater than scientists had thought. In 2008 a team from the University of Chicago published a study of seawater acidity off the coast of Washington state. The study looks at changes in ph levels since 2000, and concludes that levels increased ten times faster than was originally predicted, and that acidification could have a tremendous impact on global fish stocks.[52]

A final threat to ocean biodiversity are the many *dead zones* that are increasing in both size and frequency. Ocean dead zones are areas in which the oxygen content of the water has plummeted, creating a toxic environment in which any sea life that enters will literally suffocate and die. Dead zones can occur naturally, but can also be caused, and greatly exacerbated, by agricultural runoff and sewer discharge. These human factors introduce excess organic matter and nutrients into lake and ocean ecosystems, leading to the creation of algal blooms that feed off the pollution. When the algae die and decompose, the resulting chemical reaction sucks oxygen out of the water and turns a once vibrant ecosystem into an underwater graveyard. The number of ocean dead zones has doubled every ten years since 1960, and recent studies show that ocean temperature increases due to global warming only intensify this rate of change.[53]

The dire threats being faced by ocean wildlife today are also being faced by terrestrial plants and animals. A third of identified species are threatened with extinction today, with scientists proposing that the current rate of extinction is up to a thousand times that of the natural rate, as determined by the fossil record.[54] This massive extinction leads a growing number of scientists to refer to a new epoch of geological time, termed the *Anthropocene* by Nobel laureate Paul Crutzen, that started in the eighteenth century and continues into the present. The Anthropocene is characterized by humanity's impact on the biosphere, as evidenced by increasing levels of atmospheric carbon dioxide, ecosystem depletion, and species extinction.[55]

In her 2014 book *The Sixth Extinction*, Elizabeth Kolbert argues that the Anthropocene may well constitute Earth's sixth great extinction event,[56] on par with the Cretaceous-Paleogene extinction, in which a massive asteroid collided with the planet some 65 million years ago, destroying approximately 75 per cent of life on Earth.[57]

Toxic contamination and its legacy

A final impact of industrial civilization on the biosphere is the toxic contamination of the water we drink, the land we inhabit, the air we breathe, and the food we eat. Due to the use of chemical fertilizers and pesticides in industrial agriculture, the runoff of these toxic substances into surface and groundwater is a serious and growing concern. In Canada, the government estimates that 150 billion litres of un- or under-treated sewage is discharged each year into lakes and rivers.[58] In 2013 the US Environmental Protection Agency (EPA) recorded the production of 25.63 billion pounds of toxic waste through industrial processes. Of these toxic chemicals, 4.14 billion pounds were released untreated into the environment.[59]

Solid waste from industrial processes and household consumption is another source of pollution that has reached unsustainable levels. In 2007, each person in the United States produced an average of 4.62 pounds of garbage daily.[60] This domestic waste production is dwarfed by that of industry, which produces 70 pounds of garbage for every one pound discarded by households.[61] In Canada, 2008 saw each person generate 777 kilograms of garbage, among the highest level in the Organization for Economic Cooperation and Development (OECD). Out of this waste, 65 per cent ends up in landfills, leading to a crisis in available dumping grounds.[62] Indeed, most major cities in Canada and the United States have faced or are facing crises in landfill space. A lack of landfill space leads to illegal dumping into lakes and waterways. It is estimated that 14 billion pounds of garbage, mainly plastic, is dumped into oceans every year.[63]

Fossil fuel production is also having a serious impact on water quality, as the search for unconventional oil and gas sources through tar sands development and hydraulic fracturing increases. The Alberta tar sands is one of the largest energy development projects in the world, covering 144,000 square kilometres, or slightly less than the size of the state of Florida.[64] To process mined *bitumen* (mixed tar and sand) into oil, massive amounts of water are needed. On average, tar sands mining uses 349 million cubic metres of water per year, or double the amount used by the entire city of Calgary, Alberta's economic capital (Edmonton is the province's political capital).[65] Much of this water comes from the Athabasca River, and accounts for 65 per cent of all water removed from this waterway.

During the mining process, in particular in situ mining, in which hot steam is injected into bitumen deposits beneath the ground, water is mixed with toxic chemicals, and is not fit for return back to the watershed. A small percentage of the water is recycled, but most is either pumped deep underground, or else placed in massive *tailings ponds*. In 2010 these hazardous wastewater ponds covered 176 square kilometres.[66] The tailings water is highly toxic to humans and wildlife, containing naphthenic acids, polycyclic aromatic hydrocarbons, phenolic compounds, ammonia, and mercury. These ponds also leach toxins into the surrounding watershed, with estimates suggesting that 11 to 12 million litres of seepage occurs every day.[67] A 2014 Environment Canada study confirms that tar sands wastewater is contaminating both the Athabasca River and underground aquifers.[68] Bodies of water within the vicinity of the tar sands are found to have concentrations of toxic hydrocarbons between 2.5 and 23 times greater than before mining began.[69]

Hydraulic fracturing, or *fracking*, is replicating the ecological and health hazards of tar sands – style oil extraction on a global scale. A typical fracking well uses from 55,000 to 220,000 litres of chemicals, along with thousands of litres of water. This mixture is injected at high pressure into underground rock formations to free pockets of oil or gas. The chemicals used in fracking can cause cancer and organ damage, and can have serious impacts on endocrine, neurological, and reproductive systems.[70] Some of the more toxic chemicals include benzene, toluene, ethylbenzene, and xylenes.[71] Water contamination and health concerns from fracking the massive Marcellus Shale deposit are documented in over one thousand court cases in Colorado, New Mexico, Alabama, Ohio, and Pennsylvania.[72]

The 2010 documentary *Gasland* highlights the growing concerns about contaminated groundwater caused by fracking, and exposes the collusion of US oil and gas companies in exempting the shale gas industry from federal drinking water protection acts.[73] Today citizens groups in Canada and the United States are seeking a moratorium on further fracking development until the true risks to water quality are known, and until proper environmental regulation of the sector occurs. Despite these concerns, the industry is expanding rapidly in North America. A 2013 report by the Environment America Research and Policy Center notes that in the United States, since 2005 there have been 82,000 fracking wells dug in 17 states. Together, these wells have produced 280 billion gallons of toxic wastewater and 450,000 tons of air pollutants.[74]

Air pollution has been a concern since the early days of industrialization, when England would regularly experience "killer fogs" composed of soot and sulphur dioxide expelled from factory smokestacks. These toxic fogs routinely killed and caused illness, with a particularly horrible instance occurring in the Great Smog of 1952. During this event, a cloud of toxic pollution blanketed London for five days. Estimates are that 12,000 people died from the smog, and another 100,000 were injured.[75] Although the conditions leading to London's killer smog have since improved with changes to industrial processes, air pollution continues to be a significant health risk. In 2012, the WHO documented 1,600 cities worldwide that experience regular air quality warnings, and estimates that 12 million people die annually from air pollution.[76] In Canada alone, the Canadian Medical Association estimates 21,000 deaths per year from air pollution,[77] while research by the OECD suggests that 800,000 people die yearly from air pollution in its 34 member countries.[78]

There are countless other examples that illustrate the ways in which today's industrial capitalist civilization is critically exceeding ecological limits. The toxic effects of pesticides and chemicals on food production, the radioactive fallout of nuclear disasters such as 2011's Fukushima meltdown in Japan, the chilling implications of genetically engineered "terminator seeds" that kill themselves after a season's growth – each could easily be the subject of its own book.

Ecosystem Collapse

What is important to note in closing is that the ecological aspect of civilization's crisis is arguably the most acute, and most unforgiving, in its eventual imposition of systemic limits. It is a universal characteristic of human societies that they adapt and change, and there is immense flexibility in how we choose to organize our communities, countries, and planet. This gives us some breathing room when considering systemic limits associated with social structures such as poverty, racism, and sexism. As human constructs these can be consciously changed, and their historic impacts ameliorated through justice, restitution, and reparations. However, once the oil, fish, clean water, and forestland are gone, they are truly gone.

Nature as a whole will survive, new species will evolve to fill niches left by those casualties of the Anthropocene die-off, but this world will never again be as suitable for human habitation on the scale that we've grown accustomed to. In the end, large-scale ecological catastrophes caused by global warming, the end of fossil fuels, and ecosystem degradation will impact us all – rich and poor, rural and urban, North and South.

The magnitude of the looming ecological crisis is such that many scientists, journalists, activists, and even politicians have sounded the alarm. Science can sketch the outlines of the coming crunch and can even tell us which aspects of civilization are most responsible for its implacable onset. The problems of dissociation, complexity, and stratification are still formidable confounds to effective action, but not determining. If these were the only obstacles to averting overshoot, there would still be considerable hope in human beings making the changes required to avert disaster.

But such a conception of the crisis would be fatally incomplete. What is missing from so much otherwise sophisticated scientific analysis of the environment is the extent to which modern civilization's political structure constrains our ability to act on available knowledge and to choose available alternatives. Scientists may know exactly what we're up against, but they're not the ones deciding our society's course. An entirely different group have this dubious honour, and collectively their control over societal decision-making processes comprises the fifth and final aspect of civilization's crisis.

6

Oligarchy

> The first person who, having enclosed a plot of land, took it into his head to say this is mine and found people simple enough to believe him, was the true founder of civil society. What crimes, wars, murders, what miseries and horrors would the human race have been spared, had someone pulled up the stakes or filled in the ditch and cried out to his fellow men: "Do not listen to this impostor. You are lost if you forget that the fruits of the earth belong to all men and the earth to no one!"
>
> — Jean-Jacques Rousseau[1]

The final horseman of the modern day apocalypse is oligarchy – rule of the many by the elite few. Oligarchy was defined by Plato in *The Republic*, as "a government resting on a valuation of property, in which the rich have power and the poor man is deprived of it."[2] This final horseman represents the political structure upon which our civilization rests, and the effect that this structure has on our collective decision making. This aspect, strongly emphasized by more radical political critics of industrial civilization, is often omitted or under theorized by ecological and systems scholars.

Oligarchy can come in several different forms, each differing in terms of the degree of concentration of political power, and the nature of the ruling class. Historically, oligarchic societies have been variously ruled by dictators, monarchs, religious or military leaders, or councils of wealthy landowners. In each instance, while one or a small group of individuals assumes supreme political power, in reality they are supported by a numerically small elite class of either nobles, merchants (capitalists), military officers, priests, or bureaucrats. Without the support of this oligarchic class, dictators would be unable to seize and secure power. However, conflicting power aspirations among the elite class also make oligarchic governments prone to infighting and instability.

Since the European parliamentary revolutions, beginning with the seventeenth century English civil wars and concluding in most countries by the mid-twentieth century, European nations have moved from being pure oligarchies to incorporating some aspects of democracy into their structures of governance. This trend has been echoed worldwide, and some form of democratic election is now the norm in nearly every part of the globe. According to the Economist Intelligence Unit's 2013 *Report on the State of Global Democracy*, over half of the world's 196 countries are democracies.[3]

The proliferation of democratically elected governments and persistent use of the word "democracy" by Western politicians as an emotionally evocative but often ill-defined buzzword, can lead to considerable confusion. In its original Athenian conception, democracy meant that all citizens had an equal share of freedom and power – the opposite of oligarchy. Given this, is it then safe to say that Canada, the United States, the Eurozone members, and approximately one hundred other countries are today no longer subject to elite control?[4] An answer to this question can be found in George Orwell's 1946 essay *Politics and the English Language*:

> In the case of a word like *democracy*, not only is there no agreed definition, but the attempt to make one is resisted from all sides. It is almost universally felt that when we call a country democratic we are praising it: consequently the defenders of every kind of regime claim that it is a democracy, and fear that they might have to stop using that word if it were tied down to any one meaning. Words of this kind are often used in a consciously dishonest way. That is, the person who uses them has his own private definition, but allows his hearer to think he means something quite different.[5]

Over sixty years later, Orwell's passage arguably describes use today of the word "democracy" by politicians and elites in industrial capitalist societies. If we were to take statements by the governments of capitalist democracies at face value, we would believe their societies to be deeply and proudly democratic. Free and fair elections, open voting for all citizens, free and competitive market economies, and the rule of law are all portrayed as hallmarks of the modern democratic state and as sacred institutions to be protected at all costs.

However, the proliferation of democratic discourse by the West invites a more rigorous interrogation, for if anything, evidence suggests that calling these modern states democratic is to use the word "in a consciously dishonest way." For sure the Western democracies *are* different from countries with overtly totalitarian or autocratic governments, such as Burma, North Korea (ironically, the Democratic Republic of North Korea), or Saudi Arabia. However, much evidence exists to suggest that, in practice, they are democratic in name only, and remain strongly oligarchic when considering actual decision-making processes. The political discourse of democracy is particularly important to unpack in countries like Canada, the United States, and the Eurozone members. Average citizens in these nations are prone to a particular strain of what Marxists would call *false consciousness*, in this case the belief that they, more than any other of the world's peoples, are equal participants in a democratic society. Such a view echoes the ethnocentric bias found in popular use of the word "civilization." As populations in the West consider themselves to be civilized in relation to non-Western, "uncivilized" peoples, so they also consider themselves democratic in relation to oppressed, undemocratic others.

The ethnocentric assumptions of Western democracy, like the equation of industrial capitalist civilization with progress, are easily challenged by a closer examination of the facts. When the political systems of Western democracies are scrutinized, clear and pervasive signs of oligarchy emerge. These oligarchic features can be seen in the concentration of economic wealth, the demographic makeup of elected officials, the numerous overlaps between economic and political interests, the ability of corporate and political elites to control scientific and media information, and the intimate connections among a small, powerful group of corporations and corporate directors. The impact of these oligarchic structures is profound, and serves to lock the vested economic interests of elites into decision making at all levels of the social system.

Concentration of Wealth

The evidence for oligarchic governance in modern democracies can first be seen in the division of economic wealth. I discuss this earlier in the context of stratification, where we saw in 2015 the richest 62 billionaires possessing as much wealth as the poorest half of humanity.[6] In Canada, a 2010 study by the Canadian Centre for Policy Alternatives (CCPA) found that the top 1 per cent of income earners, 246,000 people, had an average income of $404,500.[7] This contrasts with $46,634 – the average yearly Canadian wage.[8] The extreme division between the lowest and highest paid workers in the country becomes even more apparent when looking at the Elite 100 – the highest paid CEOs of companies listed on the Toronto Stock Exchange. These executives had average incomes of $7.96 million in 2012, fully 171 times the average Canadian wage. These extreme levels of compensation have been growing steadily, as in 1998, the top 100 executives made 105 times the average Canadian wage. From 1998 to 2012, compensation among the top 100 executives increased 73 per cent.[9] Overall, in 2010 the top 1 per cent of income earners in Canada accounted for 32 per cent of all income. This is a drastic increase from 1977, when the top 1 per cent only took in 7.7 per cent of all income. The income gap today is greater than at any time in over 90 years, greater even than during the Great Depression.[10]

When examining wealth (in contrast to income), the gap in Canada between haves and have-nots becomes even larger, with the richest 86 individuals owning more wealth than the poorest 11.4 million (34 per cent) of Canadians.[11] In the United States, a similar case of extreme wealth differential can be found between the top 1 per cent and the rest. In 2010, the top 1 per cent of Americans controlled 35.4 per cent of all wealth, while the bottom 80 per cent controlled 11 per cent. The gap in incomes between the highest paid corporate CEOs and average workers is far greater than found in Canada, with CEOs of companies listed in the Dow Jones Industrial Average making 500 times the average US wage of $36,000.[12]

With their significant material wealth, it is not surprising that the oligarchic class also uses a greater share of ecological resources and produces a greater share of waste. A 2008 CCPA study shows that the ecological footprint of the top 10 per cent of income earners is almost two and a half times greater than the lowest 10 per cent. A 2011 CCPA study shows that the top 1 per cent of income earning households have greenhouse gas emissions almost six times greater than the bottom 10 per cent of households. Given the greater degree of resource use by economic elites, it is no surprise that the rich tend to favour anti-environment political parties and oppose stricter environmental regulations.

The undeniable presence of a high degree of class stratification isn't evidence itself of political oligarchy if, for instance, economic power did not translate into political power. We can theoretically envision a society in which each citizen has equal access to political office, apart from wealth. However, this is clearly not the case in Western democracies, where the link between economic power and monopoly power in political decision making is remarkably apparent. What follows are some of the key ways in which wealth and political power are linked in today's capitalist "democracies."

The Revolving Door

A common feature of Western democracies that exemplifies the link between economic and political power is the "revolving door" relationship among high-ranking politicians, executives of major corporations, and wealthy individuals and families. In Canada, this can be seen in the directorships of leading media corporations, with former prime minister Brian Mulroney sitting on the board of media giant Quebecor, former Ontario Progressive Conservative

Party leader and current Toronto mayor John Tory sitting on the board of Rogers Communications, former Saskatchewan premier Roy Romanow sitting on the board of Torstar, and ex–federal Conservative Party cabinet minister Stockwell Day sitting on the board of Telus.[13]

The door also swings the other way, with business CEOs and lobbyists regularly entering government. A recent Canadian example is Ontario federal Conservative candidate Raymond Sturgeon who left work as a lobbyist for Lockheed Martin Aeronautics, manufacturer of the F-35 fighter jet.[14] Another high-profile Canadian example is Belinda Stronach, heir to the Magna Corporation fortune, who became a federal Liberal Party cabinet member and leadership candidate.[15] The prime minister Stronach served under was Paul Martin Jr., head of Canada's largest shipping company – Canada Steamship Lines (CSL).

Entering the upper ranks of political office has definite economic benefits. While Martin was a federal Liberal cabinet minister from 1993 to 2003, CSL received $161 million in government contracts and grants. And as federal finance minister, Martin refused to close loopholes that enabled CSL, and other large, profitable Canadian corporations, to evade paying tax by using Barbados as an offshore tax haven.[16]

In the United States, the link between powerful business interests and government is even stronger. Most of the early US presidents came from wealthy land-owing families, including George Washington, Thomas Jefferson, James Madison, and Andrew Jackson. Many subsequent presidents were allied with powerful corporations, with Herbert Hoover building a fortune from mining, JFK inheriting massive wealth gained from financial services and oil, and George Bush Sr. and Jr. inheriting millions in oil and banking wealth.[17] A great deal of the Bush family's fortune was generated by Prescott Bush in his work for Brown Brothers Harriman and Union Banking Corporation. In these roles Prescott worked with powerful German industrialist Fritz Thyssen, helping him to equip the armies of the Third Reich, and making millions from the Nazi war effort.[18]

Prominent corporate leaders in numerous American industries routinely find themselves in high levels of government, often heading up legislative portfolios that directly influence their former employer's business interests. In 1992 the US Food and Drug Administration (FDA) had a former Monsanto lawyer draft the government's policy on biotechnology. A few years later this same lawyer returned to the private sector and became Monsanto's vice president. In the US oil and gas sector, fully three quarters of lobbyists have previously been in Congress or the executive branch of government.[19] According to the UK non-profit, Transparency International, in 2009 there were more than 13,700 registered lobbyists in Washington, accounting for over $3.5 billion in political donations. In the EU, the same year saw 15,000 registered lobbyists working for 2,500 different lobbying organizations.[20] In Canada, according to a 2015 report by the Shareholder Association for Research and Education, 956 government lobbyists are registered to the Toronto Stock Exchange's top 60 corporations (TSX-60). Of these lobbyists, 60 per cent represent the oil and gas industries, reflecting Canada's recent push to develop the tar sands and shale gas, and to build controversial pipeline projects. In 2014, TSX-60 lobbyists had 1,092 meetings with federal government officials.[21] Lobbying in the sector has already paid off, with British Columbia cutting provincial corporate taxes for liquid natural gas companies, and with the federal government under heavy pressure to do the same.[22]

Perhaps the most highlighted example of the revolving door in US politics is the relationship between top executives of Wall Street's major financial corporations and the US Department of the Treasury, the Securities and Exchange Commission (SEC), and the Federal Reserve Bank. Since the 1980s there has been a steady stream of Wall Street executives occupying the most prominent federal government positions overseeing financial policy and banking regulations. The current Treasury Secretary, hedge-fund manager Steven Mnuchin, worked seventeen years at Goldman Sachs before moving to OneWest Bank.[23] Mnuchin's net worth is estimated at $500 million.[24] The former Treasury Secretary, from 2013 to 2017, Jacob "Jack" Lew, was a chief operating officer of Citigroup Alternative Investments.[25] Mnuchin and Lew are simply two of a long line of Treasury heads who have come from the big private banks. His predecessor, Timothy Geithner, was a member of investment consulting firm Kissinger and Associates. Geithner replaced Henry Paulson, past CEO of Goldman Sachs, who while in office from 2006 through 2009 was one of the main architects of the bank bailouts that allowed Goldman to emerge stronger and more profitable from the 2008 financial crisis.[26] At other times in the past thirty years, chief executives from Merrill Lynch, Goldman, Citigroup, and JP Morgan Chase have occupied top positions in federal government finance organizations, including the SEC. Recent examples include Treasury Secretary Robert Rubin (Goldman, Citigroup), and Federal Reserve chair Alan Greenspan (Brown Brothers Harriman).[27]

The revolving door between Wall Street and the US government has had direct impacts on financial policy. In 1981, President Ronald Reagan hired the CEO of Merrill Lynch, Don Regan, as Secretary of the Treasury. Immediately, Regan went to work dismantling the financial regulations that had been put in place following the market crash during the Great Depression. In 1982 the savings and loan companies were deregulated, allowing them to make more risky investments. This led directly to crisis in the 1990s, where savings and loan institutions lost over $124 billion and thousands closed their doors. As a result of the savings and loan crash, the federal government paid out $220 billion.[28]

After the savings and loan scandal, Wall Street insiders presided over further deregulation, as Alan Greenspan was hired as head of the Federal Reserve Bank and Robert Rubin was hired by Bill Clinton to be head of the Treasury. This deregulation enabled mergers in the financial system and the concentration of power into fewer and fewer mega corporations. In 1999 the Glass-Steagall Act was overthrown, and the 1999–2001 tech sector bubble and 2006–2008 housing bubble were created.[29] At each step of the process the offices and mechanisms of public oversight were occupied by the leaders of corporations that had direct material interests. These interests pushed Wall Street legislators to dismantle public protections in favour of rapidly intensifying capital accumulation for themselves and their fellow financial elites.

Corruption and Criminality

Although the majority of large American investment banks were involved in deregulating the financial sector and influencing government through the revolving door, another important factor in the financial crash was the fraudulent and criminal behaviour of financial institutions. History well demonstrates that when oligarchs are not able to achieve their aims through changes to legislation, they simply break what laws stand between themselves and expanded power and profit. Goldman Sachs is an example of such sustained and systematic criminality, and in a 2010 article in *Rolling Stone*, investigative journalist Matt Taibbi traces the involvement of Goldman in every major financial catastrophe since the Great Depression. In the lead up to the 1929 stock market crash, Goldman was one of the key players in the investment trust game, in which shares in Goldman-owned investment companies were offered widely, and at accessible prices, to average Americans. Other Goldman-owned investment companies then purchased millions of these shares and succeeded in inflating their value. The Shenandoah and Blue Ridge investment trust corporations are an example of this Ponzi scheme, in which share prices were artificially inflated to the point of massive over-leveraging. When the trusts finally failed to provide the return they promised and the house of cards collapsed, the market crashed and Goldman alone lost an equivalent of $475 billion in 2010 dollars.[30]

During the early 1990s tech sector crash, Goldman was instrumental in lowering the standards used to evaluate the liquidity of new IPOs (*initial public offerings* – in which a company first offers stock to public investors). Since the Depression investment banks had only recommended IPOs from companies that had been in business for a minimum of five years and shown three years of profitability. In the 1990s Goldman threw these practices out the window and began promoting stocks from unprofitable companies, and then using its insider status to inflate their price. Taibbi documents Goldman's use of the practice of "laddering," or artificially inflating the share price of new IPOs, to make billions during the 1996 to 1999 tech sector boom.[31]

All told, the tech sector crash led to the loss of $7 trillion in assets, and created a recession in the United States from 2001 to 2002.[32] Goldman's role in the tech bubble and in the 2006 to 2007 housing bubble is an indication that oligarchic influence on government regulation was only half of the cause of these financial collapses. Equally important was the massive criminality of financial sector executives, who circumvented what laws existed, and engaged in widespread fraud. In a 2014 article in the *New York Review of Books* Jed Rakoff describes the findings of the Financial Crisis Inquiry Commission, struck by the Obama administration in 2009, and tasked with exploring the cause of the meltdown:

> As the commission found, the signs of fraud were everywhere to be seen, with the number of reports of suspected mortgage fraud rising twenty-fold between 1996 and 2005 and then doubling again in the next four years. As early as 2004, FBI Assistant Director Chris Swecker was publicly warning of the "pervasive problem" of mortgage fraud, driven by the voracious demand for mortgage-backed securities. Similar warnings, many from within the financial community, were disregarded, not because they were viewed as inaccurate, but because, as one high-level banker put it, "A decision was made that 'We're going to have to hold our nose and start buying the stated product if we want to stay in business.'"[33]

The Great Depression, savings and loan crisis, tech sector crash, and 2008 global market crash all illustrate the prevalence and normalization of criminal behaviour among the North American financial elite. Criminal oligarchs routinely cover for each other, as when savings and loan executive Charles Keating, who swindled millions from his institution, was declared "clean" by Alan Greenspan just before Keating was charged with fraud and sent to jail.[34] Oligarchs also lie for each other, as evidenced by endemic corruption in the form of false valuations of IPOs during the tech sector crash, and of derivatives in the 2008 global market crash. In fact, oligarchic lies and corruption have been key to the largest corporate crimes of the past decade, with Enron and WorldCom being two prominent examples. In both cases, corrupt executives from the corporations and their accounting firms used fraudulent "mark to market" schemes to artificially inflate company profitability.[35]

Corruption and criminality also enable wealthy individuals and corporations to avoid paying taxes. Tax evasion is a worldwide problem, estimated in 2011 to account for $3.1 trillion in missing government revenues. In 2011 the United States alone lost over $337 billion from tax evasion, while Canada lost over $80 billion.[36] Oxfam's 2016 report estimates that a total of $7.6 trillion in wealth is hidden away in offshore havens – more than the combined GDP of the UK and Germany.[37] In 2016 the issue of offshore havens became an international news sensation when a massive leak of financial information from Panama-based law firm Mossack Fonseca was printed in the German newspaper *Süddeutsche Zeitung*. The leak revealed a worldwide network of tax evasion involving over 200,000 companies and numerous wealthy individuals.[38] Known as the *Panama Papers*, they implicated power-players as diverse as Vladimir Putin, former British prime minister David Cameron, Ukrainian President Petro Poroshenko, and the former president of Iceland, Sigmundur Davíð Gunnlaugsson. Gunnlaugsson was forced to resign after he was implicated in the leak, and other political leaders have endured political crises as their involvement in offshore schemes was revealed.[39]

Observers of the Panama Papers note that setting up an offshore tax haven is technically legal. However, the leak revealed that several con men were engaged in tax evasion with Mossack Fonseca. Canadian Michael Ritter was convicted of financial fraud in 2005, and appears in the Panama Papers as a client of the Panamanian bank. Similarly, former BC lawyer Fred Sharp was a long-time Fonseca client, despite being disbarred in 1995 after pleading guilty to fraud. Sharp's overseas company, Bond and Co., helped set up 1,167 offshore accounts for wealthy clients and used several tricks to hide their identity and limit the amount of financial information that found its way back to Canada. Referencing the connections between Fonseca, Ritter, and Sharp, *Toronto Star* reporters Robert Cribb and Marco Chown Oved conclude:

> A sprawling industry of tax avoidance professionals – lawyers, financial planners, bankers and accountants – make a living advising the rich how and where to find places to lighten, or even eliminate, their tax responsibilities in Canada.
>
> They are the enablers.[40]

The extensive media attention that the Panama Papers received sparked a renewed call by progressive economists to close offshore havens. In a letter organized by Oxfam International, three hundred economists urged stringent reform of tax laws. Signatories include Jeffrey Sachs, director of the Earth Institute at Columbia University, and Tomas Piketty, author of the blockbuster *Capital in the Twenty-First Century*. The open letter, addressed to world leaders ahead of a UK-government sponsored summit on corruption, notes that tax evasion hits poor countries harder as it deprives their governments of the revenue needed to spur development and reduce poverty. The letter also notes that it is no secret why tax havens continue to be legal, as Jeffrey Sachs observes in a press release:

> Tax havens do not just happen. The British Virgin Islands did not become a tax and secrecy haven through its own efforts. These havens are the deliberate choice of major governments, especially the United Kingdom and the United States, in partnership with major financial, accounting, and legal institutions that move the money.[41]

The practice of wealthy individuals and corporations avoiding taxes shows again the ability of oligarchs to draft laws that favour their interests, and also the ease with which they subvert these laws when they become inconvenient. A final place this can be seen is in the political process itself, which has long proven vulnerable to manipulation and gaming by elites.

Electoral fraud orchestrated by elites goes back to the very genesis of modern democracies. Perhaps the best example is the history of parliamentary democracy in England, which from the signing of the Magna Carta in 1215 has evolved as a battle between democratic popular will and the oligarchic interests that seek to limit it. At first, the franchise was simply limited by law, as the first Parliaments only comprised the nobility and church leadership, and served as a bulwark for the elite class against the dictatorial power of English monarchs. Near the end of the thirteenth century the landed gentry were first invited to Parliament, later forming the Lower House in the mid-fourteenth century.[42] By the sixteenth century, there was a formal House of Lords and House of Commons, but membership in the latter was still restricted to property-owning men. Parliamentary criticism of the English monarchy's power increased throughout the sixteenth and seventeenth centuries, with a growing number of commoners wanting universal representation, and an increasing number of women arguing for their right to vote. In 1642 these tensions exploded into the English Civil War, in which the powers of King and Parliament clashed openly, leading to the execution of Charles I in 1649. For the next two centuries Parliament became entrenched in English law, but the franchise remained a severely limited and corrupt process. Until the Reform Act of 1831, many major population centres had no representation at all, while a number of scarcely populated "rotten boroughs" elected representatives at the whim of the nobles who controlled them.[43]

In the modern era, oligarchic interference in democratic elections continues, with elites influencing outcomes through their economic power, through manipulating the laws that govern the franchise, and through pure fraud. Campaign finance is a powerful lever for controlling the political process, particularly in countries like the United States where it requires vast financial resources to participate in the often empty spectacle of modern elections. In the United States, the election of 2012 saw expenditures of $2.6 billion between the presidential candidates alone, with more than $6.2 billion spent overall. The 2016 election is expected to beat even these exorbitant sums, with total spending predicted at over $6.9 billion.[44] This ballooning of election expenses can be attributed to the recent revision of campaign finance laws that makes it easier for large corporations to donate millions to their candidates. The Citizens United decision in 2010 struck down an earlier campaign finance law that had forbid corporations from paying for political ads that were made independently from candidate campaigns. With the ruling, campaign funding by outside donors for the 2014 mid-term elections was 66 per cent higher than it was the previous cycle, before the new laws came into effect. Now super-PACs (political action committees) can spend millions on political advertising, further ensuring that the message of powerful interests is reflected in the halls of government.[45]

When sheer monetary power isn't sufficient to game the political process in favour of oligarchs, recent elections in the United States reveal that outright fraud will also be used to disenfranchise millions of youth, poor, and non-white voters. In response to widespread complaints about the 2016 Democratic Party nomination race between Wall Street favourite Hillary Clinton and self-declared "democratic socialist" Bernie Sanders, Election Justice USA published a report about voter suppression. *Democracy Lost: A Report on the Fatally Flawed 2016 Democratic Primaries* reveals widespread corruption in the nomination process, including voter suppression (insufficient polling stations, voting hours, numbers of ballots), registration tampering, illegal voter purging, and fraudulent voting machine tallies. Election Justice estimates that the suppression overwhelmingly targeted Sanders supporters, and could have prevented Sanders from securing an additional 184 pledged delegates. This would have put Sanders in the lead concerning pledged delegates, and could have drastically affected the nomination outcome and the presidential race.[46]

Incredibly, the widespread electoral fraud uncovered by Election Justice doesn't even represent the full extent of elite interference in the Democratic nomination race. On July 22, 2016, just before the Democratic Party nomination meeting on July 25, transparency advocate WikiLeaks released 20,000 emails hacked from the Democratic National Committee (DNC) server. The emails show concerted efforts on behalf of senior DNC staff to ensure that Clinton was chosen as the nominee, long before any votes were cast. The emails show the staff concocting anti-Sanders stories to feed to the press and searching for ways to discredit him, including attacking his atheism and his campaign organization.[47]

Oligopoly and Political Influence

Apart from direct interference in the political process, oligarchs exercise considerable power by their control over economic sectors. The resulting market distortions can be seen when examining *oligopolies* – markets controlled by a few massive corporations. In his 2005 book *Ruling Canada: Corporate Cohesion and Democracy*, sociologist Jamie Brownlee notes that twenty-five corporations hold 41.5 per cent of all business assets in Canada.[48] Contrary to the prevailing capitalist ideology of "free market competition," most key industries in North America today are oligopolies, with very little market diversity. The resulting concentration of economic power and industry control exerts considerable influence over government decisions, economic trends, and consumer behaviour.

There are several examples of oligopoly in Canada, with one of the most prominent being in the cellular phone industry, where, in 2010, Bell, Rogers, and Telus controlled over 95 per cent of the market.[49] A similar degree of concentration occurs in the United States, where in 2011 three companies – AT&T, Sprint, and Verizon controlled close to 100 per cent of the cell phone market.[50] In Mexico, one company, American Movil, monopolizes the wireless market, controlling an incredible 70 per cent.[51] The owner of American Movil, Carlos Slim, also happens to be the richest man in the world, with assets valued at $74 billion.[52] Other important Canadian oligopolies include the banking sector, where Royal Bank of Canada, Toronto Dominion, Scotiabank, Bank of Montreal, and the Canadian Imperial Bank of Commerce dominate the market.[53] Banking oligopolies are common worldwide, with Deutsche Bank AG controlling the German banking system, France and Italy each being dominated by two banks, and Japan having a "big three" banking oligopoly.[54] In the United States, banking has also become an oligopoly, with the top five banks in 2009 (Bank of America, JPMorgan Chase, Citigroup, Wells Fargo, and P&N) accounting for over 40 per cent of all bank deposits.

In addition to banking, over half of industries in the United States today are oligopolistic. Examples include the beverage sector, in which Coca Cola, Pepsi, and Cadbury Schweppes together control 90.3 per cent of the market, and the tobacco sector, in which Philip Morris, R.J. Reynolds, Brown & Williamson, and Lorillard account for 89.5 per cent of the market.[55]

Perhaps the best-known example of a single corporation dominating an industry is Walmart, the world's largest retailer, founded by the Waltons, the world's wealthiest family. With 2012 revenues of $466 billion, Walmart's economic activity is greater than the entire economy of 157 of the world's nations.[56] If Walmart were a country, it would be the twenty-sixth largest in the world. Walmart is the largest private employer in the United States, and due to its massive size, it can have profound impacts on political decision making concerning employment conditions, unionization, and government social services. Between 2005 and 2010, the Walton Family Foundation donated more than $700 million to support the "school choice movement" in the United States. The goal of this "movement" is to undermine public education and divert money to private schools.[57] From 2000 through 2012 the Walmart Political Action Committee and the Walton family gave nearly $17 million in campaign donations, 83 per cent of which went to Republican candidates.[58] Collectively, the Walton family has more wealth than the poorest 43 per cent of Americans.[59]

Another influential oligarchic family are the Koch brothers – heirs of an American dynasty that stretches back to the late nineteenth century, when Dutch immigrant Harry Koch became wealthy in the newspaper and railway businesses. Harry's son Fred entered the oil business with partner Lewis Winkler, founding the company Winkler-Koch. Both Harry and Fred professed a far-right political ideology that was anti-labour, racist, and militantly opposed to even the most tepid reforms of the welfare state. Fred Koch became a board member of the libertarian John Birch Society, and participated in their fight against racial integration in the South. In the 1960s and 1970s, Fred's son Charles became even more deeply involved with libertarian politics, and spoke out strongly against any form of government regulation of business. In 1967 Charles took over Fred Koch's business empire, renaming it Koch Industries.[60]

Charles Koch expanded his company's oil interests, and also engaged in what would prove to be a lifetime of fraudulent business practices. In 1974 Koch Industries was compelled by the federal government to repay more than $20 million that it had overcharged its American customers. In the late 1970s the company pleaded guilty to five felonies, including fraud, for attempting to fix a government lottery for new oil exploration tracts. In 1989, a senate investigation into Koch Industries described their business practices as "grand larceny," citing the company for stealing $31 million over three years from oil fields on Native land. During this time, the political aspirations of Charles and David Koch, now co-owners of Koch Industries, continued to grow.

First the brothers poured millions into the Libertarian Party, attempting to make it a viable contender with the Republicans and Democrats. In 1980 David ran as the Libertarian's vice presidential candidate, on a platform committed to slashing government regulations and eliminating taxes on the wealthy and on profitable corporations. When the Libertarian Party strategy failed to take off, the Koch brothers instead orchestrated a takeover of the Republican Party, first through supporting senator Bob Dole. The brothers' political influence paid off when in the early 1990s they were threatened by a proposed "BTU tax" that would have seen fossil fuel companies pay for the pollution they cause. To fight the law, the Kochs created Citizens for a Sound Economy (CSE), a front group used to propagandize for the brothers via town hall meetings and anti-tax rallies. Over ten years the Kochs invested $8 million in the CSE and successfully defeated the tax.[61]

Perhaps the greatest example of the Kochs' criminality concerns the thousands of miles of oil and gas pipelines they own. Under a corporate culture that encourages risk-taking and discourages precaution, safety, and even maintenance, the Kochs rapidly expanded both their network of pipelines and their record of serious environmental disasters.

A former employee who worked on Koch pipelines in Louisiana testified that spills were regularly covered up by the company, and if reported to authorities, were always greatly underestimated. In 1994, an aging pipeline ruptured in south Texas and poured over 90,000 gallons of crude, creating a 12 mile oil slick that covered a creek, surrounding marshlands, and both Nueces and Corpus Christi Bays. In 1996, the US Environmental Protection Agency (EPA) noted that Koch pipelines had spilled 11.6 million gallons of crude oil from 1985 to 1996. The brothers were forced to pay $30 million for 312 spills in six different states, and in 2000 they were also fined $20 million for a 97 count indictment related to violations of the Clean Air Act. Despite these convictions and penalties, Koch Industries continued its pathological business practices, until in 1996 one of their pipelines near Lively, Texas, exploded and killed two teenagers. The pipeline was carrying liquid butane, was seriously corroded, and had previously failed a pressure check in 1995 and an anti-corrosion check in 1996. The family of one of the teenagers killed won a $296 million settlement against Koch Industries, then the largest wrongful death settlement in US history.[62]

The present day political and economic influence of the Waltons and Kochs is incredibly powerful, but this is not new. Oligarchic families have long dominated economic and political life in the United States. In *A People's History of the United States*, Howard Zinn describes how the late nineteenth-century industrial boom was driven by a new class of corporate multimillionaires – later known by historians as the Robber Barons. Fantastic wealth was built through mining, steel production, railways, and textiles, and while some men who made fortunes came from little or no means, a study of 1870s corporate executives reveals that 90 per cent came from middle and upper class families. The Robber Barons colluded often with government, and bribes were common – whether Thomas Edison bribing New Jersey politicians, or heads of the Erie, Union Pacific, and Central Pacific railroads spending hundreds of thousands on bribes and receiving millions in government assistance in return. John D. Rockefeller made his millions in Standard Oil, Andrew Carnegie in railroads and steel, and J.P. Morgan from banking.[63]

During the reign of the Robber Barons, federal and state governments were in firm support of oligarchic interests, and supported them with strike-breaking, deregulation, fraud, and opposition to the many attempts at reform being proposed by workers and farmers. In 1868 the US Supreme Court passed the fourteenth amendment to the Constitution, and corporate lawyers were able to extend the concept of legal personhood to corporations. This opened the door to further rights being granted to corporate entities in the century to follow. The courts did the bidding of oligarchs for years after, and in 1886 alone the US Supreme Court overthrew 230 laws that had limited the power of corporations.[64]

At the height of their power, the Robber Barons sat as directors on numerous corporate boards, creating a small network of wealthy and powerful individuals that controlled America's corporate wealth. At one point J.P. Morgan sat on the board of forty-eight corporations, while John Rockefeller sat on thirty-seven.[65] Modern sociologists refer to this phenomenon as *interlocking directorates*, and it continues to describe the connections and structural alliances among directors of the world's largest corporations today.[66] Recent studies affirm that in each of the Western democracies there is a network of powerful families and individuals who sit on several corporate boards and who play a large role in determining economic practice and policy.[67] Increasingly, these national corporate networks are influenced by multinational corporations, creating linkages that some researchers argue are giving rise to a coordinated *Transnational Capitalist Class*.[68]

The extent to which corporate networks are nationally or internationally linked is an interesting current debate in sociology and political science. However, what is clear is that in either forum they work to concentrate corporate decision-making power within the ranks of the elite. The overwhelming majority of corporate directors come from the upper economic class and the dominant culture. For example, a 2006 book by R.L. Zweigenhaft and G. Domhoff notes that in the top one hundred US corporations, 71 per cent of directors are white males.[69] Differential access to political power based on gender and ethnicity can be observed in other areas of industrial capitalist societies. In the Canadian House of Commons, after the 2008 elections only 22.1 per cent of seats were held by women.[70] Similarly, in the 2006 federal election, just 24 visible minority candidates were elected, or 7.8 per cent of the total seats. This percentage is just under half of the proportion of Canada's visible minority population.[71] In 2010, women made up only 17 per cent of corporate officers and 13 per cent of directors of Canada's top five hundred public and private companies.[72] In 2001, the Canadian Census found that visible minorities hold just 3 per cent of upper management positions in Canadian businesses, despite making up more than 13 per cent of the population.[73]

Another way in which oligarchy affects decision making is that members of the dominant class are more likely to vote. In a study of Canadian voting results from 1965 to 1984, political scientists Joseph F. Fletcher and H.D. Forbes determine that those least likely to vote have low income and low education.[74] Similar results are reported in a 2006 Pew Research Center Report, where it is found that in the United States the poor, youth, visible minorities, and those with low education are less likely to vote.[75] The likelihood of wealthy individuals voting more and having more influence on government due to money and power leads to their controlling political decision making. A 2014 study by US political scientists Martin Gilens and Benjamin Page examined 1,779 policy decisions over a period of 20 years. The researchers conclude that the top 10 per cent of income earners had 15 times the political influence of citizens with average incomes. Those in the middle of the income spectrum had "little or no independent influence," while those working class or poor below them had even less.[76]

Patriarchy and White Supremacy

The lack of women and visible minorities among elected politicians and business executives illustrates another important feature of the North American oligarchy. Not only is the political system based on a vicious classism, but it is also racist and misogynist. Women and minorities face several barriers to participation in societal decision making, and also bear the brunt of oligarchy's oppressive and repressive characteristics.

Canada and the United States, like most oligarchic societies, are based on essentialized notions of masculinity and femininity, and on the social, political, and economic subjugation of women. *Patriarchy*, the tendency of human civilizations to be male dominated, is found in historic and present day societies worldwide. In industrial capitalist civilization, gender essentialism remains pervasive in cultural representations, economic activity, and political structures – all of which remain dominated by men.[77] In popular discourse femininity is consistently denigrated, as men attack weakness in other men by calling them "bitches," "pussies," or "sissies." Stereotypically masculine traits such as strength, aggression, and rationality are valorized in mass media and political rhetoric, while stereotypically feminine traits such as nurturance, cooperation, and emotional expressiveness are devalued.[78] Men's biological status as "predators" is reaffirmed, as is women's essential identity as victims, or prey. The results of this pervasive essentialism are easily seen in male dominance of political office and corporate management, men's greater share of income and wealth, and epidemic levels of violence directed against women.[79]

The dominant culture's essentialist view of femininity as inferior to masculinity is a key aspect of civilization's crisis, first for the oppression it visits on women, but also for the binary opposition it sets up between masculine and feminine. Denigrating femininity and its associated emotions and behaviours serves to police the boundaries of a pathological masculine culture defined by asserting power over other human beings and over the natural world.[80] The result is civilization as a hyper-masculine pursuit of dominance that subjects homosexuals and non-stereotypically masculine men to ridicule and violence, that denies compassion, nurturance, and cooperation to men, and that excludes these qualities from decisions within the political and economic realms. The resulting distortion in social priorities is profound, and explains why so little political and financial capital is invested in education, childcare, and supports for society's most vulnerable populations – the elderly, the poor, and the mentally ill. In contrast, vast social and economic resources are directed toward civilization's prime masculine preoccupations – war, wealth accumulation, and professional sports.

Feminist economist Marilyn Waring highlights the resulting distortions in social priorities caused by a patriarchal culture based on essentialized notions of femininity and masculinity. In her seminal 1990 book *If Women Counted: A New Feminist Economics*, Waring notes that some of the most productive labour that happens in any country is the domestic work done to sustain families.

The vast majority of this work is done by women; and the vast majority of it is unpaid. Because this critical work of child rearing, home maintenance, food provision and production, eldercare, and emotional support is unpaid, it is considered by standard economists to be valueless, or unproductive work. In contrast, Waring notes the billions spent yearly on armaments, including such comparatively absurd expenditures as having US army personnel idly sit day-in and day-out in nuclear missile silos, waiting for a launch command. A mother working in the home to raise a family is considered economically valueless, while these soldiers, strapped into chairs and performing no productive action, are well-paid members of the military-industrial complex – an economically and politically powerful sector of modern industrial capitalism. That the sole productive function these soldiers might undertake is to annihilate life as we know it makes the comparison almost surreal.[81]

What essentialist views of women reveal is that the tendency to reduce a group of people to a simplistic and negative stereotype is in the end always about control. If we can construct a group as innately inferior – due to biology or some other immutable factor – then we can justify hierarchy and dominance. Gender essentialism has justified the exploitation of women since the dawn of recorded history, and today continues to victimize women and marginalize them from positions of power and influence. In addition, this oppression helps perpetuate a destructive warrior culture based on hyper-masculine notions of dominance and aggression. Oligarchic rule, through militaries, police forces, and economic institutions, is thus validated, and the characteristics that could mitigate its murderous excesses are safely banished.

Justification for oligarchic rule and a warrior culture is also related to essentialist constructions of race and ethnicity. As I discuss in the context of stratification, industrial capitalist civilization develops and spreads worldwide via processes of imperialism and colonialism. These processes, while clearly driven by economic gain, are sanctioned by prevalent racist and ethnocentric belief systems. These beliefs have deep historical roots, reaching back to eighteenth century European notions of a Great Chain of Being in which human "races" are hierarchically ranked, with whites being superior.[82] The notion that humanity can be divided into races and scientifically "ranked" became one of the cornerstones of European colonial ideology, and justified their imperialist subjugation of African, Asian, and Indigenous peoples.

In the nineteenth and twentieth centuries, scientific racism provided powerful support for white political and economic dominance – both in Europe and North America. Social Darwinism and eugenics were used to justify the Atlantic slave trade, and the slave economies of colonial North, Central, and

South America. By 1860 there were over four million African slave labourers working on plantations run by white owners.[83] North American colonization also saw the near genocide of the continent's Indigenous population, and their relegation to a precarious existence in a tiny fraction of their original lands.[84]

In the twentieth century, movements for the civil rights of various North American peoples succeeded in making substantial changes to the political and economic power structure, but fell far short of eliminating its racist foundations. While African Americans gained the franchise and legal rights, they continue to be underrepresented in the political and economic elite, and overrepresented in rates of poverty and incarceration. While First Nations in Canada and the United States have been able to resist the wholesale elimination of their culture, they remain locked into racist systems of law like the Indian Act, and subject to "internal colonization" on government reservations. Both groups continue to experience an epidemic of systemic racism and hate crimes. The murder of young black and brown men by US police officers, and the hundreds of missing and murdered aboriginal women in Canada are just two examples of the disproportionate violence that falls on people targeted by racism.[85]

The racist basis of North American oligarchy can also be seen in the prevalence of anti-Muslim/anti-Arab sentiment. As the largely white American and Canadian oligarchic classes engage in imperialist interventions in the Middle East, racism directed toward the region's inhabitants steadily increases.[86] The 1967 Arab-Israeli war, the OPEC crisis, the 1979 Iranian revolution, the Afghan-Soviet war, and the two US invasions of Iraq have all contributed to the sociocultural representation of Arabs and Muslims as "the enemy." This has led to discrimination and hate crimes directed toward Middle Eastern immigrants in North America, and to military repression in the form of invasion, occupation, and drone assassinations being unleashed on the citizens of Iran, Iraq, Libya, Palestine, Lebanon, Syria, and Ethiopia.

Control over Science and Information

Think tanks

A powerful mechanism used by oligarchs to affect government policy is through a series of extra-governmental advisory committees, think tanks, and industry associations. Sociologist Jamie Brownlee describes this process of corporate influence, and the way it plays out in Canada through the Canadian Council of Chief Executives (CCCE), Canadian Chamber of Commerce (CCC), Canadian Manufacturers and Exporters Association, and the Canadian

Federation of Independent Business (CFIB). These organizations build and focus elite consensus and translate it into highly effective government pressure. The result is invariably a shift in the legislative environment in the interest of each industry's major corporate players. Complementing the function of these direct business lobbying organizations is a network of think tanks including the Fraser Institute, C.D. Howe Institute, National Citizen's Coalition, and Conference Board of Canada – all of which serve to further elite ideology and policy.[87] The same is true of think tanks and NGOs in the United States. The RAND Corporation, Project for a New American Century, Center for Strategic and International Studies, American Enterprise Institute, Heritage Foundation, and Cato Institute are all examples of influential conservative think tanks. While before World War II there tended to be a relative balance between liberal think tanks and those on the right, in recent years this has changed. By 2000, in the United States, right-wing or libertarian think tanks outnumbered their left counterparts two to one, and outspent them three to one.[88]

The link between conservative think tanks and private and corporate wealth is well-documented. In 2010, the *Vancouver Observer* reported that between 2008 and 2010, the Koch brothers donated close to $500,000 to the Fraser Institute to fund research and commentary that supported their oil and pipeline interests.[89] Think tanks are funded by elite wealth, and in turn think-tank members provide right-wing intellectuals to government. George H.W. Bush appointed over a dozen members of the American Enterprise Institute (AEI) to high-level government positions.[90] Past members of the board of trustees of the AEI include Dick Cheney and former ENRON CEO Kenneth Lay. The most powerful American conservative think-tank, the Heritage Foundation, had a profound impact on the policies of both the Reagan and Bush presidencies. The foundation placed numerous members into high-level positions in both governments, and received millions annually from the largest elite family and corporate foundations, including those representing the Coors and Koch empires.[91] Another organization, the American Legislative Exchange Council (ALEC), specializes in creating business friendly government laws. ALEC pairs conservative legislators with corporations and helps them draft legislation that furthers corporate interests.[92] In Canada, the links between right-wing think tanks and government are equally clear. Past prime minister Stephen Harper was president of the National Citizens Coalition from 1998 to 2002, while Jason Kenney, one of Harper's key ministers, was past president of the Canadian Taxpayers Federation.[93]

Universities

Many of the researchers that work for elite think tanks are also linked closely with major universities, another set of institutions that plays a key role in translating elite interests into government policy. In Canada, corporate sponsorship is a growing component of the funding strategy of major universities. In turn, university research institutes and chairs provide the policy framework and ideological justification through which corporate interests are realized. An example of this network of overlapping interests can be seen in the Canadian mining industry, where the Canadian International Development Agency (CIDA), ostensibly a government aid and development agency, works closely with mining corporations and university-based research institutes and think tanks. In his excellent work of critical journalism, *The Black Book of Canadian Foreign Policy*, Yves Engler (2009) describes how CIDA worked closely with Greystar Corp., an energy and mining consulting firm, and the Canadian Energy Research Institute (CERI), based at the University of Calgary. These interests succeed in pressuring the Colombian Department of Mines and Energy to drastically weaken environmental and labour standards to allow Canadian mining companies to exploit Colombia's mineral resources.[94]

The links between mining, universities, and government can also be seen in the Munk School of Global Affairs at the University of Toronto. Founder and chairman of Barrick Gold, Peter Munk, established the school in 2000 with a $6.1 million donation, then increased his support in 2010 with an additional $35 million.[95] In the past, Munk has been a prominent supporter of brutal Chilean dictator Augusto Pinochet, praising him for deposing troublesome socialist president Salvador Allende and making the country lucrative once more for Barrick's mining operations. The Munk school ostensibly produces academic research on global affairs, but the terms of the school's founding require oversight of "programs, initiatives and activities" by the donors. At the same time, Munk and Barrick continue to lobby the Canadian and US governments to oppose proposed "responsible mining" legislation. In 2009, when the Canadian government held multi-stakeholder meetings to address ecological and human rights concerns associated with Canadian mining companies, Barrick refused to participate, and instead formed their own consultative process, the Devonshire Initiative. The Devonshire Initiative brought together mining companies and Barrick-funded NGOs, and was founded by Marketa Evans, founding director of the Munk Centre for International Studies.[96]

A final example comes from the Canadian oil and gas sector. In September of 2011, David Keith, a respected climate scientist, resigned as director of the University of Calgary's Institute for Sustainable Energy, Environment and

Economy. In an interview with the CBC, Keith expressed his fears that corporate funding from the oil industry had compromised the integrity of the institute's research. One of the institute's academic employees was removed after the university received pressure from Enbridge, and institute priorities were being redirected to suit corporate goals.[97]

Not surprisingly, in the United States we find a similar network of universities, corporations, and government agencies that combine to determine economic, social, and political policy. The financial services industry is perhaps the best example of this matrix, where powerful individuals split time between high-level university appointments, corporate management roles, and government office. During the 1980s, as Ronald Reagan's chief economic adviser, Harvard economics professor Martin Feldstein was instrumental in deregulating the financial services sector. Feldstein was also on the board of insurance giant American International Group (AIG), and made millions working in the financial sector. Harvard economist Larry Summers worked as chief economist at the World Bank and twice served as Treasury Secretary. Summers has been an economic adviser to Ronald Reagan, Bill Clinton, George W. Bush, and Barack Obama, and was instrumental in fighting the regulation of derivatives. Summers also served as president of Harvard University.

Another compelling example of the link between government, corporations, and universities is the military-industrial-academic complex. Collaboration between these three sectors has been ongoing since World War II, when the government paid out millions of dollars in weapons development contracts to the Massachusetts Institute of Technology, the California Institute of Technology, Harvard University, Columbia University, the University of California at Berkeley, and Johns Hopkins University. By 1946, the Office of Naval Research had 602 collaborative projects with American universities, employing over 4,000 scientists and graduate students. Since World War II, military research has increased dramatically, with a 2002 report from the Association of American Universities (AAU) revealing that 350 colleges and universities are conducting Pentagon-funded research. The Department of Defense is currently the third largest funder of university research in the United States, behind the National Institutes of Health and the National Science Foundation.[98]

The close collaboration between colleges and universities – key centres of intellectual and cultural production – and corporate and government interests creates catastrophic distortions in scientific practice. As the demands of economic elites assume precedence, science and scholarship move from an objective, critical stance to one that is fundamentally biased. There is a long history of corporate-funded research that at best misrepresents research findings, and at worst involves outright falsification of results and promotion of pseudo-scientific claims. The tobacco industry is perhaps the most infamous producer of corrupt research, with a decades-long record of misrepresenting the health risks associated with cigarette smoking.

Big tobacco

In their 2010 book *Merchants of Doubt*, historians of science Naomi Oreskes and Erik Conway note that a link between cancer and cigarette smoking was proven by German researchers as early as the 1930s. In the 1950s, this research was replicated in North America, leading to widespread public concern, and calls for regulation of the tobacco industry. In response, CEOs from six of the largest American tobacco companies conspired to produce their own "scientific" research that presented cigarettes in a positive light, and that countered the growing body of evidence proving their severe health impact. They formed the Tobacco Industry Research Committee with the goal of creating doubt about the science linking smoking to illness, and of ultimately protecting the profits of big tobacco producers from lawsuits. This goal would be achieved by funding research, establishing ties with doctors, medical journals, and medical schools, and working closely with major media establishments to disseminate the pro-tobacco agenda. What followed was an over twenty-year battle in which industry-funded scientists successfully countered the work of legitimate scientists at every turn. As the body of evidence linking cigarettes to lung cancer and other diseases became incontrovertible, the tobacco industry spent even more money. By the mid-1980s the industry had spent over $100 million on scientific research, and had distributed grants to 640 researchers in 250 hospitals, medical schools, and research institutions.[99]

Eventually, the tide of unbiased research overwhelmed industry-funded science, and in the 1990s "Big Tobacco" began losing lawsuits. However, due to active industry manipulation, scientific facts about smoking's hazards, known since the *1950s*, did not lead to US government regulation of tobacco until *2009*. Over fifty years of untold deaths and illnesses, along with billions in profit, is the result, and the struggle to ascertain the true impact of smoking on health continues to the present day.[100] In a 2011 study, published in the journal *Nicotine and Tobacco Research*, the authors reveal that tobacco industry researchers knew of dangerous radioactive particles present in cigarette smoke as early as 1959, and covered up the information for years.[101] Similarly, a 2010 meta-analysis published in the *Journal of Alzheimer's Disease* reveals bias in forty-three previous studies done on the link between smoking and Alzheimer's. The independent studies show that on average, smoking makes a person 1.72 times more likely to develop Alzheimer's; in contrast, research funded by tobacco companies show a risk factor of 0.86, suggesting that smoking actually *reduces* one's risk for contracting the disease.[102]

Big pharma

The pharmaceutical industry is also notorious for suppressing drug research that shows the ineffectiveness or harmful side effects of medications. Despite stated commitments from big pharma to make negative studies available to researchers and clinicians, only positive results are published in research journals, and negative results are usually available only through legal judgment, as was the case with GlaxoSmithKline's (GSK) release of negative studies for their bi-polar medication lamotrigine.[103] GSK was also implicated in one of the largest recent drug study scandals, where negative research concerning their anti-anxiety medication Paxil, a selective serotonin reuptake inhibitor (SSRI), was suppressed. The hidden studies failed to show treatment effectiveness among children and teens, while also suggesting increased risk for suicidal tendencies in this age group. After losing a lawsuit, GSK was forced to release all subsequent Paxil studies.[104] Tainted drug research isn't just limited to a handful of companies, but appears to be endemic to the entire pharmaceutical industry. A 2003 meta-analysis, published in the *British Medical Journal*, by Joel Lexchin and colleagues, examines thirty different drug studies covering a wide range of illnesses. The analysis concludes unequivocally that studies funded by drug companies are more likely to return positive results than those funded independently.[105] Other research suggests that up to 60 per cent of drug studies are never published.[106]

Merck and Company, a US pharmaceutical company with over $100 billion in assets, has been caught covering up research that shows serious side effects in two of its blockbuster drugs – Fosamax and Vioxx. Fosamax was designed to fight osteoporosis, but as far back as the early 1970s, company research revealed that it could cause bone fractures and fatal jawbone decay. This research was suppressed, and in 2007 alone Fosamax did $3 billion in sales. In December of 2013, Merck settled $27.5 million in lawsuits filed by former Fosamax users, and continues to face over 4,000 other unsettled cases.[107] Vioxx was marketed by Merck as a "wonder drug" akin to Aspirin, and made the company an estimated $2.5 billion per year from 1999 until its patent expired in 2004. In 2006 an article in the *New England Journal of Medicine* accused Merck of covering up research data showing that the medication is associated with "an array of adverse cardiovascular events." Vioxx was shown to double the risk of cardiac events, causing an estimated 27,785 heart attacks over its patent life. In 2007 Merck was forced to pay $4.85 billion to former users or their families.[108] Merck has gone even further than suppressing negative research, once creating its own forum for fake research – *The Australasian Journal of Bone and Joint Medicine*. The "journal" was funded by Merck, published from 2002 to 2005, and presented itself as a peer-reviewed scientific publication. However, the journal contained articles that focused on Merck drugs, were not peer reviewed, and presented only positive results. Elsevier, the academic publisher that produced the journal, eventually issued a statement in 2009 admitting that it had published industry-funded publications that were not, in fact, peer reviewed.[109]

Food and biotech

Biotechnology companies have employed the same strategy as tobacco and pharmaceutical companies, using their economic power to purchase political influence, generate biased research, and fight attempts at public regulation. In the United States, Monsanto, McDonald's, Kraft Foods, Kellogg, ConAgra Foods, and Nestlé provide funding to the non-profit American Society for Nutrition (ASN). The ASN publishes three peer-reviewed journals – *American Journal of Clinical Nutrition, Advances in Nutrition,* and *Journal of Nutrition.*[110] The ASN also advocates for the food industry in government policy. In Great Britain, a similar non-profit organization, the Science Media Centre (SMC), receives funding from biotech giants BASF, Bayer, Syngenta, and Monsanto. In 2014 the SMC produced a report for the UK government that argued for the safety and economic importance of GMO (genetically modified organism) foods. In addition, the organization has led attacks on researchers critical of GMO safety and efficacy.[111] Biotech and other Big Food companies have also infiltrated the field of clinical nutrition through funding the American Academy of Nutrition and Dietetics (AND) – the association of professional nutritionists. In 2001 AND had 10 corporate sponsors, while in 2011 this had grown to 38, including Coca Cola, Mars, ConAgra, and Pepsi Co. These corporate sponsorships have led to "educational" sessions at the yearly AND conference on how sugar and aspartame are not harmful for children.[112]

Criticisms of biotech-funded research have been levelled by independent scientists. A 2013 review of Monsanto-funded animal toxicology studies published in *Environmental Sciences* reveals that flawed methodology tended to bias study results in the biotech industry's favour. In addition, review authors Hartmut Meyer and Angelika Hilbeck demonstrate that Monsanto-funded studies were only criticized for poor methodology when their outcomes failed to support industry claims.[113] Biotech-funded researchers and advocates have tried to argue that there is a "scientific consensus" around the safety and efficacy of GMO foods, and that critical scientists are "deniers."[114] However, in 2013 the European Network of Scientists for Social and Environmental Responsibility (ENSSER) published a statement by ninety researchers, academics, and physicians maintaining that "This claimed consensus on GMO safety does not exist."[115] Despite the persistence of critical independent scientists and widespread public support for mandatory labels, biotech companies have been successful at preventing GMO labelling in both Canada and the USA.

Companies like Monsanto have established a near-monopoly on GM agriculture, with approximately 40 per cent of all US cropland planted with Monsanto GM seeds.[116] Adding insult to injury, Monsanto has been ruthless in pursuing farmers whose crops are accidentally cross-pollinated with their patented GM seeds, and in 2006 they were able to pressure as many as 4,500 farmers to pay approximately $160 million in crop-contamination settlements.[117] In response to a successful 2009 court challenge by non-GM sugar-beet farmers, who argued that Monsanto's GM beets were unsafe, the corporation was able to change legislation and protect itself from further suits. As a result of lobbying, in 2012 the US government passed the Farm Bill, which has since become known as the Monsanto Protection Act.[118]

Through the revolving door, Monsanto has also been able to place three of its former executives in top positions within the Obama administration. Previous Monsanto vice president Michael Taylor became a high-level adviser in the Food and Drug Administration (FDA); former Monsanto Director Roger Beachy became a director in the USDA with responsibility for allocating agricultural research grants; and former corporate lobbyist, Islam Siddiqui, became an Agricultural Trade Representative tasked with marketing US GM crops worldwide.[119]

Climate change denial

The power of oligarchs to control, suppress, and manipulate scientific research can also be seen in what has been termed the "climate denial machine" – a network of corporate funders from the fossil fuel industry, industry-friendly think tanks, and corporate-controlled politicians. The roots of the "industry" can be traced to the fake research initiatives funded by big tobacco from the 1950s to the 1980s. In 1984 a tobacco industry scientist named Frederick Seitz founded the George C. Marshall Institute, a conservative think-tank that produced research designed first to promote US military projects like the Strategic

Defense Initiative (SDI), and that later turned to anti-global warming.[120] A 2013 report by Greenpeace USA reveals how in the 1990s, the Marshall Institute, along with the tobacco industry-funded The Advancement of Sound Science Coalition (TASSC), the Citizens for a Sound Economy (CSE), and Competitive Enterprise Institute (CEI), moved beyond opposing tobacco control legislation through creating "smoker's rights" groups, and began organizing to attack the science behind climate change.[121] Apart from big tobacco companies, Koch Industries was a major funder of these organizations, and of the two associations that were the direct precursors of the far-right Tea Party movement – FreedomWorks, and Americans for Prosperity.[122]

In 1989, an organization called the Global Climate Coalition (GCC) was formed from a number of industries that stood to lose financially if carbon became regulated. Major funders of the GCC included Exxon-Mobil and Koch Industries, and members included the largest American and European automotive and oil companies. When the first Intergovernmental Panel on Climate Change (IPCC) report came out in 1990, the GCC mobilized to support global warming deniers – taking them on speaking tours and funding their research. When the second and third IPCC reports were released in 1995 and 2001, GCC members lobbied to have the report results altered, and the threat of climate change reduced. Failing in this pressure, they renewed their attacks on the science and individual IPCC scientists. When the GCC began to be perceived as a self-interested industry group, it dissolved in 2002, and the fight to deny climate science was taken forward by supposedly independent conservative think tanks. In reality, these organizations were funded by the exact same fossil fuel and tobacco industries.[123] In 2006, the Canadian Fraser Institute, flush with Koch Industries funding, produced its own "independent scientific assessment" of the fourth IPCC report. The Fraser Institute's report marshalled the usual handful of fossil fuel funded scientists, and it was clear that the deniers had leaked access to the IPCC report well before it was officially released.

The scientific consensus on human caused global warming has grown steadily from one IPCC report to the next, today reaching to over 97 per cent of published climate research. Despite this fact, the actions of fossil fuel oligarchs have succeeded in keeping doubt alive and thwarting decisive government action. They have also succeeded in creating significant levels of doubt in the general population. In the United States, a November 2013 Yale study showed that 23 per cent of Americans don't believe in climate change.[124] A similar Forum Research poll published in July of 2014 showed that while 81 per cent of Canadians believe climate change is real, 13 per cent still deny its factuality.[125] The Bush administration went from official denial, to acceptance, and Obama has continually affirmed his belief in climate change. However, the United States continues to refuse to sign onto the Kyoto Accord, or to commit to meaningful reductions in carbon emissions. Now, with Trump in the White House, climate change denial has once more become official government policy.[126]

In Canada, Stephen Harper went from calling the Kyoto Accord "a socialist scheme to suck money out of wealth-producing nations" in 2002, to saying that "climate change is perhaps the greatest threat to humanity" in 2007. Despite this change in rhetoric, Harper still pulled Canada out of the treaty, and consistently avoided committing Canada to a meaningful reduction of greenhouse gas emissions.[127] Similarly, the current Trudeau government, while paying lip service to the threat of climate change, continues to support tar sands development and pipeline expansion.[128]

Canada's previous Conservative government took extraordinary measures in changing government policy to support the interest of fossil fuel oligarchs. Oligarchic interference in the practice of science is perhaps most shockingly illustrated in the case of the Harper government's attack on Canadian government scientists. Since the Harper conservatives were elected to a minority government in 2006, until their defeat in 2015, they systematically cut funding to a wide range of research departments, muzzled government scientists, and attacked scientists critical of the tar sands.[129]

Mass media

A final way in which oligarchs distort information and impact decision making in Western democracies is through the mass media. In their seminal 1988 work *Manufacturing Consent*, Noam Chomsky and Edward Herman conduct an in-depth analysis of the supposedly "free and unbiased" American press. What their analysis shows is, despite the absence of overt government censorship, media corporations end up presenting a fundamentally biased picture of reality:

> In sum, the mass media of the United States are effective and powerful ideological institutions that carry out a system-supportive propaganda function by reliance on market forces, internalized assumptions, and self-censorship, and without significant overt coercion. This propaganda system has become even more efficient in recent decades with the rise of the national television networks, greater mass-media concentration, right-wing pressures on public radio and television, and the growth in scope and sophistication of public relations and news management.[130]

Chomsky and Herman see the media's propaganda function operating as a set of filters through which the news passes before it is disseminated in newspapers, television, and radio broadcasts. The filters relate to economic interests of media corporations and advertisers, the priorities of government elites, and widely held nationalist sentiments (anti-communism in the 1980s, anti-terrorism today). As the providers of mass media news and entertainment become more concentrated, the propaganda effect intensifies.[131] Today's mass media is at record levels of concentration, with a handful of corporations controlling the marketplace. In Canada, 72.4 per cent of media revenues are generated by only five mega corporations: Bell CTV, Rogers Communications, Shaw Communications, Quebecor, and Telus.[132] In the United States, concentration is even greater, with six massive corporations accounting for 90 per cent of media revenues: General Electric, Disney, News Corp., Time Warner, Viacom, and CBS Corp.[133]

The ability to spin and suppress news in their own interests provides economic and political elites with a powerful mechanism of control. Citizens in Western democracies may have the right to vote, but if we have limited access to critical perspectives and unbiased news sources, we will almost certainly lack the ability to cast an *informed* vote. This in turn makes it difficult to understand and effectively counter the actions of elites that are oppressive to working people and minorities, and destructive to the environment.

A caveat to the ability of oligarchs to control corporate media messaging is that on rare occasions the media *can* turn on oligarchic interests, or else become divided in their support of different elite factions. During his scandal-wracked administration, Richard Nixon strained relations with much of the mainstream press. The battle between the Trump administration and journalists is another example of this phenomenon, as major media outlets (*New York Times*, CNN, ABC, NBC, CBS) line up to criticize his far-right policies.[134] At the same time though, there are limits to how far the corporate media are willing to step beyond their elite-reinforcing worldview. In the 2016 election races, a Harvard study showed that mainstream media coverage greatly favoured Trump over Clinton, and Clinton over Sanders. In the Democratic Party nomination contest, Clinton received three times as much media attention as Sanders, and the "democratic socialist" platform and substantive issues that Sanders ran on were largely ignored.[135]

There are other limits to the ability of oligarchs to control public perception. Surprisingly, although corporate media are often successful at constraining debate on critical social issues within narrowly constructed, elite-friendly parameters, when the public are directly consulted via opinion polls, we reveal a high degree of awareness of oligarchy, inequality, and the devastating impact that both have on our societies.

In a 2015 *New York Times*/CBS telephone poll, 1,022 adults answered questions about the economy, income inequality, and worker's rights. When presented with the view that "anyone can get ahead in today's economy," 63 per cent agreed that "just a few people at the top have a chance to get ahead." When asked about inequality, 65 per cent of respondents agreed that the income gap was a problem that needed to be addressed now, while 74 per cent agreed that large corporations have too much influence on American life and politics.[136] These results echo similar responses in opinion polls that show a majority of North Americans want greater public control over the economy. A 2014 survey of seven hundred likely US voters saw 87 per cent of respondents advocating for increased enforcement of laws and regulations governing corporations.[137] Similarly, another 2015 *New York Times*/CBS poll revealed that four fifths of Americans believe money plays too great a role in political campaigns.[138]

Authoritarian and Militarized States

Depending on who we are as North American citizens, for the most part it *is* true that if we obey the law, work our job, and pay our taxes, we generally perceive life as free and the system as largely fair (if flawed). We enjoy freedom of speech and assembly, along with human and civil rights protected by the rule of law. But if we challenge the law, don't have a job, or are not part of the dominant group – that is white, wealthy, straight, and male – then we soon realize that North American society can be incredibly intolerant of difference and vicious in its defence of power and privilege. When the liberal democratic façade of the modern state is stripped away, it reveals an increasingly authoritarian and militarized social system in which civil liberties are being steadily eroded, state surveillance and repression are steadily increasing, and democratic accountability and transparency are being removed from the institutions of governance.

Police violence

The oppressive aspect of Western democracies is visible in rates of incarceration, and in routine police shootings of poor, mentally ill, and minority individuals. In 2013 Canada's prison population was at an all-time high, having grown from 12,000 to over 15,000 in the previous 10 years.[139] Over this same period, the number of visible minority inmates increased by 75 per cent, while the number of white inmates slightly decreased. The United States incarcerates more people per capita than any other country in the world. As of 2013, the rate was 713 per 100,000, with US inmates accounting for fully one quarter of the planet's prisoners.[140] Increasing authoritarianism can also be seen when union members march to protect jobs and wages, when protestors rally or occupy to push for political change, or when environmentalists attempt to protect endangered ecosystems from destruction. In all of these cases, the coercive apparatus of the state acts quickly in defence of elite interests. Police are generally the executors of this oppression, but in many countries the military also plays a large role.

For many non-white North Americans, the threat of violent assault or murder at the hands of law enforcement is a daily reality. In the United States, young black and brown men, many unarmed, are routinely killed by law enforcement. The murder of unarmed black men by police led to massive protests in Ferguson, Mississippi, in 2014,[141] and Baltimore in 2015.[142] In Ferguson, unarmed 18-year old Michael Brown was shot seven times by white officer Darren Wilson. In Baltimore Freddie Gray was killed after being arrested by a police lieutenant. Gray's neck was broken – nearly severed, and his windpipe crushed. In both communities, decades of systemic racism and brutality boiled over, leading to national media attention.

Activists in the Occupy, Quebec student, Idle No More, climate change, and Black and Brown Lives Matter movements regularly experience the violence that awaits those who challenge oligarchic power.[143] When this power is confronted by protestors, the humane surface of Western society is skinned back to reveal a hard, militarized core. Civil rights are abrogated, state violence deployed, and dissenters are expected to conform or else face the consequences. These consequences include imprisonment, assault, silencing, and marginalization. Of course, in other countries the repressive power of the state falls on dissenting citizens with far more severity. In overthrowing Hosni Mubarak, the brave protestors in Tahrir Square, most of them youth, were slaughtered in their hundreds.[144]

Military-industrial complex

The authoritarian and militaristic aspects of Western "democracies" are also reflected in military institutions themselves, and in the tendency of governments to use military force in foreign policy. Western governments continually position themselves as bringers and protectors of peace as much as of democracy. In contrast, the enemies of national elites are consistently portrayed as being aggressive, warlike, and unstable. This polarized portrayal of conflict in Western media sources is so universal as to be almost unnoticeable, and yet the picture presented is far from the truth.

In Canada there is a long history of political doublespeak covering up our country's aggressive military engagements and reframing them as "peacekeeping." Similarly, the West and its allies are generally presented by Western media as engaging in aggression, conflict, and war in pursuit of noble ends – to defend helpless victims of oppression, or to bring democracy to unfree peoples. However, any serious discussion of modern warfare soon jettisons these ideological statements, and instead focuses on the perennial causes of global conflict – competition between oligarchs and oligarchic states for wealth and power.

That oligarchic interests exert strong control over foreign policy can be seen in the US government's hostile stance toward states seeking to pursue their sovereign interests in defiance of the world superpower's wishes. Governments in Venezuela, North Korea, Cuba, Iran, Libya, Syria, Russia, and China have been encircled by military bases,[145] threatened by provocations and sabre-rattling rhetoric, and subjected to destabilizing economic sanctions and military interventions. Since World War II, the US government has intervened militarily in other states over seventy times. These conflicts were documented by William Blum in his 2003 book *Killing Hope: U.S. Military and CIA Interventions Since World War II*. Much of these interventions were done covertly as part of the hidden struggles involved in realpolitik. Others, such as recent invasions of Iraq, Afghanistan, and Libya, were done overtly under the auspices of a moralist incitement to defend freedom and democracy against the threat of hostile, amoral others (Al Qaeda, Terrorists), or to liberate people from oppressive dictatorships.[146] Canada has a similar, if less extensive history, intervening often in support of US imperial objectives, or else to support national interests. Canadian interventions in Haiti, Afghanistan, and various countries in Latin America have expressed equal parts realpolitik (usually corporate interests) and a moralist narrative of "peacekeeping."[147]

The result of oligarchic conflict in the modern era has been particularly devastating. World War I was fought among the imperial powers of Europe, North America, and Asia for control of colonial fiefdoms. The toll of this bloody conflict included over 8 million dead soldiers, 21 million wounded, and over 6 million civilian deaths.[148] World War II continued the imperial power struggle with the slaughter of approximately 55 million people, or 3 per cent of the entire world's population. Over half of these deaths were civilians.[149] During the Cold War between Russia and the United States, the Vietnam conflict alone is estimated to have caused 3,800,000 deaths, with most casualties being civilians.[150] More recently, UK researchers from polling company Opinion Research Business released 2008 data suggesting that over 1 million Iraqis had been killed since the 2003 US-led invasion.[151] This invasion was ostensibly launched to prevent Iraqi dictator Saddam Hussein from attacking the West with "weapons of mass destruction." This idea continues to be perpetuated, no matter that serious analysts have thoroughly refuted it, and instead point to the United States' desire to control Iraqi oil wealth, project military power into the Middle East, and protect Israel from regional competitors.[152]

Corporations in the military armaments industry and government are inextricably linked in most Western democracies, a condition described as the "military-industrial complex" by former US president Eisenhower in his 1961 farewell address. In this now famous speech, Eisenhower warned:

> This conjunction of an immense military establishment and a large arms industry is new in the American experience. The total influence – economic, political, even spiritual – is felt in every city, every Statehouse, every office of the Federal government. We recognize the imperative need for this development. Yet we must not fail to comprehend its grave implications. Our toil, resources and livelihood are all involved; so is the very structure of our society.
>
> In the councils of government, we must guard against the acquisition of unwarranted influence, whether sought or unsought, by the military-industrial complex. The potential for the disastrous rise of misplaced power exists and will persist.[153]

Militarized spending

Since Eisenhower's speech, the US military budget has grown astronomically, accounting in the 2016 federal budget for 45 per cent of all government expenditures, or $1.3 trillion (including new military spending and debt service of past spending).[154] Even though US military spending decreased slightly in 2013, due to troop reductions in Iraq and Afghanistan, it still accounted that year for over 36 per cent of the entire world's military spending.[155] Worldwide, over $1.7 trillion is spent on armaments alone, making the arms trade one of the world's largest industries. As Eisenhower, and many others have warned, this economic power has translated into political power, and serves to guide government spending and foreign policy. In terms of domestic spending, military budgets eat up revenues that could otherwise be spent on education, healthcare, other social programs, and the transition to a green economy. In the United States alone, close to half of government expenditures go toward defence. In Canada, military expenses are a far smaller share of overall government expenditures, but in 2011 Canada still had the thirteenth largest military budget in the world at $22.3 billion. This represents a level of spending 18 per cent higher than the country's Cold War maximum.[156]

In North America, the military power of states has increasingly been deployed outside of any ostensibly public or democratic frameworks. In the United States, since 9/11 there has been a significant expansion of covert government operations, directed by what has been termed the *shadow government* or *deep state*. In a 2014 interview, former Republican congressional staff member Mike Lofgren described the deep state as "the thread that runs through the history of the last three decades. It's how we had deregulation, financialization of the economy, the Wall Street bust, the erosion of our civil liberties and perpetual war."[157] Lofgren cites the main players in the deep state as the Pentagon, Homeland Security, the State Department, and the US Treasury. He argues that these branches of government have combined to ensure that the corporate interests backing a perpetual war economy are able to control federal policy. One example of this collusion is the privatization of defence functions, with 70 per cent of the current intelligence budget going to private contractors. Another example is that the act of war itself has also become privatized, with the US Department of Defense employing 155,826 private contractors in Iraq in 2008, and only 152,275 troops.[158]

Along with having a largely privatized fighting force, the US army is increasingly operating in secret. In 1987 the US Special Operations Command (SOCOM) was formed to carry out special operations and secret missions, including assassinations, counterterrorism, and psychological operations. As of 2013, SOCOM personnel were deployed in more than 120 countries.[159] As of 2014, approximately 72,000 troops were active with SOCOM, half of which were SEALS, Rangers, Special Operations Aviators, or Green Berets. SOCOM soldiers work inter-operably with the militaries of 106 nations, and in 2014 a Northern Command, SOCNORTH, was created to operate in the United States, Canada, Mexico, and parts of the Caribbean.[160] SOCOM operatives also run propaganda websites that masquerade as official news sources, and are embedded in North American academic institutions to monitor potentially subversive intellectuals.

In addition to the proliferation of covert military operations worldwide, the US government has been operating a global program of extrajudicial assassinations by unmanned drones. The drone program started under the Bush presidency, with 51 strikes. The program expanded dramatically under Obama, with over 330 strikes launched as of 2014. Finally, under George H.W. Bush, the CIA established several "black sites" around the world in which suspects in the global "war on terror" could be illegally incarcerated and tortured.[161]

The oligarchic and militaristic character of Canada, the United States, and other Western democracies presents a powerful countervailing force to movements working for change. Attempts to act on scientific and humanistic imperatives concerning ecological sustainability and social justice are blunted, diverted, or outright crushed. A fatal distortion of societal decision making results, as the narrow interests of oligarchs become fixed as "national interest." Far from being noble or refined, the spectrum of oligarchic interest is the most predatory, immoral, wasteful, and ecologically destructive. For this reason, it represents the fifth, and most intractable aspect of civilization's impending crisis.

The Crisis in Focus

I began chapter 2 with a passage from the Book of Revelation – an evocative description of the forces that John of Patmos believed would herald the end of the world. The story of Revelation presents a rich metaphor for our current predicament, but I've presented a story of potential collapse based in scientific analysis.

The purpose of my argument in the previous chapters has been to support three premises. The first premise is that the crisis of modern civilization can't be geographically isolated, and instead presents a global problem. The second premise is that the crisis is dire, having reached a terminal phase that leads, if the current trajectory holds, toward collapse. The third premise is that the crisis is not amenable to reform, and instead presents a problem that necessitates radical change.

Supporting these premises, I describe five patterns of interaction within the overall system of civilization – the Five Horsemen of the modern day apocalypse:

1. *Dissociation:* Globalized production and distribution processes affect people's ability to put their own actions, and the actions of elites, into a coherent causal and ethical framework. These actions by our civilization's members, institutions, and systems of governance are therefore disconnected from their effect on the natural world and on other peoples. Without this critical feedback, even well-intentioned actors can't make rational and ethical choices regarding their behaviour.
2. *Complexity:* The world-spanning nature of industrial capitalist civilization, and the massive number of interrelationships it represents, mean predicting the effect of any given change on the system as a whole is devilishly

difficult. Because the crisis cannot be isolated in one part of the globe, the dysfunctions can't be dealt with individually.
3. *Stratification:* A profoundly unequal distribution of wealth leads to mass human misery and death through displacement, political instability, and continuous conflict.
4. *Overshoot:* The economic practices of industrial capitalism exceed ecological limits. Industrial capitalist civilization is critically degrading the biosphere, burning through non-renewable energy sources, and shifting the entire climatic balance.
5. *Oligarchy:* Political decision-making systems worldwide are controlled by a numerically small, wealthy elite. This serves to lock in patterns of conflict, oppression, and ecological destruction. The insular culture of elites makes it difficult for them to understand the impact of their choices on less powerful groups and on the biosphere.

The scale and complexity of industrial civilization clearly indicate that the threat of its collapse entails a global threat. While it's true that countries differ substantially in their degree of industrialization and degree of integration into global economic systems, these differences do little to inculcate them from the effects of industrial civilization's collapse. Because the reach of the world's most powerful countries, corporations, and oligarchs is global, their actions will eventually affect every other nation. A current example of this is the Middle East, a region that has been suffering decades of warfare and oppression due primarily to the energy scarcity of the world's military and economic powers. As the energy available to powerful political and economic interests wanes, these interests will stop at nothing to control and extract every remaining resource, no matter its location. Richard Heinberg, author of *The Party's Over: Oil, War and the Fate of Industrial Societies*, describes the likely impact of energy scarcity on the United States:

> As energy from fossil fuels starts to decline, the people in control of our political and economic systems will take increasingly desperate measures to keep their hold on power and to keep the privileged lifestyle of their social class intact.... They will step up repression of dissent and wage war on any country that might have resources they want. They will blame "terrorists," "foreign enemies," and "liberals" for our mounting problems and will increasingly erode our constitutional rights.... Theirs is the path of war, environmental degradation, and ultimately the collapse of our industrial society.[162]

The past fifteen years of US foreign policy provide compelling evidence that Heinberg's predictions are already coming to pass – two invasions of Iraq; the invasion of Afghanistan; the overthrow of Libya's Muammar Gaddafi; the close alliance with the oppressive House of Saud; the conflict with Iran; the destabilization of Venezuela, owner of some of the world's largest proven oil reserves; the civil war in Syria; the military encirclement of oil-rich Russia – all of these indicate that the oligarchic game to control the earth's remaining fossil fuels is well afoot. This same drive to extract all available resources is playing out within powerful countries as well, as evidenced by the proliferation of projects seeking to exploit unconventional sources of fossil fuel. The Alberta tar sands, deep-water oil drilling, hydraulic fracturing, and mountain-top removal coal mining are all examples of how the logic of industrial capitalism will not stop until every chance for resource extraction or capital accumulation is exhausted. Within this logic, all the newly exploited regions can do, both domestic and foreign, is either acquiesce or fight for their survival.

My second premise speaks to the late stage of civilization's crisis. There is very little time left to act, and catastrophic tipping points, both ecological and sociopolitical, are looming. Ecologically, the end of cheap fossil fuels will begin exerting steadily mounting pressure on every aspect of life. Despite the momentary spike in production caused by the exploitation of unconventional oil, the era of the peak is likely now, and will soon be followed by an even more acute ecological limit – that of peak fresh water. Scarcity of oil and water will be the two most powerful forces pushing human civilization into escalating cycles of internal and external conflict, a fact that national intelligence agencies are already taking very seriously.[163] Climate change and other forms of ecosystemic degradation will also work synergistically with other limits to exacerbate the overall crisis. These ecological limits are linked intricately to limits in the sociocultural, economic, and political realms, in which catastrophic tipping points include the rise of fascism in several currently "democratic" countries, and another global military conflict. A world war III or IV, depending on how one counts, is an increasingly likely outcome as oligarchic regimes become more authoritarian and ecological limits ripple out through the social system. If oligarchs and militaries continue to monopolize decision-making control, such an outcome appears likely.

My final premise follows logically from the first two. If one desires to avert the crisis of civilization, to avoid collapse, and to transition into a sustainable and humane global system, then one must address the *fundamental dynamics* of the current system. No localized or limited reforms will be sufficient to shift the system's trajectory from collapse to sustainability. No "green capitalism" or "sustainable growth" model will get us there, nor will our current systems of accounting, trade, production, consumption, or decision making. Equally inadequate is the dominant societal consciousness that separates individuals from their environment and from other human beings. Only a process of radical transformation can pull us through the current age of crisis and create the possibility for an ecologically viable and humane future.

Part II
Radical Transformation

7

The Death System

> A society that has lost its life-values will tend to make a religion of death and build up a cult around its worship.   — Lewis Mumford[1]

If oligarchy is the primary force leading civilization to the point of crisis, then it follows that avoiding catastrophe necessitates replacing elite rule with a different system of political decision making, and a different approach to socioeconomic organization. Easy to say, but not so in practice, as generations of political radicals have learned. The power of oligarchs to subject populations and secure their rule is formidable. While oligarchic governments are often unstable, and fall regularly to internal competitors, the oligarchic system itself is remarkably durable. This durability comes in part from the ancient nature of oligarchy, which first emerged over eight thousand years ago, and which soon after spread outward to dominate the planet.

But there was a time prior to the emergence of oligarchy when democratic cooperation was the order of the day. To radically transform oligarchic societies into democratic, sustainable societies, it helps to understand how elite rule first arose and what its defining characteristics are. In this chapter I will consider what anthropological and archaeological research can tell us about the earliest human communities. What was the evolutionary shift that took us from democratic cooperation to the relations of dominance and exploitation that we are now all too familiar with?

The Crisis and Human Nature

When considering the emergence of oligarchy, it is first important to challenge a popular myth. The myth holds that elite rule is ubiquitous because it emerges *naturally*. Prevalent among the Western world's major religious and political philosophers, this belief holds that human societies based on inequality, selfishness, aggression, and violence exist because these are the dominant characteristics of human nature. This can be called the *Hobbesian thesis*, after the seventeenth century English philosopher who claimed: "in the first place, I put for a general inclination of all mankind, a perpetual and restless desire for power after power, that ceaseth only in death."[2] According to Hobbes, humanity's nature was inherently selfish, and the only way that human civilization was possible was for a powerful sovereign to enforce peace.

The idea that oligarchy is based in human nature suggests that it is *inevitable* – and as good as it gets. It's the only form of society that can keep us from the chaotic and violent alternative that would ensue if our nature was allowed to run free, what Hobbes describes as "a time of war, where every man is enemy to every man."[3] This pessimistic sense of human nature has deep historical roots, reaching back to Plato and to early Church philosophers such as Augustine of Hippo. For thousands of years this thesis has been used to justify oligarchic rule, and it continues to have considerable popular appeal today. For many Christians, students of classical economics, and adherents to the secular philosophy of political realism, inherent selfishness seems to elegantly explain the ample evidence of humankind's cruelty and destructiveness. Indeed, if we consider only the dysfunctional social dynamics described in the book so far, then the Hobbesian thesis seems undeniable, and the possibility of building a different civilization appears bleak. However, this picture would be incomplete, and would miss the equally potent moral, cooperative, and democratic impulses that have always formed the basis of human communities.

Modern civilization's crisis is driven by a destructive political and economic system dominated by elite interests, but society did not start out this way. What archaeological and ethnographic research affirms is that the earliest human communities were egalitarian, cooperative, hunter-gatherer bands. This form of society emerged organically from our evolved biological capacities for intelligence, sociality, and empathy. These characteristics formed a *primordial adaptive complex* that enabled the creation of language, culture, and technology. These discoveries made humans one of the most adaptive species on the planet, and enabled us to overcome incredible threats to our survival. Hunter-gatherer communities represent the earliest forms of political democracy, and of ecocentric and sustainable cultures. For tens of thousands of years we lived in these small, highly adaptive bands, until a complex process of environmental and cultural co-evolution led to greater social complexity and eventually to emergent political hierarchies.

First humans: Ethnographic perspectives

Scientists have been able to reconstruct the process of early human evolution by using two lines of evidence. The first concerns the archaeological record, comprising over a hundred years of intensive excavation, analysis, and interpretation by a global community of scientists. The consensus from this research affirms that for about 180,000 years of our approximately 200,000 year history, anatomically modern humans lived in cooperative groups with few noticeable status differences and no clear evidence of inter-group violence or warfare.[4]

The second line of evidence deals with ethnographic studies of modern era pre-state societies. These relatively small-scale cultures, including hunter-gatherers, horticulturalists, pastoralists, and agriculturalists, have long been read as living examples of ancient human societies. While the idea of looking at modern non-state societies as "living fossils" somehow frozen in time is problematic, it *is* valid to draw cautious and limited conclusions from their ethnographic study. Most importantly, these two lines of evidence are used together – with new archaeological discoveries continually rewriting the story of human origins, and ethnographic accounts helping fill in the inevitable interpretive gaps.

The human communities living most closely to the ways of our distant ancestors are known as immediate-return foragers. These groups lack sedentary communities, agriculture, and food storage, and live off of what they immediately hunt and gather from the land. Research shows that the great majority of these groups are *egalitarian* in nature. Anthropologist Polly Wiessner defines egalitarian groups as "societies that maintain equal access of individuals, within age-sex categories, to resources and status positions."[5] Anthropologist James Woodburn notes that in these societies, "individuals have no real authority over each other," and there is no dominance hierarchy among adult male members. Woodburn lists four basic characteristics that define egalitarian immediate-return foraging societies:

1. Social groupings are flexible and constantly changing in composition.
2. Individuals have a choice of whom they associate with in residence, in the food quest, in trade and exchange, and in ritual contexts.
3. People are not dependent on specific other people for access to basic requirements.
4. Relationships between people, whether relationships of kinship or other relationships, stress sharing and mutuality but do not involve long-term binding commitments and dependencies of the sort that are so familiar in delayed-return systems.[6]

Relationships in immediate-return hunter-gatherer societies are not without role distinction and status differences concerning age and gender. Gender roles and relationships are variable among the groups that have been studied, but Woodburn notes that "in all of them women have far more independence than is usual in delayed-return systems."[7] What is common is that a set of behavioural norms bind group members together into a cooperative and highly equal society, in which generosity is encouraged and selfishness, laziness, and domineering behaviour are actively discouraged. Anthropologist Christopher Boehm calls this "moral community" and argues that all human societies exhibit its characteristics to varying degrees.[8]

Ethnographic studies of contemporary and historic egalitarian bands reveal that the equality they experience isn't simply a default extension of human nature, but is actively and creatively enforced through cultural means. Positive social relations are not haphazard, but exist within a framework of cosmological beliefs, moral rules, behavioural sanctions, and creative levelling mechanisms. What these cultural systems accomplish is to create groups that are cohesive and cooperative, with a minimum of disruption caused by conflict, jealousy, or individual power-plays. Christopher Boehm suggests that the main role of this societal type is to manage the disruptive effects of a narrow range of aggressive, "alpha male" behaviour.[9] To Woodburn the ultimate effect is to break people's relationship to personal property and wealth accumulation.[10] In reflecting on the Ju/wasi, a tribe of Kalahari hunter-gatherers, anthropologist Elizabeth Thomas notes the importance of egalitarian social structures in maintaining the bushmen within their ecological niche. Their gathering didn't exhaust the plant life, and their hunting didn't exhaust the animal population. Their subsistence economy maintained a stable population, thus reducing pressure on resources and eliminating conflict due to overcrowding. Ultimately, she argues, through processes of social and ecological feedback, a highly effective, cooperative, and environmentally sustainable culture was created.[11]

Egalitarianism: Archaeological perspectives

The archaeological record provides compelling evidence that environmental conditions have been a key driver of human evolutionary change, and that the emergence and development of egalitarian human cultures involved a process of gene/culture/environment co-evolution, in which all three factors are recursively linked. The first humans evolved in Africa during the Middle Paleolithic (between three hundred thousand and forty thousand years before present, or BP). This period was marked by harsh and rapidly changing climatic conditions that pushed our ancestors to the very brink of extinction.[12] In the face of this environmental challenge, a high degree of cooperation became imperative for group survival. The genetic aspects of cooperative co-evolution involved uniquely human biological adaptations, including an increase in brain size, the development of language ability, and the development of strong social emotions or instincts.[13] An additional impetus for the evolution of egalitarianism came from the empathic and social character of our primate and early hominid ancestors.[14]

What the emergence of cooperative cultures did was to accelerate and intensify the development of our innate social and empathic capacities. Culture allowed humans to take advantage of social learning, and to accumulate and disseminate discoveries and innovations over time.[15] In addition, the non-human environment we developed within provided a constant stream of feedback, as our ability to adapt to changing conditions through biological and cultural means kept us in a state of dynamic equilibrium. The stable populations and low environmental footprint of foraging societies is a testament to this state of sophisticated ecological balance. Of course, saying this is not to assert that pre-agricultural human communities had *no* impact on their environment. As fully modern humans moved into new areas, their hunting would have affected animal populations, as would the entry of any new predator into an established ecosystem. However, the argument that prehistoric hunters had a catastrophic impact on megafauna populations in North America, Asia, and Australia has been seriously challenged. The most recent research shows that climate change was most likely the reason why such species as the woolly mammoth, the giant sloth, and the marsupial lion became extinct.[16]

Moral Community: An Emerging Life System

The social system of ancient egalitarian societies balanced our innate intelligence, empathy, and sociality with moral community and ecological sustainability. Moral community – the original social contract – was a complex and effective means for individual human beings to survive, thrive, and express their unique developmental potential. These societies developed strategies to address the problem of *power-over*, the tendency of a small percentage of hyper-aggressive males to assert dominance over the group. These strategies to check the assertion of dominance included *counter-power*, through political coalitions, and *power-with*, the individual and collective benefits accruing from democratic cooperation. Moral community was able to balance our innate sociality, expressed in a desire to conform to group norms, with our creative intelligence and individuality, expressed in our desire for autonomy, status, and innovation. The blending of these factors formed the crucible of human culture, the most powerful adaptive force ever produced by evolution. Through culture and cooperation early human communities survived and advanced for over 180,000 years. I call this the *Life System*.

Moral community was a highly successful system of adaptation, and yet, not perfect, and early egalitarian societies were also far from perfect. Despite their incredible accomplishments, the struggle for life in the late Pleistocene would have been harsh, and it would be a stretch to assume that communities operated under a sense of enlightened humanism. To say that early human societies were all based on moral rules still leaves many questions about what those rules were. How did they deal with gender differences, mental illness, physical handicap, advanced age, or alternative sexualities? These are all critical concerns inadequately answered by the archaeological and ethnographic records. Because of this, it would be naive to argue that our first human communities were idyllic, or that to solve civilization's current crisis we should seek to "return to the stone age."

We can, though, confidently assert that these first human societies were neither Hobbesian nor despotic. They were structured in a remarkably equal, functional, and ecologically sustainable way. Archaeological evidence suggests a considerable degree of gender equality, with studies suggesting that Neanderthal women may have hunted,[17] that the majority of hand-prints in Paleolithic cave paintings were made by women,[18] and that both women and men likely looked after children.[19] There is also evidence that even very early human communities cared for the elderly and injured. As early as 1.5 million years BP, a female Homo ergaster find demonstrates advanced skeletal pathology that would have rendered her incapacitated, and necessitated years of care.[20] When considering the evidence of cooperation and compassion in human prehistory, it is clear that while there's little to be gained through a literal return to the past, there is much to be gained by understanding the past, and by applying its important lessons to present and future dilemmas.

The irreducible minimum: Adequate food, shelter, and clothing

Moral community is based on the principle that each member of the group has fundamental rights to safety, security, and material sustenance. In *The Ecology of Freedom*, Murray Bookchin refers to the concept of "the irreducible minimum," first proposed by anthropologist Paul Radin to describe the communal nature of early hunter-gatherer societies. After several decades of research, Radin concludes that "all aboriginal peoples accepted the theory that every human being has an inalienable right to an irreducible minimum consisting of adequate food, shelter, and clothing."[21] Bookchin notes that this norm of solidarity was a critical precondition for the free and democratic association found in egalitarian societies:

> Radin's concept of the irreducible minimum rests on an unarticulated principle of freedom. To be assured of the material means of life irrespective of one's productive contribution to the community implies that, wherever possible, society will compensate for the infirmities of the ill, handicapped, and old, just as it will for the limited powers of the very young and their dependency on adults. Even though their productive powers are limited or failing, people will not be denied the means of life that are available to individuals who are well-endowed physically and mentally. Indeed, even individuals who are perfectly capable of meeting all their material needs cannot be denied access to the community's common produce, although deliberate shirkers in organic society are virtually unknown. The principle of the irreducible minimum thus affirms the existence of *inequality* within the group – inequality of physical and mental powers, of skills and virtuosity, of psyches and proclivities. It does so not to ignore these inequalities or denigrate them, but on the contrary, to compensate for them. Equity, here, is the recognition of inequities that are not the fault of anyone and that must be adjusted as a matter of unspoken social responsibility.[22]

Bookchin calls the communal solidarity found in early moral communities the *equality of unequals*, and juxtaposes it with modern, legalistic notions of justice that presuppose equal capability. When the concept of the irreducible minimum is discarded, state-level societies can sustain levels of inequality that would seem completely *inhuman* to the members of egalitarian societies. Under the modern principle of justice in which every person is viewed as equally responsible for their conduct and as equal in their abilities, poverty can be viewed as an individual failing, with the effects of gender and ethoracial prejudice dismissed as "excuses," and the elderly, disabled, and youth viewed as inconvenient "burdens."

A further effect of the irreducible minimum is to enable the democratic participation of all members in group decision making. Democracy can only function when there is equality of access among participants. With guarantees of material sustenance for all, and no inequalities in wealth and power that can be used to assert control over the group, the broadest range of political participation is ensured. The democratic revolutionaries of ancient Athens realized this critical link between economic equality and democracy when they passed laws that required all elected magistrates to be paid. This countered the previous tendency for the wealthy to dominate politics. Before the reforms of Cleisthenes, commoners were too busy working to take time for political action, while the rich man's time was freed by the labour of workers and slaves.[23]

Democracy and adaptive culture

Early human societies reveal that the extent to which a culture is adaptive is directly related to the extent to which its political organization is democratic. Culture has immense power – both for the creation and sustenance of sustainable, moral communities, and also for their potential destruction or exploitation by selfish elites. Culture provided survival benefit to early human groups as long as their social conventions and institutions were adaptive, and as long as reproductive success and high status were associated with ecologically sustainable and altruistic behaviour.

Hunter-gatherer bands lived in intimate contact with the land that sustained them. This gave them immediate feedback in terms of their behaviour, and thus resolved the modern problems of information flow associated with dissociation, scale, and complexity. If a band over-hunted a certain game animal and crashed its population, the feedback was immediate. This could include hunger, the need to relocate – even starvation. With such direct ecosystemic feedback, it is no wonder that most Indigenous cultures contain a powerful sense of the interconnectivity of all beings, and a deep respect for the animal and plant resources that sustain human life.

Democratic hunter-gatherer bands share knowledge equally among their members, creating the ideal environment for cultural innovation. There are no patents or intellectual property rights among hunter-gatherers, and the free and democratic exchange of knowledge gave them the best possible chance of developing new, adaptive cultural practices. This relationship between the production of culturally useful knowledge, in essence *science*, and democracy, remains true to this day.

While egalitarian societies were highly adaptive, cultural evolution also opened a door to the development of maladaptive conventions and institutions. For example, if social conventions dictated that a prestigious lineage of leaders needed to remain "pure" by only allowing marriage among relatives, the resulting genetic degeneration of the lineage would lead to decreased intelligence and increased congenital health defects among leaders, with potentially catastrophic effect. In fact, this maladaptive social convention has arisen several times throughout human history, as pressures to contain political power and economic wealth within a ruling bloodline led to inbreeding, the eventual collapse of the noble line, and significant social turmoil. A historical example is the Spanish Habsburg dynasty, which after eleven generations of mostly in-bred marriage, produced a final heir, Charles II, who was impotent, disfigured, and mentally incapable.[24] In previous chapters I argue that modern civilization is based on a complex web of such maladaptive cultural conventions, from a reliance on dwindling, non-renewable energy sources, to a disposable consumer culture that prioritizes convenience over sustainability. As soon as culture becomes the arbiter of what is considered "desirable," or "good," people can be quite willing to embrace conventions that are ultimately destructive.[25]

Foraging bands were exposed to immediate social, empathic, and environmental feedback mechanisms, and these guarded against maladaptive cultural institutions developing within moral communities. However, as social complexity increased, these feedback mechanisms could become disrupted, allowing maladaptive cultural norms and beliefs to proliferate. The ultimate implication is that as humans increasingly relied on cultural evolution, then control over cultural resources – both cognitive and material – would become an increasingly important source of power. While this knowledge was shared among the members of egalitarian bands it retained its primarily adaptive character, but with increasing social complexity and role specialization, it could be monopolized by elites, and turned into a source of destructive belief and practice.

Competition, group dynamics, and leadership

Early egalitarian societies weren't devoid of competition, conflict, or status differences. Murray Bookchin argues that "organic societies" had status differences, but that these didn't constitute hierarchies.[26] However, research doesn't support this claim, with egalitarian bands having noticeable distinctions in status among adult men, between men and women, and between young and old.[27] My use of the word *hierarchy* reflects these differences in status and prestige, and yet it is not indicative of relationships based on political domination, or on institutionalized inequalities in wealth. Early foraging societies may have been hierarchical, but they were undoubtedly minimally hierarchical, and most importantly, politically egalitarian. In contrast, oligarchic societies are characterized by relations of domination and institutionalized inequalities in wealth.

A similar caveat applies to my description of the primordial adaptive complex. As a species human beings may be best described by our cooperation, empathy, and creative intelligence, but as individuals and groups we can also be xenophobic, selfish, aggressive, lazy, dishonest, and a host of other less-than-noble traits. Our very nature makes our behaviour heterogeneous and unpredictable. Similarly, democratic community doesn't imply homogeneity, stasis, or a lack of conflict. The genius of early egalitarian societies wasn't that they were inhabited by somehow different, "better" versions of our modern selves, but that our natural tendencies to jockey for status and prestige were consciously directed toward group-sustaining ends, while simultaneously preventing prestige leadership based on influence and persuasion from turning into oligarchic leadership based on dominance and coercion.

The kind of leadership present in egalitarian societies is instructive. First, from the available evidence, it seems that what made egalitarian societies politically equal wasn't necessarily a lack of leadership. While it's true that some egalitarian groups like the Hadza appear leaderless, it's also true that many others had recognizable leaders in the form of big men, or of shamans and elders who could be either male or female. The important element of egalitarian societies is how leadership was constituted – what qualities led to one being considered a leader, and what duties, powers, and responsibility were attributed to leadership.

Research has shown that leaders in egalitarian societies tended to be the members who most embodied altruistic and cooperative values. Individuals who expressed selfish or domineering qualities were considered unfit for leadership. As well, leaders lacked coercive power, and instead acted as facilitators of a democratic group decision-making process. Leaders used persuasion within the decision-making process, but their influence went only so far as their perceived prestige within the group. Other members would listen to leaders to the extent that they respected them, and felt the leaders represented their individual and collective interests.[28] Of course, even this limited, persuasive power of leadership could be potentially dangerous if used for personal gain, or in ways that impair the function of the group. These are very real threats, and this is why egalitarian societies also developed checks and balances to the power of leaders in the form of political levelling systems (such as norms governing the distribution of food and the resolution of conflicts).

The secret of success for egalitarian societies doesn't necessarily lie in the material conditions that facilitate their development. Although environmental pressures played an important role in encouraging cooperation and egalitarianism as gene/culture adaptations, the adaptive complex that resulted is not tied to a particular level of technology or system of economics. Egalitarian bands are adaptive because their moral relationships embody the concept of *interbeing*, a term coined by Vietnamese Buddhist monk Thich Nhat Hanh. Interbeing is the knowledge that one's existence, self-identity, and self-fulfillment are inseparable from other human beings and from the natural world.[29] For our ancestors this concept of self and community was the conscious embodiment of a fundamental scientific fact, and this is what gave it such adaptive power.

The Life System

Ultimately, human nature and moral communities combined to enable early humans to adapt, survive, and thrive in the face of incredible threats to their existence. The resulting pattern of interaction can be considered a Life System that maintains human communities in ecological symbiosis with their natural environment, and balances our innate autonomy and individuality with the good of the group. The Life System –

- Emerges from the primordial adaptive complex, the three key aspects of human nature that spurred on cultural development:
  1. *creative intelligence:* complex consciousness that enables creativity, individuality, behavioural innovation, and behavioural diversity
  2. *empathy:* well-developed social instincts, including the ability to sense the emotional state of others and to be impacted by this state
  3. *sociality:* an inclination honed through the learned advantage of living in highly cooperative groups
- Is reinforced through *moral community*, that is cultures based on democratic political association, in which potentials for competitive, selfish, and antisocial behaviour are managed and directed toward adaptive, group-supporting ends. Social controls are primarily non-coercive, and coercive only in the face of severe anti-social behaviour that threatens the survival and viability of the group. Moral community protects human individuality and creativity while balancing them with cooperation, stability, and ecological sustainability.
- Has an ecologically sustainable economy; it does not destroy the land base on which it survives.
- Is based on the *irreducible minimum* in which all have free and equal access to the means of subsistence and production, and in which each individual is free to pursue their unique developmental potential.
- Is based on *transparency* and *accountability* of leadership, decision-making processes, and social institutions.
- Has free and equal access to cultural information.
- Has leadership based on prestige, not domination.

- Is based on *interbeing*, that is, empathically based collective identities that bind members of the group to each other and to the biosphere. This sense of interconnection can lead to tribalism, but it can also be expanded to embrace those once considered "the other." In the latter case, interbeing can lead to *biosphere consciousness* in which we consider all human and non-human lives as members of our extended family and as having inherent value.[30]

The Life System describes the pattern of social interaction prevalent at the dawn of human societies. We are uniquely equipped to live in these egalitarian, democratic communities. Our ability to do so, however, depends on our conscious regulation of the material conditions and cultural norms under which we live. We don't have to exist at a stone-age level of technology to re-establish moral community in the present day, but we do need to ensure that any political and economic system, including the nation state, adheres to the principles of the irreducible minimum and the social-ecological fact of interbeing.

This intentional structuring of relationships is critical, because human behavioural diversity and complexity means that our actions can vary significantly under different social contexts. If we are raised in a culture that glorifies conflict, competition, and individual gain, then our natural empathy and sociality will be twisted, and we will tend to manifest these anti-social behaviours. Indeed, such a cultural shift is what happened with the emergence of formal hierarchies and fully oligarchic societies.

The Fateful Turn

There are numerous theories concerning how inequalities in wealth, status, and political power first emerged from egalitarian moral communities. For Murray Bookchin, as he argues in *The Ecology of Freedom*, it was inherent social divisions based on gender, age-ranking, and religion that were the first to destabilize equality. Bookchin argues that these three forms of social differentiation were present in primordial organic societies, with each of them containing the potential to promote hierarchy and inequality. When combined with the radical changes in social structure and practice brought on by sedentary living and economic surplus, the result is the flowering of latent status distinctions into full-fledged class distinctions. Bookchin argues that this transition didn't occur until Neolithic villages evolved into or were subsumed by more complex and socially stratified chiefdoms and archaic states.[31] However, several other scholars trace the pivotal moments of oligarchy's genesis to earlier, less complex tribal societies. The anthropological literature describes these transitional forms between egalitarianism and oligarchy as *transegalitarian*, and research has provided key insights into this critical period of cultural evolution.

Transegalitarian research points to a number of possible "pathways to power."[32] Each of the proposed theories involves the interaction between *structure* and *agency* – the power of social institutions and environments to mould behaviour, and the power of individuals to in turn influence social institutions in their own interests.[33]

Sociologist Anthony Giddens provides a useful concept to express the dialectic between structure and agency, and to show how this interaction can lead, over time, to radically different social institutions. He describes a process of *structuration*, whereby individuals are able to use their personal power, or agency, to achieve positions of influence within society, and to use this influence for their own benefit.[34] A proficient hunter in an egalitarian band, for example, may use the honour of distributing meat as an opportunity to build power within the group by disproportionately rewarding his close kin. If the "big man" is successful in creating a kin-based network that supports his desire for increased decision-making and wealth-distributing power, there is a chance these relationships can become hereditary, and passed on to subsequent generations. Over time, this can lead to institutionalized inequality between an elite family and other families in the group. In this way an individual act of agency has become a social structure – a cultural institution that shapes future behaviour. To subsequent generations, this changed relationship can be perceived as "just the way things are done."

Researchers identify several potential mechanisms through which egalitarian moral communities could transition into unequal, hierarchical societies. Following Bookchin, one mechanism highlights the primordial status differences that exist, in managed form, within egalitarian societies. These status differences can involve gender, age, lineage, or group prestige.[35] Another mechanism focuses on how class divisions can arise from increasing social complexity caused by economic and environmental changes.[36] Researchers have also hypothesized that inequality could emerge from a division of labour and role specialization that initially benefited the group, but which later enabled political domination.[37] In contrast, other researchers point to the role of aggressive, domineering individuals as consciously manipulating social institutions to their benefit.[38] Finally, some researchers highlight the importance of ideological changes in supporting emerging inequality. In particular, the role of religion is focused on, and the power of early religious specialists, or shamen, to monopolize spiritual and cultural power.[39] Complex interactions between these variables, research conclusions suggest, were likely responsible for the transition from egalitarianism to social stratification. This process was variable, uneven, and marked by defeats and reversals. Eventually though, a combination of structural pressures, combined with despotic agency, gave birth to the first truly oligarchic societies.

What most researchers agree on is that powerful sources of stress that acted to disrupt early egalitarian societies included changes to climate, to the mode of economic production, to dwelling patterns, and to population size. The production of greater amounts of food on a more reliable basis led first to an increased population carrying capacity among communities that had switched to plant and animal domestication. Increased population tends to necessitate more complex forms of political coordination and decision making. It can also lead to more conflict, especially if a lack of room to expand leads to significantly higher population density. Anthropologists call this pressure for spatially concentrated resources *circumscription*, and prominent theorists of emerging social complexity, like Robert Carneiro, argue that it was a key motivator of Neolithic cultural evolution.[40] Increased conflict due to circumscription can then lead to the need for more sophisticated mechanisms of social regulation. In anthropological terms, these early communities began moving from a *band* level of social organization to a *tribal* level. This occurs when a number of bands come together or when a band settles down, shifts to a sedentary horticultural lifestyle, and experiences population growth. Early tribal societies made distinctions between different groups within the community based on kinship, and the coordination of different groups within settlements necessitated more active participation by leaders, and more formal processes of decision making and dispute resolution.[41]

Combined with the development of storage technologies, surplus production in early horticultural societies could also become a potential source of inequality. Individuals or groups that were able to control the productive surplus would be able to influence political processes and to amass wealth in the form of personal property. Surplus could also be used to support non-food-producing members of the group, thus enabling increased social complexity in the form of political, economic, administrative, military, and religious specialists. With the increase in social complexity, conflict and warfare between groups also emerged for the first time as a regular threat.[42]

With the evolutionary feedback system created by increased food production, storage of surplus food, population growth, sedentarism, and increasing social complexity, egalitarian societies were faced with an incredible challenge. The factors that had caused moral community to flourish – harsh climate, scarce and unreliable food resources, small groups, sparse population, nomadic existence, no surplus production – were all irrevocably changed. Unchanged, however, were our evolved sociality, empathy, and creative intelligence. Cooperative cultures were still the life-blood of human societies, but these societies were now buckling under pressures they had never before encountered, and under time scales that were incredibly rapid. In response to these pressures cultures adapted as best they could, but tragically, many of the cultural adaptations to environmental and economic pressures generated new pressures that communities were equally ill-equipped to withstand. This positive feedback effect has been described by archaeologists as an "evolutionary ratchet," a dialectical process of change that tends to push societies in a given direction, and to make it more difficult for them to revert to earlier forms.[43] In this case, the ratchet effect of increasing social complexity led to an increase in hierarchy, and eventually to the emergence of full-blown oligarchy.

One of the ways in which evolving complexity might have led to institutionalized social stratification is through a process that has been described as *power-to*, in which individuals or groups within a community are tasked with special social roles. These roles may start out as functional for the group, but their specialized status and exclusive access to resources and information creates a danger of the role being exploited for selfish benefit.[44] Examples of groups afforded power to fulfill important social roles include people tasked with conducting trade; groups who produced certain items or did certain work – such as weavers, potters, masons; groups who performed administrative functions, such as priests who oversaw and accounted for agricultural surplus; and leaders who organized ritual practices. Finally, an important group that was given power-to by the community were warriors. With the advent of increasing between-group conflict caused by sedentary living and growing population, having an effective defensive and offensive capacity would have gained in importance. As the need for warriors intensified, their status within the group would increase as well.

Rise of the Oligarchs

Working through the archaeological and ethnographic evidence, we begin to get a sense of the immense pressures that sedentary living and agriculture began to place on prehistoric societies. These pressures spur changes to social structures, create new opportunities for exploitation by aggressive alpha males, and in some communities lead to the eventual emergence of formal hierarchies and institutionalized inequalities in wealth. To understand the evolution of political power as bands transitioned into ranked tribal societies, and then into chiefdoms and later archaic states, some additional theoretical context is helpful.

In the collection *Studying War*, anthropologist Stephen Reyna presents a framework that categorizes different societal types based on their "mode of domination," or the particular way in which social, political, and economic power is exercised by societal elites. Reyna starts his analysis by defining political power in a Hobbesian sense, as the ability of a person or group of people to control the actions of another individual or group. Implied in this definition is the ability to enforce behaviour that others would prefer not to engage in, or which is against their objective material interests. This definition is similar to that used by several critical sociologists and political theorists, including Marx, and is often synonymous with the idea of *domination* – in which power is exercised with coercive force.[45] Another term for this is *power-over,* and it aptly describes the forms of political power exercised by the seventeenth century absolutist monarchy, or, in modified form, by government in the nineteenth century "democratic" capitalist state.

However, when considering *egalitarian* and *transegalitarian* societies, the notion of power as domination doesn't accurately describe social relations. In egalitarian bands, power is instead expressed in a consensual and directly democratic way, as *power-with*. This form of power describes the ability of a group to work together in accomplishing common goals. It may involve certain individuals being persuaded or even pressured to endorse a particular course of action, but no one is forced to accept a decision, and every member of the community has input into making and implementing decisions. As philosopher Joanna Macy writes, "Power-with . . . is not a property one can own, but a process one engages in."[46] It describes individuals and groups who accomplish their objectives without using coercion or force on others. Reyna argues that within these kinds of societies, leaders actually have *no* capacity for domination, and no ability to use violence to force compliance.

Where power begins to take on more of a Hobbesian cast is when persuasive egalitarian leadership turns into the more coercive persuasion of big men in ranked societies. These leaders have more resources and greater personal prestige with which to influence group decision-making processes, and as a result their application of power moves closer to domination. As the ability of leaders to force compliance is still weak in these contexts, leaders accomplish selfish goals primarily through the use of deceit. Actions ostensibly taken in the public good conceal aggrandizing intentions, and allow leaders to amass more influence than previously possible. However, this application of power is still highly mediated by a need to provide community benefit and to accede to the wishes of less powerful group members. In transegalitarian societies, power is constantly negotiated, regularly questioned and challenged, and often unsuccessfully mobilized. Big men have limited ability to directly enforce their will over others by violence, and must therefore rely on prestige and guile to achieve their ends. The leaders' ultimately selfish goals can be realized to the extent that they can convince their subordinates that they (the leaders) are acting in the interests of their subjects.[47]

The power wielded by aggrandizing big men in tribal societies begins taking on a *hegemonic* character. Recalling chapter 1, hegemony refers to a form of political power in which elite authority is based on a mix of both coercion and consent. As articulated by Italian Marxist philosopher Antonio Gramsci, the concept of hegemony reflects the realization that even the most brutal and despotic states – in Gramsci's case the Fascist government of Benito Mussolini – maintain their power at least in part by the perceived legitimacy of rulers in the eyes of those they rule. Gramsci was one of the leaders of the Italian Communist Party, and was captured and imprisoned by Mussolini. While incarcerated he wrote extensively on philosophy, art, and politics, producing a collection of manuscripts that have become known as *The Prison Notebooks*. Central to Gramsci's writing was the question of how socialist movements failed to take power during the governmental crises that swept Europe after World War I. In his reflections, Gramsci concludes that a key reason for this defeat was that revolutionaries had failed to fully realize the ideological and consensual nature of power in nominally democratic, capitalist states. When combined with the state's capacity for coercive force, the ideological nature of hegemonic power proves remarkably durable, and necessitates different strategies if it is to be resisted and eventually overthrown.[48]

If rulers in hegemonic societies exercise power through both consensus and coercion, then tribal societies with decentralized leadership can't yet be considered fully hegemonic. Lacking coercive power, aggrandizing leaders instead had to rely on building a kind of "rigged consensus," in which subordinates were encouraged, or tricked, to participate in exploitative schemes. As noted by anthropologist Brian Hayden, this process is similar to the Marxist conception of *false consciousness*, where subordinate classes are convinced to act in ways that are against their own interests.[49] However, this scenario only captures one aspect of hegemonic consensus. The other aspect involves the actual benefit that leaders provide to their communities as a result of public pressure, counter-power coalitions, gossip, and other forms of democratic control. Part of the reason hegemonic power is a negotiated process is because it *has* to be. Elites can only maintain their position by giving in to some of the demands made by those they rule.⁵⁰ In *Marxism and Literature* Raymond Williams writes about this quality of hegemonic power: "it does not just passively exist as a form of dominance. It has continually to be renewed, recreated, defended, and modified. It is also continually resisted, limited, altered, challenged by pressures not at all its own."⁵¹ The concept of hegemony sees elite domination as a process, as a set of different strategies and structures of power, each involving a dynamic and shifting mix of consensus (power-to) and coercion (power-over).

Gramsci contrasts power formed through hegemony with rule through force, or dictatorship. Rule by force is based purely on dominance and coercion, and in such cases the elite class lacks legitimacy in the eyes of the ruled and is generally unresponsive to subordinate interests.⁵² An example would be a colonial government within an empire, such as the British Raj in India. The government of Vichy France represented rule by force, as do modern conditions of military occupation, such as the NATO mission in Afghanistan, or the Israeli occupation of the West Bank and Gaza strip. With rule by force, the coercive power of elites is at its most despotic, and is also displayed in its most naked form. The ruled have no illusions that their masters share their interests, and the only things maintaining structures of governance are the threat and application of violence. In situations of rule by force, there is generally constant rebellion, often violent and implacable, on behalf of the subordinate population. In contrast, elites in hegemonic societies, while still utilizing coercion, maintain supremacy primarily through the power of cultural legitimacy, and also through negotiation. As a result, political power in hegemonic societies is much more stable. Even if the objective material relationship between ruler and ruled is despotic and predatory, this quality of domination is largely veiled to subordinate groups. In this sense, hegemony functions most effectively when it makes despotic power "invisible," presenting structures of domination and inequality as merely "common sense" or "tradition."⁵³

Research has shown how aggrandizers in transegalitarian societies began the process of constituting what would later become fully hegemonic power. Growing control over the accumulation and distribution of economic surplus, and over trade and warfare, developed new capacities for coercion. At the same time, elaborate feasting, kinship structures, and religion were used to increase the ruler's legitimacy, and to veil their exploitative intentions.⁵⁴ As the positive feedback system of circumscription (scarcity of territorially specific resources), population explosion, and growing social complexity accelerated, this pre-hegemonic modality of power evolved into fully hegemonic form in the first chiefdoms and archaic (early) states. It is important to stress that this evolutionary process was not *unilineal*, and does not represent a *necessary* series of stages that all societies moved through. If anything, research shows that it was exceedingly rare for the nascent hierarchies of rank societies to transform into *oligarchic* societies in which a small elite class was able to establish hegemony over a much larger group of subordinate classes.[55] In many cases complexity did not lead to oligarchy, and even the early city-states of ancient Sumeria appear to have maintained several egalitarian characteristics.[56] However, once oligarchy had been established in just a few agricultural communities, the trajectory of human evolution was forever altered.

In oligarchy, an elite class assumes hegemonic control over society, largely directing the productive capacity of that society toward elite interests. Contrary to the Hobbesian thesis, oligarchy does not constitute *productive* power, so much as it constitutes *exploitative* power. The productive capacity of societies remains grounded in the Life System, in the empathic familial relationships that reproduce necessary social labour, and in the cooperative institutions that enable complex economies and provide the basis for shared identity, cultural innovation, and cultural adaptation.

What oligarchy *does* constitute are increasingly pervasive and determining structures of domination and exploitation.[57] The impetus for evolving structures of domination arises as societies fall under this *oligarchic imperative* and resistance to the elite agenda grows. Democratic pushback, including open rebellion, necessitates oligarchs developing more effective means of controlling the populace they are exploiting. Historically this has led to developments in elite capacities for surveillance, social and economic sanctions, ideological manipulation, and violence. At the same time, oligarchs strive to make the basic economic relationships within society more effectively exploitative. This has involved devising more efficient means of extracting surplus value from the labour of subordinate classes, whether by work obligations, slavery, wage economies, taxation, military service, or fines.

There is strong evidence that the need to manage antagonisms between elite and subordinate classes played a key role in the emergence of the state – with its codified laws, monopoly on violence, and formalized systems of exploitation (slavery, taxation, conscription, feudalism, wage labour), as Engels describes in the *Origin of the Family, Private Property and the State*:

> As the state arose from the need to keep class antagonisms in check, but also arose in the thick of the fight between the classes, it is normally the state of the most powerful, economically dominant class, which by its means becomes also the politically dominant class and so acquires new means of holding down and exploiting the oppressed class. The ancient

state was, above all, the state of the slave owners for holding down the slaves, just as the feudal state was the organ of the nobility for holding down the peasant serfs and bondsmen, and the modern representative state is an instrument for exploiting wage labour for capital.[58]

Two tools used by oligarchs to assert their power over subordinates are *essentialism* and *reification*. Elites in archaic states began distinguishing between commoner and aristocratic classes, and asserting that differences between the two groups were innate, or ascribed. Similarly, the fluid, gendered division of labour found in egalitarian societies was re-cast as an essentialized divide between men and women, with women seen as innately inferior.[59] As chiefdoms and states expanded through military conquest, subjected people were also seen as innately inferior, and as "natural" slaves.[60]

Reification is a process whereby a social construction is presented as natural, eternal, and necessary. Elites reified the nation, state, religious, and leadership structures that ensured their power. Oligarchic rule was affirmed as the natural "order of the universe," and was equated with society itself.[61]

Contradictions of Oligarchy

Once the oligarchic imperative takes hold within a society, elites strive to increase powers of exploitation and domination to maximize their wealth and political power. Feedback processes resulting from these twin priorities then give rise to two contradictions – one social, the other ecological.

Social contradiction

The desire by elites to intensify exploitation of subordinate classes leads to increasingly onerous demands placed on society's producers, growing inequalities in wealth and property, and growing poverty. The drive to extract as much social wealth as possible begins degrading the capacity of society's life-sustaining structures, leading to ruptures in kin relationships and cooperative systems. This assault on the collective "social fabric" is similar to Marx's argument that capitalism led to the progressive immiseration of the working class.[62] It is also echoed in philosopher John McMurtry's *The Cancer Stage of Capitalism*, in which he argues that the profit motive, delinked from any moral or ecological constraint, acts as a self-replicating, cancerous growth on the Lifeworld – the cooperative and life-sustaining aspects of human societies.[63]

However, this corrosive effect of increasing inequality isn't just limited to capitalist modes of production, but is an incipient characteristic of any oligarchic system. The ultimate effect of the drive to increase exploitation is that the hegemonic basis of elite power is destabilized. Increased hardship for subordinate groups fractures the value consensus between elite and subordinate. The ideological veil of power-to (that elites rule in the interest of subordinates) is stripped back to expose a stark core of power-over, and hegemony is revealed as dictatorial rule. As a result, through social contradiction the oligarchic imperative actively undermines the conditions for its own existence.

This tendency for oligarchic societies to collapse under elite domination and exploitation has been noted by several theorists. Archaeologist Jonathan Haas points out that elite power is costly to maintain, requiring significant economic resources. Should these resources diminish, the ability of elites to project power is undermined:

> In a state with a weakened economic power base, exercising power over the population is not only more expensive and less effective, but the power structure itself is more open to internal conflict and strife. Such a state is thus more susceptible either through self-destruction of the power structure, revolution of the population, or a combination thereof.[64]

In a seminal study of imperial civilizations, sociologist Shmuel Eisenstadt makes a similar argument to Haas – noting that two of the main factors leading to the destabilization or collapse of empires include the aggrandizing political goals of elites and their over-exploitation of resources obtained from subordinate classes. Both can lead to the de-legitimization of elites and the widespread desertion or rebellion of members of the exploited class.[65]

The social contradiction of oligarchy deepens when deteriorating conditions caused by hyper-exploitation lead to resistance and rebellion from subordinate groups. This challenge to elite rule then primes the second part of the imperative, as oligarchs seek to stabilize their power and improve their capacity for domination. This second feedback cycle tends to lead to increasingly authoritarian forms of governance and to "police states" in which surveillance, oppressive law, and repressive violence become more important tools of maintaining social order. Building up elite capacities for domination then further intensifies exploitative pressures, as extra resources go toward the military, internal security forces, and mechanisms of punishment and control (courts, prisons). (For an illustration of the social contradiction of oligarchy, see figure 7.1)

The social contradiction set in motion by intensifying cycles of exploitation and domination generally puts excessive demands on the polity's productive and reproductive capacities. This excessive demand can result in a number of possible outcomes. The first entails a reformist strategy by elites designed to re-establish hegemonic balance. A segment of the oligarchic class negotiate a de-escalation of their desire for wealth accumulation and political control in return for social stability. An example of this strategy is the post-war compromise between capital and labour in North America following World War II. In exchange for recognizing trade unions and enacting labour laws, capitalists were able to continue profiting from the exploitative industrial wage economy. This example shows that negotiation by elites can lead to objective improvements in the lot of subordinate classes; however, it serves primarily to maintain the essentially despotic relationship between rulers and ruled. This is the strategy favoured by elites seeking to rule more by consensus than coercion. It can re-stabilize a polity, but is generally a short-term condition due to the continued presence of the oligarchic imperative and the desire of elites to increase wealth. As such, after a time, the social contradiction reasserts itself, social resources are once more overtaxed, and the hegemonic balance is once more threatened.

Figure 7.1. Social contradiction of oligarchy

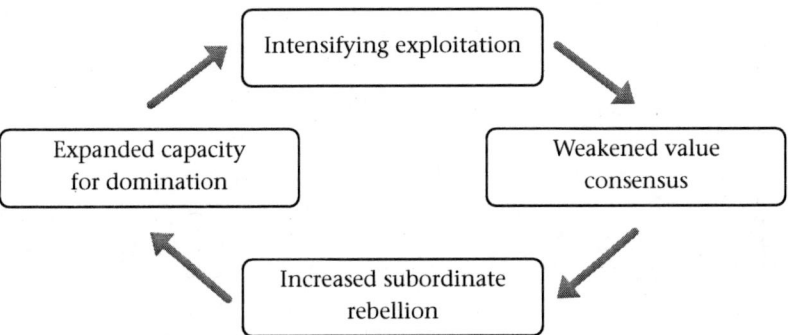

Because the reformist strategy implies a diminution of elite wealth and power, it is often unpopular among the ruling class, and can lead to a schism within the class and internal competition between reformist and predatory camps. This danger leads oligarchs to favour a second strategy to resolve excessive resource demands that involves extracting wealth from other societies through intimidation or violent conquest.

Waging war provides several benefits to oligarchs. First, unlike the strategy of hegemonic negotiation, which actually diminishes the exploitative and despotic capacities of oligarchs, waging war tends to increase both. As oligarchs are always in control of the military structure, allocating resources to warfare enables leaders to directly benefit in terms of personal wealth (derived from salaries, pillage, or production of war materiel) and increased repressive capability. Creating standing armies, increasing their ranks, and improving their weaponry allows rulers to extract resources through conquest, but also enables more effective use of violence to control their own populace. Second, the ability to successfully wage war enables oligarchs to capture land, extract tribute, capture slaves, and eliminate potential political and economic competitors. Finally, mobilizing for warfare enables elites to exploit group-related empathic boundary markers and to create an "us against them" mentality that builds social cohesion and increases the perceived legitimacy of rulers.[66]

When examining historic examples of chiefdoms and states, it soon becomes apparent that the strategy of oligarchic war-making, while generally attractive and productive for elites in the short-run, over the long-term proves just as unstable as the strategy of hegemonic negotiation. Attempting to solve the social contradiction of oligarchy by ever greater violent expansion creates its own insurmountable contradictions. As such, oligarchic societies regularly fall prey to either a revolutionary overthrow of elites, or else the complete dissolution of the polity. In the first case elites are deposed either by a competitor group within the ruling class, or else by a counter-hegemonic coalition of non-elite social groups. Depending on the political bent of the usurping group, such revolutions can radically shift the hegemonic basis of society, either temporarily resolving the social contradiction, or in other cases exacerbating it. The latter case can occur when an elite group pursuing a strategy of hegemonic negotiation is overthrown by another elite faction, which considered the old rulers to be "too weak." Twentieth century Fascist coups in Germany, Italy, and Spain are examples of this form of reactionary revolution.

Ecological contradiction

What I argue is that ultimately, oligarchic societies throughout history have collapsed under their internal contradictions. Anthropologist Joyce Marcus has identified this tendency in seven archaic states – the Maya, Zapotec, Central Mexican, Andean, Mesopotamian, Egyptian, and Aegean. Her "dynamic model" describes a cycle in which early states form through competition and warfare between oligarchic chiefdoms, collapse into sub-state polities through continued warfare and competition, and then potentially reform in second or third generation states.[67] The cycle of collapse noted by Marcus is partly due to the social contradiction, but also to an equally powerful ecological contradiction. For, as the oligarchic imperative places excessive demands on the socioeconomic system, it also places excessive demands on the biotic systems that sustain it. As subsistence and other economic production intensifies to meet elite demands for wealth, ecosystem resources like food-producing land, water, energy, raw materials, and wildlife are critically depleted. The resulting scarcity of environmental inputs leads to economic and social crises, and can cause intense unrest and political instability. In response to the resource-crunch, oligarchs invariably respond with the strategy of waging war to acquire new territory and necessary resources.

As can be seen in figure 7.2, the ecological contradiction results in a vicious circle of environmental crisis followed by territorial expansion and intensified environmental exploitation. These cycles eventually end when resources become circumscribed, either by an oligarchic society encountering neighbours it can't defeat militarily (political circumscription), or by natural limits to resource availability (such as, exhausting the supply of a given raw material, wiping out a population of game animals, or using up all the available arable land in a region). A historical example of the ecological contradiction is the Easter Island civilization, which destroyed its forests in a competition between oligarchs.

Figure 7.2. Ecological contradiction

```
         Intensifying exploitation
         of ecosystemic resources
        ↗                        ↘
Warfare and territorial      Critical depletion of
     expansion               ecosystemic resources
        ↖                        ↙
         Economic, social, and
            political crises
```

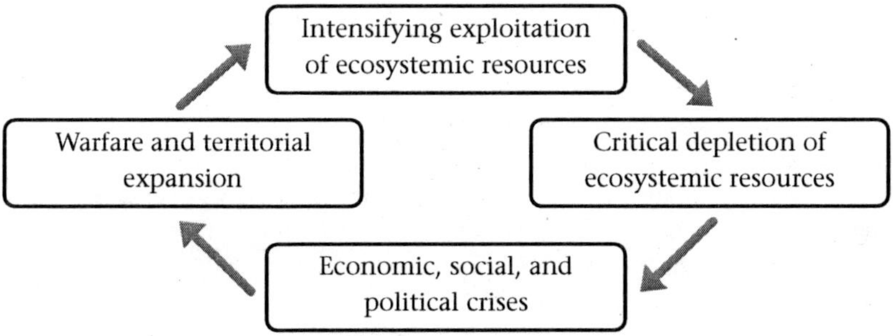

To revisit the analysis presented in chapters 2 through 6, the oligarchic imperative leads inexorably to both ecological overshoot, and to deepening social crisis. In the present day these two factors, when combined with the global scale of industrial capitalist civilization, will lead to the same ultimate end. A globalized economy entails the ultimate resource circumscription, as space quickly dwindles in the face of relentless expansion by numerous oligarchic polities.

When considering their recurring social and ecological crises, and their near-inevitable tendencies toward collapse, oligarchic societies can be considered manifestations of a *Death System* that preys upon and undermines the earlier social structures of moral community. While the term may seem dramatic, it precisely captures the inherent contradictions that drive oligarchies, along with their ultimate outcome. For human beings, the result is intensifying cycles of exploitation, violent repression, and war. For the biosphere, it is mass extinctions and ecosystemic collapse.

Collapse

Once oligarchic societies emerged, social life was changed drastically and irrevocably from its egalitarian origins. Whereas the first humans lived remarkably free and equal lives in cooperative and supportive groups, citizens in archaic states were rigidly stratified into social classes. For the aristocracy this meant unprecedented wealth and power – the finest food and clothes, palatial residences, personal servants, lives free from toil, and the power of life and death over their subordinates. For the great majority this meant some measure of servitude with life controlled by the whim of superiors in the socioeconomic hierarchy. For the underclass that made up the bulk of state inhabitants, life also became an exercise in harsh toil, brutal exploitation, and diminished health.[68] This sharp increase in material inequality is arguably the most noticeable change from egalitarian to oligarchic societies. Inequality has steadily increased as hunter-gatherer bands developed into tribal societies, chiefdoms, and agrarian states.

Oligarchic states tend to be politically unstable, environmentally destructive, and prone to collapse. The oligarchic imperative for increasing power and wealth leads to two contradictions – one social, the other ecological – that put unsustainable pressures on the social, economic, political, and ecological foundations of civilization. These same contradictions are driving modern industrial capitalism to collapse, a prediction supported by numerous historical examples.

When discussing this historical tendency toward collapse, two caveats need to be mentioned. First, throughout history, societies at various levels of complexity have faced collapse. Oligarchic civilizations may be particularly prone to this fate, but not predestined to it. Similarly, politically decentralized societies are much less likely to collapse, but are also not wholly immune to it. A second caveat is that any society collapses due to several different pressures that act on it and that combine to overcome its organizing and stabilizing capacities. Warfare with surrounding neighbours, environmental catastrophe, climate change, human-made environmental destruction, energy scarcity, internal revolt, and oligarchic power struggles have all contributed to the collapse of politically centralized societies throughout history. This is why archaeologists like Joseph Tainter argue that what leads to collapse isn't one pressure, but a constellation of pressures that eventually overwhelms a society's adaptive capacity.[69]

Complexity vs. Oligarchy

If you recall from the introduction, Tainter maintains that civilizations, like all human societies, are "problem-solving organizations" that have to constantly contend with internal and external challenges to their viability. He argues that what historical civilizations have done in response to challenges is to enact solutions based on increasing complexity. This has meant more intensive agricultural production, more government hierarchy and bureaucracy, more intensive resource extraction (minerals, fish, water), more intensive technology use, and more intensive information collection and processing. These strategies work well at first, but as civilizations increase in size and complexity, intensification in each of these areas is subject to the law of diminishing returns. In essence, with each unit of effort spent in complexity in any of these areas, one gets increasingly less payoff in terms of viability. This is because complexity is energy intensive, and therefore solving a problem of energy scarcity with solutions that increase energy demand leads eventually to the social and ecological contradictions just discussed.[70]

Tainter's understanding of collapse is echoed by Jared Diamond. Diamond subtitles his book on societal collapse *How Societies Choose to Fail or Succeed*, and focuses on the ability of societies to make crucial decisions in the face of serious threats to their sustainability. In their writing, both Diamond and Tainter make the point that, while several threats are always implicated in societal collapse, its actual occurrence is due rather to the failure of the society, as a "problem-solving organization," to adapt to the challenges it faces. Tainter does include inequality and oligarchic governance as variables contributing to societal collapse, but diminishes them in favour of the central contradiction between societal complexity and available energy. While this is an important insight, what I've argued in this book, and what Tainter and Diamond overlook, is the profound constraint that oligarchy places on collective decision making and the resulting impact this has on our ability to respond to crisis. Without this realization, Tainter's argument about complexity serves to hide more than it reveals.

Tainter makes the assumption that added complexity always entails greater energy usage – an assumption worth critiquing. Yes, this relationship holds for many cases, such as when expanding populations run out of locally available resources and decide to import resources using energy intensive trade networks, to secure them using technologically intensive strategies such as irrigation networks, or to seize them using military means. This is a dynamic that has played out since the dawn of cities and archaic states and *does* lead to diminishing returns on energy invested.

However, Tainter misses that there are other options available to societies. They can choose between *different kinds of complexity*, or even between solving a problem with complexity, or solving it in a way that is *non-complex*, or even *less complex*. As an example, we can look at the contemporary United States – a massive, highly industrialized state with an equally massive demand for energy. For years this energy has been provided primarily by fossil fuels, which until the 1980s were largely produced domestically. However, as domestic production of conventional oil peaked in the 1970s, the reliance of the United States on foreign oil began to increase, reaching a height of 60 per cent in 2006.[71] From an energy perspective, the United States was facing a severe crisis at this point – a challenge to its viability and a test of its decision-making systems.

In the face of such an energy crisis, Tainter's model would suggest only one option – more complexity, and a slide further down the diminishing returns on energy complexity slope. However, is this really the case? Isn't it possible, in the face of a 60 per cent reliance on foreign oil, to imagine several different societal responses? One is to launch military adventures overseas to secure oil resources. One is to invest massive amounts of capital into attempts to extract "unconventional" fossil fuel sources such as deep-water wells, shale oil, and shale gas. One is to undertake a massive campaign to promote energy efficiency and reduce energy consumption in industry, transportation, and residences. One is to begin the massive process of shifting the US economy from a reliance on fossil fuels to one based on renewable solar and wind energy. All of these options can be seen as adding "complexity" to the US social system, but clearly not all of them have the same implications for the diminishing returns on energy trap. By focusing only on complexity, Tainter is unable to explain what actually happened in response to the US energy crisis – how the first two responses occurred, and how the last two are still struggling to be realized against stringent systemic opposition.

Considering the powerful US families and corporations that are represented in fossil fuels, the military, and the upper levels of government, then decisions to deceive the public into an Iraqi invasion and to spend billions to extract less energy-rich unconventional fossil fuels become easy to understand. The important question is really *why* certain kinds of complexity are chosen over others, and to answer this we have to contend with oligarchic control over societal decision making.

Clearly, societies can utilize different kinds of complexity to deal with existential crises – some more energy intensive than previous system-states, some actually less so – and this speaks to the distinction between appropriate versus inappropriate technology. In Tainter's view, it would seem as though all new technologies represent greater energy use; however, in practice appropriate eco-technologies can drastically reduce energy use through benefiting from the latest scientific and technological research and innovation. Examples include passive solar design, more efficient photovoltaic technology, geothermal heating, and efficient, renewably powered public transportation systems. Many contemporary responses to energy scarcity involve both high *and* low complexity aspects. An example would be major cities like Copenhagen in which a highly complex cycling infrastructure has facilitated unparalleled levels of bicycle use – a technologically simple, almost carbon net-zero form of transportation.[72] Other responses to modern civilization's eco-crisis will undoubtedly involve the same combination of high complexity and low-technology, such as replacing clothes dryers with clotheslines, expanding urban agriculture and community gardens, and increasing rainwater collection, to name only a few. Each of these strategies involves changes to municipal bylaws and urban planning approaches (increased complexity), yet each will ultimately lead to much lower energy use.

An uncritical use of "complexity" doesn't just hide differences between types of technology and social organization and the real forces that affect their use. It also obscures the causes for many of the incredibly wasteful, destructive, and oppressive aspects of modern civilization. Oligarchic control over societal decision making means that crucial knowledge and expertise are not factored in to possible solutions to crises. The reason, quite simply, is that the various solutions to pressing social and ecological problems directly contradict elite desires for ever-increasing wealth and political power. In the present context ecologists, social scientists, philosophers, and other critical intellectuals are often muzzled and politically neutralized by elite monopolization of political and economic power structures. Critical popular input into societal decisions is blunted through ideological manipulation, misinformation, fraud, and repression. The net effect is to ensure that civilization's ability to act on quality information is fatally compromised, and practically and technologically easy alternatives become impossibilities. In Canada this constraining effect of oligarchy was recently exemplified by the Harper government's silencing of federal climate scientists. The oligarchic government, supported by millions of dollars from the fossil fuel industry, worked tirelessly to discourage independent science and promote anti-scientific viewpoints.[73] The same threat now faces the United States under a Trump presidency, with a climate change denier presiding over dismantling of the Environmental Protection Agency.[74]

However, oligarchy's effects are not just limited to political decision making. It is true that we're not able to act on knowledge of impending collapse and make required changes, but it's also the fact that every facet of our civilization is shaped by the oligarchic imperative of power concentration and wealth extraction. The very *culture* of industrial capitalism promotes antihuman and anti-ecological dysfunction, and this places a constant and suffocating burden on all of our social, economic, political, and ecological systems. It might help to think in terms of an "oligarchic tax" manifesting in monstrous inefficiencies when every social interaction has to become an opportunity for private profit accumulation and surplus value extraction. Some tangible examples include the *planned obsolescence* of consumer products via disposable design, and the *perceived obsolescence* promulgated by advertising.[75] The burden is also felt in corporate interests that continue to drive wasteful energy practices, promote personal gas-powered automobiles, and expand destructive pesticide and fertilizer-intensive mono-crop agriculture.

Finally, the oligarchic tax can also be seen in massive social, energy, and ecological investments in the arms industry, in maintaining standing armies, and in financing military campaigns and colonial occupations. In *The Rise and Fall of the Great Powers*, historian Paul Kennedy argues that all empires from 1500 CE onward have declined due to "imperial over-extension":

> It sounds crudely mercantilist to express it this way, but wealth is usually needed to underpin military power, and military power is usually needed to acquire and protect wealth. If, however, too large a proportion of the state's resources is diverted from wealth creation and allocated instead to military purposes, then that is likely to lead to a weakening of national power over the longer term. In the same way, if a state overextends itself strategically – by, say, the conquest of extensive territories or the waging of costly wars – it runs the risk that the potential benefits from external expansion may be outweighed by the great expense of it all.[76]

At first glance Kennedy's argument seems to fit within Tainter's complexity versus energy framework. Military rivals and the need for more resources and power are challenges that a society responds to with added complexity – a larger and more organized military and new military hardware. Over time, the investment of societal energy into military complexity bears diminishing returns, leading to a decline and possible collapse of the society. So far, there is no contradiction with Tainter; however we must immediately consider the additional implications of Kennedy's analysis. It isn't just *any* complexity that leads to civilization crisis, but over-investment in the most catastrophic manifestation of oligarchic competition – total war between states. This is an insight completely in line with the earlier historical research of scholars like Eisenstadt and Marcus, in which ancient states were both built and destroyed by imperial warfare. It is also in line with countless modern day examples of imperial warfare – whether the expansion of the British and French empires at the behest of power-hungry monarchs, Hitler's quest to dominate Europe in World War II, the threat posed to US elites by Communism in the Vietnam War, or the desire by a subsequent generation of elites to secure oil wealth in the US invasion of Iraq. In all instances these wars were given their impetus and organization by the interests of the oligarchic class – political elites, corporations, wealthy individuals, and the military elite. As well, in all instances these wars proved immensely profitable to a small sector of their populace, and ultimately damaging to the nation as a whole.

Constitution of the Oligarchic Class

A final argument of Tainter's that it is important to challenge is his assertion that left critical theories of collapse are "psychologizing," and therefore somehow unscientific and worthy of dismissal. In *The Collapse of Complex Societies*, he argues that these theories forget that elites have a rational interest in maintaining the subject populations that they dominate and exploit, and therefore it is "irrational" for them to act in ways that undermine the viability of the entire society and that paradoxically undermine their own interest.

Tainter notes that elites do act irrationally at times (in ways that clearly lead to societal breakdown), but that at other times they act rationally (in ways that maintain their elite position within a stable social form). He then maintains that because there is no way to understand this apparent contradiction, that "the use of greed and self-aggrandizement (e.g. among landed gentry or entrenched bureaucrats) as explanations for economic weakness and collapse really take us nowhere." They are unproductive because "both are psychological factors whose expression, to the extent that it is variable, needs explanation."[77]

From a left critical tradition, Tainter's understanding of class stratification and political oligarchy is simplistic and wholly omits the extensive scholarly tradition on social class and political-economic systems starting from the writings of Marx and continuing to the present day. However, the criticism of a "psychologizing" explanation for crisis is important to contend with. Am I simply saying that civilization's crisis is because of "bad people" at the top of the social hierarchy that are making "bad decisions"? Is my theory of oligarchic control just another way of smuggling in an essentialist conception of social classes that are homogeneous in thought and action? Is it the case that all oligarchs think and act the same way? Finally, could I be accused of reducing the problems of modern civilization to a tiny cabal of elite string-pullers? Am I suggesting that our crisis is essentially conspiratorial in nature, or that behind every act of environmental damage or oppressive social practice there is a monocled, moustache-twirling oligarch?

To address the issues raised by these questions, I begin by stressing that political oligarchy is a *system* and that its elites, the oligarchs, are a *class*. By my definition earlier in the chapter, the Death System is "a social formation in which a small, exploitative elite have gained positions of determining power, and have structured human social relations in their interests." I argue that this is a description true of all oligarchic societies. However, it is equally true that the constitution of oligarchic classes varies greatly across space and time. We can see this illustrated in a description of the class's modern manifestations, and the ways in which its collective identity and interests are constituted. The main characteristics of today's oligarchic class include different institutional locations of power, multiple and overlapping systems of ranking, shared interests, intraclass conflict, and a *systemic* structure, as opposed to a *conspiratorial* or *essential* one.

Intersectional power

The oligarchic class exercises its power through the political state, and also through those social institutions existing outside of the state, or what social theorists call *civil society*. In terms of the state, oligarchic power is present at all political levels – municipal, regional, national, and international. This power is exercised by direct political participation by elites as city councillors, members of regional or federal legislatures, or members of judicial bodies. However, much oligarchic control over government comes from the impact of corporations and wealthy elites on the political process. This influence comes in the form of economic contributions to political campaigns, lobbying of government for legislation favourable to oligarchic interests, and the "revolving door" between business and political elites, as corporate directors and CEOs spend time in government, while politicians rotate from government office into high-level directorships, lobbyist positions, and lucrative consulting contracts.

In many states key structures of oligarchic power also include the military and religious institutions. Theocratic states such as Iran integrate a powerful priestly class into the oligarchic hierarchy, whereas military regimes such as the governments in Egypt and Pakistan express oligarchic power through military rank. In other states oligarchic power is primarily expressed through ethnic/nationalist structures, such as the Alawite Muslim minority backing the Syrian regime of Bashar al-Assad, the hegemony of the House of Saud in Saudi Arabia, or the Sinhalese Buddhist regime in Sri Lanka. In many modern states the structure of the oligarchy is heterogeneous, and includes a network of elites from different economic sectors, the military, different racial/ethnic groups, and religious hierarchies. The North American oligarchic class is an example of such heterogeneity, being defined by accumulated wealth from different sectors (finance, natural resource extraction, media, manufacturing, military contracting), by European ethnicity, or "whiteness," and by Judeo-Christian religion. Barack Obama and Condoleezza Rice aside, racialized minorities and members of non-Judeo-Christian religions are rarely represented among the North American elite.

A final defining feature of the oligarchic class in all modern states is its patriarchal character. In most countries women exist as a separate, subordinate social class. Effects of this ranking lead to lower socioeconomic status, restrictions to political and economic participation, and restricted access to health, education, mobility, legal protection, and a host of other human rights. Having said this, it is true that the strength of patriarchal culture varies greatly among different oligarchic societies, and in countries like Canada and the United States, women have won a significant degree of access to social, political, and economic power. It is also true that in many societies women among the oligarchic class have rights and access to power far greater than that attainable by working-class women, or even working-class men. As such, while patriarchy and female oppression are a defining feature of all oligarchic societies, the actual experience of gender is strongly determined by specific sociocultural contexts.

Apart from the structural subordination of women, oligarchic classes tend to have a patriarchal character that derives from their historical status as warrior cultures. In an attempt to evoke the ancient justification of oligarchic rule as power given to a protective warrior class, oligarchs tend to valorize dominant, violent masculine ideals and behaviour, and to maintain close symbolic and functional ties to military power. Historically the sons of the ruling elite spent time in military service, and even in the modern era this can be seen in George Bush Sr.'s military service, and the service of Prince William and Prince Harry, heirs to the British House of Windsor. When oligarchs are not comfortable risking themselves in actual enlisted service, military rank is often worn like a Halloween costume, such as when George H.W. Bush appropriated military attire to announce pyrrhic victory in Iraq,[78] or when Canadian prime minister Stephen Harper and defence secretary Peter MacKay donned combat fatigues to visit Canadian troops during their occupation of Afghanistan.[79] Despite this strong militaristic tradition, it is also true that a number of modern oligarchic families, especially those without connection to the aristocracy, do not encourage actual military service. Instead, they express hyper-masculine values in their focus on achievement, hard work, toughness, ruthlessness, and discipline. These values are seen as ensuring victory in the capitalist marketplace, today an arguably more important arena of power than the actual battlefield.

A key feature of the oligarchic class is thus its *intersectional* nature – it is defined in various times and places by a multiplicity of overlapping systems of ranking. The constitution of oligarchic and subordinate classes within a specific country is determined by the socially constructed nature of power relations in that particular place and time. These relations are constructed through ideology and practice, and based on essentialist beliefs, but not on *actual* differences in nature or capacity. Despite their ideological claims to superiority, the oligarchic class is not dominant due to the inherent or essential characteristics of its members. To take an example particular to North America, there is nothing inherently dominant or superior about "whiteness" or European descent, just as there is nothing inherently subordinate or inferior about "blackness" or African descent. At earlier times in history white Europeans were dominated and enslaved by other ethnic groups.[80] Similarly, at times in history dark skinned Africans dominated and enslaved other ethnic groups. In another context, Christianity is one of the defining features of the oligarchic class in North America, whereas in Egypt, Libya, or Syria, Christianity is associated with subordinate status.[81] As such, there is nothing inherently dominant or subordinate about a Christian religious identity. What determines these power relationships – whether one is a member of a dominant or subordinate group – is our unique social location and the particular historical and social context we find ourselves in.

Although the systems of social ranking that construct its identity are fluid, changing in different times and places, the oligarchic class is ultimately defined by its position within the socioeconomic and political hierarchies. In all places and all times the oligarchic class is that possessed of the greatest economic wealth and political power. It always constitutes a small percentage of the overall population, and is always strongly represented in the highest positions within government and the key institutions of civil society. In many cases individual oligarchs or oligarchic families extend influence into both spheres, such as media magnate and former Italian prime minister Silvio Berlusconi. This is also widely apparent when considering former US presidential candidates – including George Bush Sr. and Jr., John Kerry, Ross Perot, Mitt Romney, and Donald Trump – all of whom combine massive wealth and corporate power with high-ranking political positions. It is no surprise that President Trump is a billionaire, or that he has staffed his government with other billionaires.[82]

The oligarchic class is unified through its position on the top of the social hierarchy. This gives oligarchs within a given country, and even across different countries, a shared culture and sense of class interests. These collective interests are expressed in political values, policy positions, voting patterns, and various forms of economic and social behaviour. More so than poor or working people, the wealthy elite tend to vote in line with their class interests, supporting candidates, parties, and policies that enable the oligarchic imperative.[83] The economic decisions of the elite tend to be focused on maximizing wealth, and they are also more likely to act in predatory ways that sacrifice the welfare of others to increase their own wealth.

Oligarchic consciousness

In the past few years there have been some revealing studies that point to critical differences in the psychology and behaviour of the very wealthy in relation to the middle class, working class, and poor. In a study conducted by Berkeley researchers Paul Piff and Dacher Keltner, the behaviour of drivers is observed at a crosswalk. Results show 90 per cent of drivers obey the law and stop at the crosswalk. Of the 10 per cent who don't stop, drivers of luxury vehicles are four times more likely to run the stop than drivers of less expensive cars. Another study they conducted observes class differences in generosity, and shows that when given the chance, wealthy subjects take twice as much candy from children as do poor subjects. A final study shows wealthy individuals as four times more likely than poor people to lie about dice scores in a game when money is at stake. A possible neural explanation for this phenomenon is suggested by a recent study by researchers at Wilfrid Laurier University in Kitchener, Ontario, who find that subjects asked to reflect on feeling powerful then show less neuronal mirroring. Mirror neurons are the brain structures that enable us to subjectively feel the experience of others.[84] It could be that the feelings of superiority experienced by elites lessens their empathy and increases their likelihood of exhibiting anti-social behaviour.

The elite culture is status-obsessed, defined by what sociologist Thorstein Veblen describes as *conspicuous consumption*, or accumulating items of material wealth as status symbols.[85] From the earliest oligarchic kings building ostentatious palaces and aggrandizing public monuments, to the modern rich with luxury yachts and private jets, the prominent display of material wealth both accentuates the elite's superior power and sharpens the boundaries between ruler and ruled. The oligarchic class constantly defines its identity in relation to those it dominates, taking signifiers of difference such as heredity, ethnicity, or religion, and mobilizing them as group boundaries and ideological justifications for rule. This tendency is robust throughout history, whether considering the ancient Greek *eupatrid*, "sons of good fathers"[86]; the "men of best quality" who opposed the democratic demands of levellers during the British parliamentary revolution; or the oligarchic founders of the American Constitution, who ensured the continued rule of "the more responsible set of men" (white property owners).[87] Through this historical continuity we can see a *class* essentialism underlying the various essentialist signifiers used by oligarchs to define themselves. In a case of circular reasoning, the wealth and power of the oligarchs is empirical *proof* of their inherent superiority, and their inherent superiority in turn justifies their greater wealth and power.

Internal competition

The unifying characteristics of the oligarchic class are contradicted by its tendency toward internal competitiveness. Elite individuals and families compete with each other for status, wealth, and power. Corporations also exist in this constant competitive environment, as do oligarchic states themselves. Inherent competitiveness leads to constant schisms within the oligarchic class, and is another structural feature that leads to political instability and the collapse of oligarchic polities. Competition between oligarchs can reflect both reformist and predatory approaches to the exercise of hegemonic power, and from the time of ancient Greek tyrants there have been oligarchs who have embraced populist politics to overthrow elite rivals, or to stave off popular rebellion that would endanger the entire class's capacity for exploitation.[88] Franklin Delano Roosevelt is an example of such a reformist political leader among the oligarchic class, and it is unsurprising that his reformist policy was challenged in 1935 by a conspiracy of predatory capitalists including the Rockefellers, JP Morgan, the Du Pont family, and Prescott Bush.[89]

As a result of their highly competitive culture and egocentric belief in exceptionalism and divinely appointed rulership, oligarchs also tend to be tribal in their politics. The tribal mentality can manifest in a family's desire for wealth and power, such as the dynastic struggles that have historically plagued monarchies worldwide, or the competition between wealthy corporate families in contemporary capitalist societies. Tribalism can also lead to fault lines among the oligarchic class based on national, religious, or ethnic lines. These tribal conflicts among elites often lead to populist strategies in which oligarchs from one national or ethnic group appeal to their subordinates in an attempt to mobilize their support in a conflict with out-group rivals. This consciously created "us against them" framework has been used repeatedly in conflict between oligarchic societies, leading exploited classes, more often than not, to tragically rally behind their very oppressors.

Intraclass competition is not the only source of variation among the oligarchy, and it is important to note that the common characteristics I've just described are not embodied in a uniform manner by all members of the elite. There are variations among oligarchic consciousness and practice, just as there are among members of any defined social group. As Raymond Williams argues, "no dominant social order and therefore no dominant culture ever in reality includes and exhausts all human practice, human energy, and human intention."[90] For example, there are members of the elite that engage in considerable charitable work, such as Ted Rogers or Bill and Melinda Gates. There are also oligarchs who have sincere and even passionate concerns for ecological sustainability or human rights. Al Gore's climate change activism is an example, as is George Soros's humanitarian endeavours. And there are obvious variations in the consciousness of oligarchs, especially in terms of how they understand their wealth and power, and the societal inequalities they rest on.

Many members of the elite express a naive and self-justifying narcissism, exemplified by Georgina Rinehart, CEO of Australian mining corporation Hancock Prospecting, who has been quoted saying, "There is no monopoly on becoming a millionaire. If you're jealous of those with more money, don't just sit there and complain; do something to make more money yourself – spend less time drinking, or smoking and socializing and more time working."[91] This statement, from the inheritor of an old money family business, and a woman with a net worth of 22 billion dollars, reveals a profoundly distorted picture of reality that eliminates Rinehart's obvious privilege. This worldview is reflected in psychological research in which the elite are much more likely to attribute their wealth and power to personal qualities such as talent, intelligence, and hard work. In contrast, the middle and working class are much more likely to perceive socioeconomic constraints as contributing to their status in life.[92] To Rinehart, her fabulous wealth has nothing to do with her inheritance (presumably she considers herself hardworking and morally upright); so, conversely, that others aren't as wealthy has to do with their laziness and moral degeneracy.

Of course, in addition to this kind of "magical thinking," there are expressions of oligarchic consciousness that are far more brutal, such as the racism that fuels multiple genocides (always elite-driven), or the vicious classism that allows for exploitation of child and sweatshop labour, the violent suppression of striking workers, or the murder and torture of political enemies.

System vs. conspiracy

Despite the noted variations in oligarchic consciousness and behaviour, it is extremely rare for elites to detach completely from the *imperative*, and from an at least tacit support of economic and political policies that ensure their continued wealth and power. As such, while Georgina Rinehart visits girls' schools in Cambodia and works with several women's charities, she also uses her fortune to fight regulation of the mining sector that would protect Indigenous families and sensitive ecosystems. This is generally true of oligarchs with humanitarian and ecological interests. Bill and Melinda Gates built their charitable fund through predatory and illegal business practices that devastated countless small technology firms. Even Al Gore, whose environmentalism and climate change championing are clearly sincere, remains a multi-millionaire venture capitalist who in no way challenges the basic capitalist framework that ensures his family's continued wealth and power. In the best cases, when elites truly espouse a progressive vision, they still tend to both protect their business and class interests, *and* pursue philanthropic goals.

The paradoxical character of the oligarchic class as an objectively definable socioeconomic group with shared interests, yet also a group with a high degree of variation and internal competitiveness, can lead to confusion concerning the class's structure and motives. In particular, a tension exists between conceptions of oligarchic society as a complex social system, having an existence apart from any conscious direction by individual agents, or as a conspiracy that is consciously controlled by powerful, omniscient interests. This question has become particularly important in the current North American political climate, which has seen the rapid growth of a previously marginal "conspiracy culture" that is politically right libertarian and fundamentalist Christian in nature. This culture is prominently embodied by media personalities like Alex Jones, whose radio and internet-streaming television programs preach a global conspiracy to create "a new world order," or a global totalitarian government. Jones is joined by televangelist Pat Roberts, David Icke, Lyndon LaRouche, the far-right John Birch Society, and a legion of imitators and followers, in their focus on a number of themes, including, their assertions of the yearly Bilderberg Group meeting as a gathering of the "Illuminati"; the United Nations as the vehicle for the new world order; the UN sustainable development project Agenda 21 as a pretext to control world economies; the existence of a global communist plot to abolish Christianity and "freedom"; anthropogenic climate change as a hoax perpetrated by the Illuminati; the all-pervasive influence of the Rothschild family and a cabal of Jewish bankers as directors of world history; banking and the monetary system as the key lever of the Illuminati's power; and an apocalyptic Christian millenarianism that sees the "End Times" ever looming.[93]

Today this eclectic mix of ideas has reached a disturbing level of mainstream acceptance, with the internet making previously marginal theories, such as the belief that reptilian beings from the centre of the earth are controlling the world's corporations and governments, more widely accessible. As bizarre as most of these theories may seem to any sober, scientifically minded thinker, their proliferation is cause for serious concern. In the United States, the immensely popular religious doctrine of "dispensationalism," which holds that we are living in the end times and expecting the biblical rapture, has been linked to the highest levels of US political and economic elites. The late right-wing fundamentalist pastor Tim LaHaye became a bestselling author and cultural power-broker by writing the *Left Behind* series – a fictionalized account of the Rapture with over 65 million copies sold to date. LaHaye's following consisted of a large segment of the evangelical Christian population in the United States, and he exerted considerable influence on US foreign policy. A 2003 Time/CNN poll indicated that 59 per cent of Americans believe the events in biblical Revelations will come true, showing the impact of LaHaye and other dispensationalist preachers.[94]

In contrast to theories of a secret cabal that controls the world, various schools of institutional analysis instead focus on the systemic and socially constructed nature of societies. Institutional analyses come from the political left, right and centre, however they all share a common view of modern states, and the global system of nation-states, as complex, socially constructed, and having real and constraining effects on human agency. Left institutional analysts, whether socialist, communist, or anarchist, describe dysfunction within social systems in terms of inequalities in power and wealth caused by class struggle or other forms of social stratification. Political centrists tend to envision a more neutral field of "political opportunity structures" that various interest groups contest. Like the left's institutional analysts, those on the right, theorists like Samuel Huntington, Zbigniew Brzezinski, and Henry Kissinger, tend to focus on power struggles between different groups defined by their cultural, racial, ethnic, or class character. The difference is that right analysts attribute systemic dysfunctions to the destabilizing influence of subordinate groups, and back the interests of power and privilege in the name of social stability.

My analysis of modern civilization is institutional in character, and shares with other left theorists the conviction that institutionalized inequalities in wealth and power are the cause of social dysfunction and possible global collapse. This is the Death System, and it is driven by the interests of the oligarchic class. However, as I mention in previous chapters, there are other aspects of the Death System that are important in understanding its critical dysfunction, including spatial and temporal dissociation of actors from the consequences of their actions, the unprecedented scale and complexity of social systems, global economic stratification, and the tendency of industrial economies toward ecological overshoot. These other factors combine with oligarchic governance to create the crisis we now face. In this view of civilization, oligarchy is itself a system of relations, not a discrete group of people with essential characteristics. In my analysis *it is the relations of domination themselves, rather than the individual agents who enact them, that are the locus of systemic dysfunction.*

A standard claim of "new world order" conspiracy theorists is that present sociopolitical realities are the result of conscious manipulation by ancient, unbroken, and secret traditions of elite power (whether Templars, Masons, Merovingians, Rothschilds, Illuminati, etc.). As a system, oligarchy certainly does have historically continuous characteristics; however it's equally true that it has evolved in significant ways and has varied greatly in its specific manifestations in given places and times. As a definable group within industrial capitalist civilization, the oligarchic class has been as much *influenced by* these macro-systemic forces as they have been *the conscious architects* of them. Civilization-level changes including religious and nationalist movements, technological innovations, ecological changes, and new social and cosmological understandings have all shaped the worldview, behaviour, and physical constitution of the oligarchic class. For example, as steam-, oil-, and electrical-based technologies emerged, they were all incorporated as tools in service of the oligarchic imperative. However, these successive revolutions in industrial production also changed the composition of economic and political power, leading some members of the oligarchy to fall from the heights of status and wealth and others to ascend.

When the industrial revolution began in Europe and a new class of factory-owning capitalists gained power, the aristocratic oligarchy was ruptured, many aristocrats were bankrupted, and newly powerful manufacturing and banking interests secured entry. Working from Marx, economic theorists like Joseph Schumpeter and David Harvey describe this accelerated pace of technological change, and its disruption of social systems, as capitalism's tendency toward "creative destruction."[95] Social upheavals can also be associated with changes in ethnic or racial politics, as when the South African revolution in the 1990s broke open the white oligarchy and enabled the emergence of a new black elite.[96] History shows that the aspirations of elites are often thwarted, that even the most powerful can be pushed around by broader social forces, and that today's oligarchic conspirators are often tomorrow's political exiles or economic failures. In other words, when looking at the development of oligarchy, what has been continuous is the reality of institutionalized oligarchic power, not a specific manifestation of this power in the form of a single ethnic group, political organization, family, or secret society.

Another feature of the Death System that contradicts "new world order" conspiracies is that the System's effects, while driven by the oligarchic imperative, are not all initiated by the oligarchic class itself. The hallmark of the Death System is a society in which social relations are structured in the interests of elites. Under these conditions every social and ecological atrocity doesn't need an elite prime mover, because the entire social system is set up so that members of subordinate classes, acting freely and rationally, tend to further oligarchic interests in their actions. For example, most workers at munitions factories are just doing their job, raising their families, and trying to get by in a tough economy. They are not oligarchs, not conspirators, and not conscious proponents of the *imperative*. However, due to the economic environment they exist within, their livelihood is linked directly to oligarchic processes of exploitation (from wage labour), domination (from political influence by the state-military-industrial complex), and violent expansion through warfare.

Oligarchy vs. psychopathology

A final error that can be made in understanding the nature of the oligarchic class involves an essentialist view of the relationship between its psychopathic characteristics, and the psychological normality or abnormality of its actual members. As I argue earlier in this chapter, there is solid evidence that individuals exhibiting a narrow range of aggressive alpha male behaviour have been a problem for human communities since the Paleolithic era. Aggrandizers or aggressive alphas, and at the extreme end psychopaths, present unique challenges to egalitarian, democratic communities, and can be sources of disruption, violence, and emergent oligarchic relations. However, the actual incidence rate of this extreme range of behaviour has likely been stable throughout the past one hundred thousand years of evolution, consisting of about 1 per cent of the total adult population exhibiting clinical psychopathy (with the condition being slightly more likely among men).[97]

Throughout history many elites and oligarchs *have* been aggressive alphas, and many have not; however, through processes of structuration, stratification, and class formation, the impact of psychopathic leadership has been to shape the interests, consciousness, and behaviour of the entire elite class in psychopathic ways. In essence oligarchy creates a *culture of psychopathy* among the elite, into which new members are socialized (whether born into the culture or ascending to its membership as adults). For this reason it is accurate to say that the oligarchic class exhibits classically psychopathic tendencies, while still realizing that most of its members would be considered psychologically "normal." Having said this, it is also the case that actual aggressive alphas and psychopaths do seem to be over-represented among the elite (such as corporate executives and stockbrokers), perhaps because they are able to most faithfully embody the calculating, amoral, and egocentric values of the oligarchy.[98]

There are countless examples of oligarchic culture's psychopathological characteristics, and its ability to elicit inhuman behaviour from otherwise psychologically "normal" individuals. History and social analysis show us that humanity's great collective atrocities – genocides, pogroms, wars, or systems of racial oppression and segregation – have been the result of psychopathic social structures. Noam Chomsky notes this when referencing the anti-social and ecologically destructive behaviour of corporations, or the inhuman behaviour of southern US slave owners. Corporate behaviour that knowingly harms workers, customers, and the environment is undoubtedly a monstrous and inhuman thing, as is the behaviour of slave owners.

And yet, Chomsky asks if all of the corporate executives and slave owners were unfeeling psychopaths? In fact, he argues, most slave owners likely went home to their families after a day's work, were loving to their spouses and children, and considered themselves to be moral beings. They were not inherently inhuman, rather they carried out monstrous acts by virtue of the fact that slavery is itself an inherently monstrous institution.[99]

These social-systemic effects on human behaviour, exhaustively documented by sociological and psychological research, show the considerable power of culture and institutions to shape our actions. To suggest that modern humanitarian atrocities or acts of ecological destruction need to be explained by an all-powerful, evil conspiracy, or by mental illness, is to deny what scientific and historical study tell us. It is to drastically oversimplify, personalize, and essentialize the pathology of civilization, and ultimately to disrupt serious efforts to change it.

8

Toward a System of Life

> If there is no struggle, there is no progress. Those who profess to favor freedom, and yet deprecate agitation, are men who want crops without plowing up the ground. They want rain without thunder and lightning. They want the ocean without the awful roar of its many waters. This struggle may be a moral one, or it may be a physical one, and it may be both moral and physical, but it must be a struggle. Power concedes nothing without a demand. It never did, and it never will.
> — Frederick Douglass

Saving the Valley

Radical Transformation opens with a story – an account of the battle to save a natural river valley in a North American steelmaking town. This conflict in turn reflects the broader story of life within industrial capitalism – the daily struggle of regular people to protect our lives, autonomy, and ecosystems from predation by the forces of money and power. In country after country, in decade after decade, this narrative plays out its themes of oppression and ecological devastation. In fact, this cycle is incredibly ancient, going back to the struggle of prehistoric communities to preserve cooperative, egalitarian, and ecocentric cultures in the face of immense environmental and demographic pressures. Ending this destructive cycle is the collective challenge that we all face, and in this final chapter I explore how we might meet the challenge and change the trajectory of human development from collapse to sustainability.

One of the goals of *Radical Transformation* is to question the story told to us by elites since the dawn of history. This story is one in which elite control of civilization has led to stability, order, and cultural advance. In opposition to this narrative, I've argued that the dynamics that have led to societal collapse throughout history can be traced to the oligarchic control of moral community and its social, psychological, and ecological feedback mechanisms. With cooperative cultures gamed and yoked to the selfish interests of elites, the framework of moral regulation either breaks down or becomes twisted in its application and effects. The protective social functions that once guarded the lives and interests of all community members become tools used by elites to oppress, exploit, and disenfranchise. The ascendance of elites to power in oligarchic societies, what Rousseau terms an act of "adroit usurpation," is facilitated, as it has been from ancient times, by a powerful myth: *the benevolence of the oligarchs*.[1] This deception presents oligarchic rulers not as parasitic exploiters of our human community, but as the very founders, nurturers, and protectors of that community.

Upon examining the evidence, the myth of oligarchs as a progressive social force is quickly dispelled. In chapter 2, I list five major sources of our civilization's crisis, "the five horsemen of the modern day apocalypse," as dissociation, complexity, stratification, overshoot, and oligarchy. Dissociation and complexity describe how citizens in industrial, capitalist states are generally cut off from feedback concerning the morality of our actions due to consequences occurring in faraway places, or far off times. We are also cut off from empathic connection to the suffering caused by civilization. These various forms of dissociation are in no way accidental, or simply unintended side effects of industrial civilization's massive scale and complexity. Instead, they emerge directly from the desire for oligarchs to avoid censure and regulation from their domestic populations. If raw materials are needed for increasing production and expanding profits, they are ripped first from the hands of marginal groups – First Nations, or the poor in developing countries. If oil is needed to keep the industrial machine churning, it is secured through military adventures in far off lands, and paid for by the countless lives of their faceless denizens. Outsourcing, externalizing, deliberate destruction of regulatory regimes – all of these phenomena are the conscious and calculated results of the oligarchic imperative, of the parasitic direction of civilization's creative powers toward elite gain.

Stratification refers to the massive and growing inequality that exists between the global oligarchs and their subordinates. Again, this state of affairs is in no way natural, and instead speaks to the deliberate and predatory action of oligarchs in usurping wealth from the poor and defenceless and hoarding it in ever greater amounts. This inequality is enforced by both structural and direct violence at all levels – in schools, law courts, prisons, police forces, and militaries. A system of oligarchic law locks in inequality and also ensures a steady cycle of poverty, crime, illness, and social upheaval. The most brute expression of stratification is outright slavery, where oligarchs are able to completely strip away the humanity of certain groups or individuals, and turn them into disposable property. Under capitalism, the introduction of wage labour (called *wage slavery* by workers in the eighteenth century) and factory production slightly alters this original exploitative relationship, allowing some among the subordinated a chance at more freedom and wealth, meanwhile also ruthlessly extracting surplus value, and turning many into human machines. Finally, competition between oligarchs seeking to maximize exploitation leads to constant warfare. In warfare humanity's inherent sociality and intelligence are turned toward truly monstrous ends, as empathic boundary markers (delineating "us" from "them") are used to manipulate the subordinate into killing each other en masse in pursuit of the oligarchs' interests.

Overshoot refers to civilization critically degrading the earth's biosphere. Under the oligarchic imperative, life-sustaining ecosystems are pillaged as "resources" and "raw materials" for industrial production. Conservation efforts are undermined, ecological science is suppressed, information is manipulated, and private profit is continually placed above community good. The Death System deliberately builds legal, economic, and political systems to speed up the destruction of ecosystems and to crush nature's defenders.

For all of these reasons, I identify oligarchy as the final, and ultimate cause of civilization's crisis. It overarches the other systemic pathologies as it provides their organizing framework and their continued impetus. The imperative of conquest, accumulation, and domination that drives oligarchic competition is deadly precisely because it harnesses moral community – the Life System – for its own ultimately destructive ends. In the hands of oligarchs, human culture, the most powerful adaptive mechanism life on Earth has yet produced, becomes the most deadly weapon directed against life itself. This relationship represents a complete inversion of the Hobbesian narrative – where oligarchy provides moral regulation to our essentially depraved nature. Instead, oligarchy is a system that directs our essentially social and intelligent nature toward depraved ends. It survives parasitically on the older, deeper manifestation of moral community – the Life System – and this gives modern civilization its dual character.

Confronting the Crisis

Realizing the interaction of Life System and Death System has implications for how we approach the multiple challenges we now face. First, although the Life System remains a potent force, the current ascendancy of the Death System cautions that reformist approaches to crisis that don't confront the problem of oligarchy have little hope of success. Like Joseph Tainter and Jared

Diamond argue, civilizations *are* problem-solving organizations, and must react to constant challenges to their survival. However, it is rarely the case throughout history, and particularly in the modern era, that civilizations have lacked the cultural knowledge sufficient to meet challenges to their viability, and to overcome them. From even our earliest histories in ancient Sumeria we have evidence that the predatory schemes of elites were questioned and challenged by democratic forces, and that cultural alternatives to the oligarchic cycle of expansion and collapse were available.[2]

The first important implication is thus that civilization's crisis is not *technical* in nature. It doesn't consist in us lacking the knowledge, capability, or technology to address the challenges we face in sociocultural, political, economic, or ecological realms. Today's scientists, activists, and social entrepreneurs detail the challenges exhaustively, and provide an equally exhaustive list of potential solutions. Participatory democracy, passive solar construction, distributed generation of renewable energy, small-scale organic agriculture, public transit, trade unions, restorative justice, demilitarization, guaranteed minimum incomes, progressive taxation, fully public health, welfare and education, nationalization of banks, energy infrastructure, and key industries – all of these solutions and more are easily available, extensively researched, and fully achievable. And almost all are being implemented today, in varying degrees, in a handful of countries around the globe. The problem civilization faces is not a lack of options. The problem lies in our inability to choose the best available options and to make the right decisions. While we remain captive to the oligarchic imperative, civilization's creative problem-solving potential is throttled, and actions that are both necessary and possible are rendered impossible.

Reformist writers tend to undertheorize these political and economic constraints on decision making, and also succumb to the functionalist fallacy of viewing societies and civilizations as undifferentiated wholes that make decisions collectively. An example can be found in Bill McKibben's bestselling *Deep Economy*, in which he ends a brilliant deconstruction of constant-growth economics by appealing to entire nations to change their economic practices. McKibben realizes that collapse will come from limitless growth and consumption, and yet there is no mention of transforming the political structures that perpetuate this model and that also frustrate the many inspiring examples of local, sustainable production mentioned in his book.[3]

A related fallacy present in reformist work is to minimize the impact of institutionalized power relationships and instead focus on admonitions to modify our individual behaviour. Thus David Suzuki's powerful work on humanity's connection to the biosphere, *The Sacred Balance*, ends with a list of ten things people can do to avert ecological catastrophe. The first nine suggestions are all about changing personal behaviours, from using local food to riding a bicycle. Only the tenth suggestion, "Get involved, stay informed," hints at any kind of collective action. This action is to join an environmental group, but not necessarily to become politically involved in elections, corporate boycotts, alternative political parties, or radical social movements.[4] In neither McKibben's nor Suzuki's books, nor in similar reformist literature, is there mention made of capitalism or oligarchy as systems in need of fundamental questioning.

The tendency to personalize societal dysfunction and to prescribe individual responses is a key feature of reformism. It is present in the concept of "voting with one's dollar," or the idea that one's ethical consumer choices are somehow a more effective means of creating systemic change than is collective political action. The Fair Trade, organic, sweat-free, and eco-product movements are all aspects of this individualized activism. These initiatives are all positive, and can have important effects, like pressuring large producers to become more ethical in their business practices, raising awareness of injustice and inefficiency, and pressuring governments to regulate markets more effectively. Despite these benefits, these kinds of individual approaches are also highly susceptible to commodification by large corporations who can engage in "greenwashing" – making merely cosmetic alterations to fool consumers, evade regulators, and avoid substantial change.[5]

To make this critique of authors like Suzuki and McKibben, or of movements like Fair Trade, is to take nothing away from the useful contributions they make to understanding the crisis we face. The changes they suggest – local, zero-growth economies, connecting spiritually with wild nature, re-energizing community, creating ethical systems of exchange – are exactly what we need to be doing. My critique of reformism asks: "What needs to occur for these eminently sane and insightful alternatives to *actually* be implemented?"

In a small way, reformists contribute to answering even this question, in that encouraging individuals to raise their environmental and social consciousness via small, personal actions *can* create a more favourable cultural climate for later, large-scale change. In addition, it is possible that some people who have a direct material interest in the current exploitative and ecocidal system might be swayed by the moral appeal made by reformist authors and movements. There are examples of this, such as CEO and environmental activist Ray Anderson. Anderson founded Interface, the global carpet-manufacturing company, and had an ecological awakening in 1994 in which he committed the corporation to a path of sustainability. The accomplishments of Interface since this change have been impressive, and suggest that ecologically sustainable manufacturing might be possible on a large scale.[6]

However, as inspiring as Interface's story is, it represents an extremely rare occurrence, and one that can't be relied on to change civilization's trajectory from collapse to sustainability. The reality is that the majority of corporate CEOs, top-level politicians, and wealthy individuals are committed to maintaining the status quo, and will actively seek to thwart the kind of change that Anderson embraced. In the face of this harsh fact, movements need to realize that to modify elite behaviour, and to change the institutions that elites govern, the oligarchic monopoly on decision-making power must be broken. To avoid this difficult truth, and to leave the question of transforming political power out of their prescriptions for change, reformists risk achieving only minor concessions from elites.

Similar limitations can be seen in reformist institutions like labour unions and most environmental and social justice NGOs. These institutions do important work; however, they rarely present fundamental critiques of industrial capitalism's political or economic foundations. In the case of unions, this is a far cry from their origins, when in the nineteenth and early twentieth centuries North American labour created some of the most radical and confrontational organizations in existence. Unions like the Industrial Workers of the World (IWW), and federations like the Congress of Industrial Organizations (CIO) were on the forefront of battles that forced government recognition of the rights of workers, and that broke down barriers between working men and women, and between workers of different racial and ethnic groups. The IWW was committed to overthrowing capitalism, and many of its members were also involved in communist, socialist, and anarchist political organizations. IWW members organized against US involvement in World War I, and inspired other unions to utilize direct action to achieve their workplace and political objectives.[7] Early unions often took radical action, like the 1936 Flint Michigan Sit-down Strike, in which the United Auto Workers occupied a General Motors' factory, winning union membership for its workers and leading to the unionization of the entire US auto industry.[8]

Today's unions still provide crucial support for workers in Canada and the United States, and also contribute to important campaigns for civil rights, social justice, and the environment. Unions remain the most important institutions in combating income inequality, and in protecting public services like healthcare, education, and social assistance.[9] Despite these many contributions, it is also true that the political stance of unions has become essentially reformist, and presents no foundational critique of capitalism, industrialism, or constant-growth consumer economies.

The same can be said of mainstream political parties worldwide, including the Democratic Party in the United States, the Labour Party in Britain, and Canadian parties like the Greens or New Democratic Party (NDP). Despite their rhetoric, none of these parties question the basic logic of oligarchy, and none of them provide practical solutions to the social and ecological contradictions that elite dominance creates. Instead, mainstream political parties tend to play a strongly hegemonic role by diverting popular unrest into reformist dead-ends, leaving the public disillusioned with the entire process of electoral politics. One caveat to this bleak assessment is that history has also shown reformist parties to be susceptible to more radical, insurgent movements. This strategy was exemplified by the 2016 Democratic Party nomination race, in which Bernie Sanders came very close to securing the nomination, and the presidency. Such campaigns are full of possibility, and I will revisit them later in the chapter.

The Crisis and the Left

With reformism failing to address the root causes driving civilization to collapse, any serious theory and practice of change must confront the ability of political and economic inequality to determine societal decision making. The left tradition excels in this analysis, and yet its many variants are also hampered by theoretical and practical weaknesses. These issues are important to examine, as the history of radical resistance to oligarchy, while full of inspiring victories, is also full of flawed strategies and tragic reversals. As the stakes of our current predicament are particularly high, the critique of radical perspectives that follows is intended to improve the chances of future transformative movements, not to dismiss the importance of their predecessors.

Totalizing categories

A first problem found among traditional left theorists is their tendency to use totalizing categories that obscure differences within social groups. Whether "masses," "workers," or "proletariat" – these labels miss the important fact that throughout history, social stratification and oligarchic power structures have always been based on several characteristics. Race, gender, nationality, sexual orientation, and religion all play an important role in defining who has access to political power and economic wealth. Social scientists refer to this as *intersectionality*, and failing to take it into account obscures real differences in power found within the "working class" or other essentialized revolutionary subjects.[10] For example, anti-civilization activist Lierre Keith points out the rampant sexism that plagued New Left movements of the 1960s and 1970s. Keith notes that several female members of the Students for a Democratic Society (SDS) left the movement due to a widespread culture of gender discrimination and harassment. Similarly, the Black Panther Party was also rife with misogyny, and prominent leaders like Eldridge Cleaver and Huey Newton saw rape as a tool of revolutionary struggle. In both instances, movements organized around an essentialized and totalizing social identity (social class or race) masked important intra-group heterogeneity and allowed for serious abuses of power.[11] A final problem with essentialist conceptions of social groups is that they make us less effective at organizing the real, diverse citizenry of modern states.[12] A focus on the "working class" as a unified, historically necessary agent of change misses the ways in which people in modern oligarchic societies are variously marginalized by their age, gender, race, ethnicity, and relation to the land. All of these people are potential allies in a project of radical transformation, and our theoretical and political language must reflect this fact.

Capitalism or oligarchy

Another problem with totalizing categories concerns the left's attribution of today's crisis to a single force – *capitalism*. Although capitalism is a horrendously exploitative and ecologically destructive social formation, it is unable to explain the entirety of civilization's crisis. While capitalism is surely a manifestation of socioeconomic life under the Death System, it is also a very recent social formation, having emerged in its modern sense during the eighteenth and nineteenth centuries.[13] The relationships associated with capitalism represent an evolution in the much older phenomenon of oligarchy, and describe a shift in the nature of pre-existing oligarchic relations. However, when looked at from an evolutionary perspective they do not constitute *novel* relations. In other words, capitalism is a specific aspect, or subcategory, of the higher-order category of oligarchy. Marx and Engels suggest as much themselves in the *Communist Manifesto*:

> In the earlier epochs of history we find almost everywhere a complicated arrangement of society into various orders, a manifold gradation of social rank. In ancient Rome we have patricians, knights, plebeians, slaves; in the middle ages, feudal lords, vassals, guild masters, journeymen, apprentices, serfs; in almost all of these classes, again, subordinate gradations.
>
> The modern bourgeois society that has sprouted from the ruins of feudal society, has not done away with class antagonisms. It has but established new classes, new conditions of oppression, new forms of struggle in place of the old ones.[14]

The categorical distinction between capitalism and oligarchy is not just pedantic. On the contrary, it allows us to see the underlying factors that give rise to systems of elite domination, and that perpetuate these systems in the face of repeated democratic rebellion. Appreciating the full spectrum of elite strategies of domination and exploitation takes us far beyond the Marxist idea of economically determined classes. Elite ownership of the means of production is an important factor, but equally important are the roles played by increasing social complexity and hierarchy, a lack of government transparency and accountability, deceit, coercion, ecological destruction, and ideology.

Another issue with capitalism is that it presents a moving conceptual target, having never existed in a "pure" form, and having changed drastically since its emergence as an identifiable social formation. Today we can speak of industrial, post-industrial, consumer, finance, state, ecological, transnational, global, green, and numerous other variants of capitalism. This categorical diversity is useful in illuminating different aspects of economic relations; however, the coherence of these forms, their vitalizing energy and ultimate effects, are explained more accurately by the ancient and historically continuous system of political oligarchy.

An additional problem with using *capitalism* to describe modern civilization's dysfunction is that the concept comes with significant limitations and considerable historical baggage. An analysis of capitalism alone is not enough to understand the manifestations of political oligarchy based on authoritarian communism, theocracy, ethnically based dictatorship, fascism, or any number of hybrid political structures. Focusing on the many and acute dysfunctions of capitalism risks minimizing the other destructive socioeconomic forms that oligarchy can take. Capitalism isn't sufficient to explain race-based regimes of slavery in the pre-Civil War American South, the apartheid regime in South Africa, the enduring conflict in Palestine, or the Iranian revolution. Inequalities in wealth and control of the means of production certainly play a role in these historical situations, but the structures of domination and exploitation present in each require an analysis much broader than one based solely on socioeconomic class.

Ecological crisis

The failure of traditional left analysis is arguably greatest when considering the ecological crisis. To doctrinaire Marxists, industrialism's destructive impact on the biosphere is all but absent from theory and practice. If anything, Marx and his early twentieth century followers revelled in the creative power of industrial capitalism, and saw in the growth of mechanized production the primary tool to remove scarcity and inequality.[15] The toxic legacy of state communist regimes is ample testament that both left and right political-economic paradigms can be based on completely unsustainable practices, and that wealth redistribution or state control of production alone are not protection against ecological overshoot, crisis, and collapse.[16] Although recent years have seen several movements to integrate ecological concerns into communist, socialist, and anarchist theories, there is still a tendency on much of the left to place issues of redistribution above issues of sustainability. As long as capitalism remains the single overarching cause of crisis recognized by left theorists, ecological, gender, and ethno-racial aspects of the crisis will continue to be overlooked.

Traditional left use of capitalism to describe civilization's crisis is also problematic in that it tends to present the task of social change as a binary struggle of "capitalism" versus "socialism." In this dichotomy, everything labelled "capitalist," in some cases including ideas of democracy, liberalism, localism, and free economic exchange, is labelled oppressive. Conversely, everything labelled "socialism," at times including authoritarianism and imperialism, is labelled liberatory. This danger can be seen in the writing of some Cold War era left intellectuals, who argued that there is a moral difference between "capitalist" atrocities and "communist" atrocities.[17] A similar difficulty appears with revolutionary communist theorists who distinguish between good (proletarian) and bad (fascist) forms of dictatorship. According to the values of the Life System, of democratic moral community, *all* human rights atrocities are worthy of condemnation, whether the deaths of one million Iraqis caused by the 2003 US invasion and subsequent occupation, or the millions who died through forced agricultural collectivization in Maoist China and Stalinist Russia.[18] Similarly, *all* forms of dictatorship are destructive and undesirable, regardless of whether they are justified by right-wing, left-wing, nationalist, or religious ideologies. If "capitalism" is the only label we have to describe social dysfunction, then how do we confront and critique the oligarchic tendencies of ostensibly "socialist" or "communist" societies? Focusing on the system of political oligarchy enables these analytical false dichotomies to be avoided, and keeps attention squarely on the phenomenon of elite political dominance and economic exploitation – the two factors that have been driving societal collapse for the past eight thousand years.

Insurrectionism

Another issue with traditional left politics concerns its insurrectionist tendencies. Insurrectionism is the belief that social change will only come through revolution, or the overthrow of the existing order through armed conflict.

Although not held by all leftists, this perspective is shared by many communists and anarchists, and also by a number of radical activists who might not explicitly identify with either political label. Revolutions are important events in the history of social movements, and serve as potent reminders of our collective potential for radical change, even in the face of fearsome repression and overwhelming odds. Despite this, the dynamics of revolution are also complicated and often contradictory, while the track record of armed revolutions in accomplishing greater democratization and ecological sustainability is decidedly mixed.

The usefulness of revolution as a strategy of social change is highly dependent on the particular social context. In societies with major class inequality and an oligarchic elite with little legitimacy, insurrection can be a viable strategy. This speaks to the success of revolutions in Russia, Cuba, and China, and in countless former European colonies after World War II. These independence movements were catalyzed against the naked dominance of imperial rule, and thus were able to mobilize the mass political will and material support needed to overthrow colonizers through armed struggle. However, in Western democracies, the presence of welfare states, the middle class, and much higher levels of oligarchic legitimacy make revolution, in the present context, a non-starter.

In highly hegemonic states like Canada and the United States, insurrectionists continually run up against the concrete gains that people's movements have made in the past, and the real and powerful manifestations of the Life System that exist in the present day. This puts insurrectionists in the difficult position of advocating that subordinate groups destroy not just the structures and institutions of the Death System, but also those pro-social aspects of the Life System. As a result, for most North Americans the common anarchist cry of "Smash the State!" appears deeply contradictory. Do they mean smash public libraries, public parks, public schools, and social welfare systems? In Canada, do they mean to smash the public health care system that looks after their ailing relatives? A similar problem faces anti-civilization activists when they entreat citizens to "bring down civilization." Do they mean bring down access to clean water, shelter, food, and transportation?

The problem is that beneath insurrectionism lies an essentialist view of the modern state as totally oppressive; a view that is unsupported both theoretically and empirically.[19] Beyond this, I argue that insurrectionists miss the very qualities that first made cooperative human cultures possible. Research suggests that the evolution of egalitarianism was neither haphazard, nor inevitable. Instead, it represented a conscious, organized, collective response to critical challenges of individual and group survival. It represented a remarkably successful attempt to deal with the potential of aggressive alphas, cheats, and free-riders to disrupt cooperative cultures, and open the group to destructive internal conflict. The Life System is based on cooperation, and cooperation requires social stability, predictability, and moral rules of conduct and interaction. In contrast, the psychopathological Death System thrives on chaos and social breakdown. This is why war has historically been the most effective means of expanding oligarchic power both within and between societies, and this is also why history shows that societal chaos and collapse tend to reinforce oligarchy, not to lessen it. The rash of recent "revolutions" in countries like Serbia, Ukraine, Honduras, Brazil, Libya, Syria, and Egypt shows that elites can use insurrection as effectively as the left – if not more so.

Vanguardism

A final problem with many left theories is their tendency toward pessimism concerning people's ability to both understand their own interests and to act to change them. While activists on the left generally affirm the capacity of "the people," in practice their interactions with those outside their immediate sects can be elitist and alienating. Left activists are often "vanguardist." They see the "masses" as incapable of providing their own liberation, and as needing an elite party (a vanguard) that will lead a process of social revolution and dictate the terms of a new "worker's society."[20] That these authoritarian tendencies risk reproducing oligarchic relations under a different name is seldom acknowledged by followers of Lenin, Mao, Trotsky, and other authoritarian communists. Ironically, many activists inspired by anarchism also possess these elitist tendencies, which can lead to a "voluntarist" politics that focuses on the action of small radical groups, dismisses the concerns of non-radicalized citizens, ignores legitimate public fears of an overly confrontational and ideologically driven politics, and ultimately proves to be as vanguardist as the authoritarian left.

These problems with left theory and practice have long histories, but have been particularly prevalent in North American movements from the 1960s onward. While many activists in the student anti-war, civil rights, and women's movements were focused on reaching out to regular citizens and building a broad-based struggle, a significant number were caught up in vanguardism and "ultra-radicalism" that saw groups split along sectarian lines, pursue increasingly alienating and violent tactics, and end up infiltrated and destroyed by state operatives.[21] The US government COINTELPRO program, and similar Canadian operations run by the RCMP were highly successful at compromising activist groups that turned to underground, illegal, small-group struggles.[22] The Black Panthers, Weather Underground, and American Indian Movement all suffered this fate. Yet despite the failure of these groups to create fundamental change in the 1970s, contemporary radicals like Derrick Jensen, Aric McBay, and Lierre Keith espouse similar tactics in their 2011 book *Deep Green Resistance*.

Anti-civilization activists like Jensen, McBay, and Keith, more than any other writers, show how flawed analysis can lead today's radicals to make disastrous political decisions. These three writers have created a Deep Green Resistance (DGR) organization based on their understanding of civilization's crisis and their prescriptions for action. (McBay later left the group after a disagreement with the other founders).[23] Although not the only active anti-civilization organization, DGR is among the most prominent, and its founders are the most recognizable faces of contemporary anti-civilization thought. Earth First! and the Earth Liberation Front are other influential organizations with cells in several countries, and both work in sometimes uneasy alliance with Deep Green activists.[24] DGR derives its philosophy primarily from Jensen's writings in *End Game*, and *End Game: Resistance*.[25] Before discussing those aspects of DGR's theory and practice that are deeply misguided, there is first much to agree with.

DGR is very clear about the extent to which industrial capitalism is destroying the biosphere. In the preface to *Deep Green Resistance*, Jensen states:

> The dominant culture – civilization – is killing the planet, and it is long past time for those of us who care about life on earth to begin taking the actions necessary to stop this culture from destroying every living being.[26]

From this idea of civilization leading to dire and impending ecological destruction, Jensen then affirms that simply trying to slow the process of destruction is ineffective. Instead, members of DGR need to proactively work to destroy civilization before it destroys the biosphere:

> People routinely approach each of this book's authors – Aric, Lierre, and Derrick – and tell us how their hope and despair have merged into one. They no longer want to do everything they can to protect the places they love, everything, that is, except the most important thing of all: to bring down the culture itself. They want to go on the offensive. They want to stop this culture in its tracks.[27]

So far, what Jensen is saying is in line with my analysis in *Radical Transformation*. While civilization remains captive to the logic of the Death System, ecological destruction and human misery will continue and intensify. Reform of this system won't work, and instead it needs to be dismantled completely. So far, so good, but where my analysis and that of DGR sharply diverge is when considering what the "dominant culture" consists of and in assessing people's capacity to change.

In *Deep Green Resistance*, Aric McBay describes the "dominant culture" that is destroying the biosphere. He is first careful to state that the crisis doesn't stem from human nature, but instead is related to "the mode of social and political organization we call civilization."[28] McBay then goes on to detail this culture as being reliant on machines and technology, being based in cities, having an extensive division of labour, being militarized and patriarchal, relying on industrial agriculture, being politically hierarchical and centralized, and requiring massive human labour and ecosystem resources to sustain itself. McBay also notes that numerous historical civilizations have collapsed, and that ours is headed for the same fate. I echo this picture in my description of civilization, in chapter 7, as held within the grip of political oligarchy and its imperative of domination and exploitation. Like McBay, I maintain that this structure needs to be completely dismantled; however, McBay, Jensen, and Keith see no reality apart from this destructive and anti-human force. To them, *all* of modern civilization is violence, oppression, insanity, and ecocide. As such, the entire thing must be destroyed.

At this point DGR runs into the same problems that other left insurrectionists do. My research suggests that civilization evolved from two discernable patterns of interaction – oligarchy and moral community – and that both forces continue to be active in the present. Given that the Life System still exists, not all of civilization is destructive and oppressive, and there is much that still speaks to our innate sociality, empathy, and creative intelligence. This means that there are many structures and institutions in the world today that embody the best parts of our evolved nature. They include the accumulated knowledge in science, philosophy, art, music, and architecture; the emancipatory technologies like computers and the internet that connect global communities and enable knowledge to be shared more freely than ever before; and the universalist notions of human rights and democracy that inspire movements for justice worldwide. The presence of these things means that there is great transformative potential in contemporary civilization. Because of this, it's also true that most citizens of modern nation-states will be reluctant to see their societies destroyed.

Not that DGR is apparently looking for wider support or broader buy-in. The movement maintains that all of civilization is psychopathological, an over-simplification that on its own doesn't preclude building a movement to change civilization into something life-sustaining as opposed to life-destroying. However, DGR quickly forestall this possibility by saying categorically that people are either unwilling to or incapable of making this change. In discussing the perspective of those committed to "militant resistance" against civilization, McBay asserts:

> Humans aren't going to do anything in time to prevent the planet from being destroyed wholesale. Poor people are too preoccupied by primary emergencies, rich people benefit from the status quo, and the middle class (rich people by global standards) are too obsessed with their own entitlement and the technological spectacle to do anything.[29]

In the preface to *Deep Green Resistance*, Jensen says that he's asked thousands of people "whether this culture will undergo a voluntary transformation?" to which the great majority have responded "No." He then takes this as confirmation that a large-scale movement to transform civilization's trajectory from collapse to sustainability is impossible. However, when faced with such a loaded question, would we expect any answer other than "No"? Cultures don't change themselves – they are changed by the actions of human agents. The real question that Jensen should be asking is "Are people capable of transforming this culture?" In response to such a question, I would think anyone with a basic knowledge of progressive social movements would answer "of course we are."

If anything, the history of civilization is itself the story of constant change, and recent history has seen massive cultural shifts that have occurred over relatively condensed timeframes. The transatlantic slave trade – in the mid-eighteenth century the most lucrative economic activity in the world – was abolished in the British empire by 1807, with the institution of slavery itself being abolished in 1834. This epochal social change started with small groups of religious abolitionists and freed African slaves, eventually building to a massive social movement with broad public support. This widespread support eventually forced Parliament to act, over the committed resistance of economically and politically powerful slave traders.[30] Similarly, in 1790 New Jersey became the first American colony to grant women the vote, and in 1919 the Nineteenth Amendment was passed granting women the vote nation-wide.[31] The same monumental changes occurred when African Americans won the franchise and full legal rights, and when unions won recognition by the state and workers won rights.

The DGR position that a large-scale movement to transform civilization is impossible flies in the face of movement history and reveals a deeply pessimistic view of human intelligence and agency. It also appears *defeatist*, a term used to describe theorists and movements that have given up on the possibility of radical change, and this is why to many on the political left the DGR flow of (il)logic is baffling.[32] Because DGR's founders don't think that the systems of industrial capitalism will voluntarily transform themselves they appear to simply give up. To most leftist activists, the unlikelihood that systems of dominance and exploitation will voluntarily change is not only the most elementary of insights, but also precisely the point where a revolutionary's real work begins. To anyone that believes in people's ability to change their culture, then the central question becomes: "How can we facilitate this change?" If we believe in our innate intelligence and capacity for transformation, then this means we need to appeal to our reason and intelligence when enacting strategies of change. Revolutionaries must be perceived by the people they want to influence as legitimate, capable, and trustworthy. They – we – must also be seen as grounded in the values of the Life System – in equality, fairness, compassion, democracy, and the collective good.

To be fair, DGR's philosophy is not completely defeatist, in the sense that it *does* advocate for a certain strategy of change. However, by denying people's capacity and agency, Jensen, McBay, and Keith believe they don't need to worry about how their actions will be perceived by most citizens. Instead, DGR advocate a campaign of sabotage that will, in industrial capitalist states, make the vast majority of people's lives more precarious and more miserable than they currently are. As communications, energy, and transportation infrastructure are destroyed, the effects will fall disproportionately on society's most vulnerable – the poor, the sick, people with disabilities, the elderly, and children. In contrast, the wealthy will be best equipped to buffer the negative impact of an anti-civilization eco-war. These facts constitute the uncomfortable shadow aspect of DGR's calls to "bring down civilization," and in response to them, how would the majority of citizens not rationally and reasonably turn against the saboteurs? How will people not protect their own lives and livelihoods, and that of their families and community?

The prospect of DGR winning mainstream support for a campaign of covert eco-war is thus highly unlikely, and yet Jensen, McBay, and Keith suggest that an aboveground movement will organize to cheer on each piece of exploded infrastructure and to celebrate as all of the decadent trappings of the "dominant culture" are lost forever – things like computers, the internet, advanced medical technology, transportation and communication networks, and emergency services. This deeply contradictory picture is only one such problem with DGR's political strategy.

Logic also doesn't support DGR's strategy to "bring down civilization" by destroying modern science and technology, since science is the main methodology that Jensen, McBay, and Keith rely on for their appraisal of the ecological crisis. More glaringly, they completely ignore the massive potential of ecologically appropriate science and technology. They dismiss the rapid advances in renewables technology and the innovations in design that drastically reduce the amounts of energy, raw materials, and waste in production processes. They don't deal with renewables at all, and instead attack a straw man of their own construction, woven with every myth proffered by a fossil fuel industry desperate to discredit its inevitable successor. Wind power is too intermittent. Solar is a pipe-dream that won't work during the winter (an old fossil-fuelled chestnut that has long since been disproven).[33] In one "change is impossible, technology can't help" paragraph, Keith goes so far as to equate wind farms with tar sands bitumen extraction and mountain-top removal coal mining.[34] These statements deal serious blows to DGR's credibility.

Meanwhile, today's researchers doing serious work around renewables and sustainability are talking about distributed power generation coupled with massive energy efficiencies gained through economic relocalization and intelligent design. This design includes passivhaus technology and breakthroughs in photovoltaics, but also low-tech innovations like geothermal heating and cooling, thermal mass, passive solar, and water recycling "living machines."[35] Earthships are an incredible example of the promise held in low-tech intelligent designs that are cost-effective and utilize a high degree of recycled material and items previously considered "waste" (discarded tires, old glass bottles).[36] While it is true that renewable energy and eco-design, production, and construction aren't enough to avert the crisis of civilization, to say they have no place in this process is absurd.

Some insurrectionist philosophies, including DGR's, claim that their small-scale militant struggle can build a broad, supportive, "aboveground" movement. It is true that many movements against domination and exploitation have involved a dialectical relationship between aboveground mass mobilizations and underground guerilla campaigns. Keith mentions some in *Deep Green Resistance*, including the WSPU, a militant wing of the British women's suffrage movement. We could also mention the South African revolution against apartheid, the Irish independence struggle, the Cuban revolutionary war, and numerous other examples. These instances all indicate that aboveground movements and underground movements can work successfully together, and that this relationship can be a more powerful motivator of change than either tendency working in isolation.[37] However, where Keith and DGR as a whole get their history seriously wrong is in understanding how militant underground resistance arises, and under what conditions it is able to work effectively with mass, aboveground movements.

There are two main problems with the DGR perspective. The first is that in all of the examples referenced by them, and in the examples I have also given, the social struggle that led to resistance was one in which the subordinate group suffered from clear, harsh, and long-standing oppression from the dominant group. Thus, the women's suffrage movement arose from the subjugation of *all* women in society – a fact that had been long and widely acknowledged before the militant WSPU was formed.[38] Similarly, in the South African, Irish, and Cuban examples, movements emerged in response to the military domination of a nation by foreign powers. In each case, oppression had real, material effects on people's lives and led directly to violence, dehumanization and despair. It was also clear to the oppressed that they were the objects of vicious repression for outrageous, unjust, and illegitimate reasons. These characteristics of oppression – that it was widespread, harsh, clearly unjust, and clearly apprehended by the oppressed – created fertile ground for mass resistance against the oppressors. These same characteristics are necessary today for a serious large-scale movement, let alone an underground guerilla struggle, to emerge.

The second problem is that, apart from low-intensity individual acts of non-cooperation and sabotage that always occur among oppressed populations, widespread resistance generally first translates into movements for reform. Thus the first generations of the suffrage movement built a widespread social consensus that convinced most women, and even a great number of men, of the legitimacy and rightness of the suffragist cause. Without this broad-based understanding of the cause, and without a mass movement pursuing resistance in a way deemed legitimate by society at large, the more militant wing of suffragists would not have received the support they did, and would not have had the invigorating effect on the broader movement that they did. One could argue that the militants wouldn't even *exist* without this first phase of mass-movement building.[39] In their analysis, Keith et al. seem to lose sight of the need for even those in the resistance movement to feel legitimate by first trying to work "within the system," or to win their cause by being reasonable and making moral appeals. History shows that these first moves will often fail in the face of oligarchic power; however this process of attempt and failure is critical for raising the level of militancy in the movement as a whole, for mobilizing people and bringing them onside with the movement's goals, and for de-legitimizing the powers they are fighting.

The insurmountable problem that DGR faces is that today, the movement to "bring down civilization" – with its call to blow up public infrastructure and rapidly induce a global population die-off – has absolutely *no* popular legitimacy. Keith as much admits this herself:

> The radical environmental movement is largely white and well-assimilated into the noncommunity of the corporate-controlled, mass-media dominated, industrially produced culture of the contemporary United States and its colonies. Community has been destroyed to the point where we don't know the names of the people living twenty feet from us and communication has been reduced to keystrokes of consonants. Those of us from that world are not even starting from scratch; we're starting from negative.[40]

From my experience with radical environmentalism in Canada, this is a fair, and rather bleak assessment. Of course, it also describes the same daunting task faced by many radical movements seeking to create fundamental change in current social systems. At any given time the bulk of the population are – and this should surprise no one – socialized to accept and support the current system, and to resist changes to it. Realizing this fact is generally the point at which most radicals roll up their sleeves and begin working to combat oligarchic cultural indoctrination, to promote alternative understandings that delegitimize the elite, and to build the capacity of a large-scale movement for change. As this movement grows and becomes more successful, and as elites push back with increased repression, underground and guerilla wings may very well emerge, and will likely be supported by the majority of aboveground resisters as a justified response to legitimate demands unreasonably denied. As such, the challenge of building movement legitimacy and movement participation are the basic problems of social change that confront any radical organization, and yet those in the DGR movement seem to think they can just bypass the entire process and get right to blowing stuff up. Far from a political strategy, this is a prescription for political suicide, and it will only succeed in sending a small group of mostly young, white, middle-class activists straight to jail.

Successful direct action

In contrast to the kind of ill-considered eco-war espoused by DGR, there are numerous examples of militant resistance to environmental destruction that are strategically effective. Direct-action land defence has been instrumental in protecting embattled ecosystems from corporate exploitation. Historic battles fought over Clayoquot Sound, British Columbia, succeeded in protecting this old growth forest from clear-cut logging. Thousands of protestors from across North America were arrested at the Sound while participating in non-violent direct actions. Blockades in solidarity with the Tla-o-qui-aht and Ahousaht First Nations succeeded in backing down MacMillan Bloedel – one of the world's largest logging corporations. Over the most intense five months of the stand-off, 859 protestors were arrested. The conflict was eventually resolved when the British Columbia government signed an agreement with the First Nations that banned clear cutting. In 2000 the Sound was designated a UNESCO World Biosphere Reserve.[41]

Similar struggles for environmental defence are being waged by Native peoples in Canada, the United States, and worldwide. Recent Canadian examples include the conflict over Native fishing rights at Burnt Church, the struggle against clear-cut logging and toxic contamination at Grassy Narrows, the anti-fracking resistance at Elsipogtog, and resistance to the Northern Gateway and Line 9 pipeline developments.[42] Indigenous resistance is often militant and committed, and can be a powerful catalyst for broader opposition to destructive government and corporate behaviour. In the United States, Indigenous resistance to the Keystone XL pipeline, in conjunction with mass protests organized by 350.org, Greenpeace, and other environmental NGOs, put significant pressure on the Obama administration, leading the president to veto a bill approving the pipeline in February of 2015.[43] In Canada, the James Bay Cree were able to successfully fight the Great Whale hydroelectric development by organizing with environmental activists in Vermont. The land defenders were able to convince the state to cancel its contracts to purchase power from the Great Whale project, thus destroying its financial basis and halting its development.[44]

More recently, the inspiring action of the Standing Rock Sioux and their Native and non-Native supporters show the true potential of direct action when combined with legislative and economic pressure. I will revisit the Standing Rock protest later in the chapter, as an example of how a movement of movements can be successful in effecting radical, democratic change.

Hegemony and Counter-Hegemony

If the evidence I've presented so far about human nature and sociocultural evolution is taken seriously, then the approach to social change proposed by vanguardists, insurrectionists, and Deep Green resisters needs to be completely reconsidered.

What is needed to effect the radical transformation of oligarchic societies is not an authoritarian revolution or an ideologically "pure," militant vanguard. First, these strategies have little hope of working in modern democracies where the history of democratic struggles has strengthened the Life System and given elite power a strongly hegemonic character. Second, even if these "radical" projects manage to succeed, they risk simply replicating the cycle of oligarchy under the guise of progressive revolution (as in North Korea, Iran, Russia, and China). Authoritarian revolutions, even when inspired by noble goals, have often led to even more centralized political control, and to continued oppression. Even the French Revolution, rightly lauded as a powerful expression of democratic struggle, gave way to the *Terror*, the Thermidorian reaction, and the dictatorship of Napoleon Bonaparte. Such outcomes won't free us from the Death System's contradictions, and they won't resolve civilization's crisis.

What *can* resolve the crisis is the creation of a directly democratic and ecologically sustainable society – a revitalization of the Life System in which every person is brought within the bounds of moral community, and in which critical information from scientists, activists, and subordinate groups is factored into political decisions. The good news is that human beings are *built* for democracy. We are among the most cooperative and social species on the planet, yet our great intelligence also makes us creative, innovative, and autonomous. The blend of these characteristics enables language and culture, and also enables science, which depends on the free and democratic sharing of discovery and innovation.

Our ability to extend empathy – to recognize the interconnectedness of human and non-human life – creates the possibility of true solidarity across social divisions created by gender, class, race, ethnicity, and sexual identity. Our creative and collective capacity is a continuous thread running through the story of human evolution, and it can guide us in the present. The drastic changes since our origins have been in the scale and complexity of modern industrial societies. The challenge then, is to express the Life System in modern nation-states through a process of radical and progressive democratization that ultimately dismantles oligarchic power.

The history of social change reveals that oligarchy is in fact vulnerable to large-scale, committed opposition. Many historical examples exist of successful resistance to oligarchic rule, from ancient popular uprisings in Sumerian city-states to the democratic revolution in ancient Athens.[45] This capacity for large-scale resistance is also very possible in the present context, as evident from the past five years, in which massive popular uprisings have swept the globe. The Arab Spring, the European anti-globalization and anti-austerity movements, the global climate justice movement, the North American Occupy and Black Lives Matter movements, and resistance to the Dakota Access Pipeline are all manifestations of this renewed radicalism. Even the wasteland of mainstream electoral politics has seen promising shoots of radical growth in the past decade, with electoral victories by radical governments in Haiti, Venezuela, Bolivia, and Uruguay, as well as radical insurgencies in otherwise moribund political parties, such as Jeremy Corbyn's victory in Britain, the Bernie Sanders campaign in the United States, or the Leap Manifesto movement in Canada's NDP. These recent struggles, along with historic victories, prove that there is no justification for defeatism in the present moment, and no reason why the dire crisis we face can't be successfully met with a large-scale movement for radical change.

The history of movements against oligarchy also reminds us that in all times and places, elites are greatly outnumbered by the populations they rule over. In modern nation-states it is really the top 1 per cent of income earners that can properly be considered members of the oligarchic class, while approximately 20 per cent have close ties to this ruling elite, and benefit handsomely from the current political and economic set-up. This leaves approximately 80 per cent of citizens in Canada and the United States who would directly benefit from an end to oligarchic control. Of course, the privileged 20 per cent will also benefit from an end to the ecological devastation caused by oligarchy, but as they stand to lose a measure of political and economic power, they will tend to resist substantial change to the status quo.

The reason why the 80 per cent of citizens who would directly benefit from radical change *don't* realize this fact, rise up, and overthrow the Death System is due to the hegemonic nature of modern nation-states. Hegemony is a theory of political power developed by Italian Marxist Antonio Gramsci. Gramsci noted that oligarchs in industrial capitalist states rule primarily through providing "intellectual and moral leadership."[46] This concept has parallels to a founding myth of the Death System – the benevolence of the oligarchs – and thus describes an ancient phenomenon. For millennia oligarchs have been utilizing cultural narratives like the "divine right of kings" to legitimize their domination and exploitation of subordinate classes. What makes a modern hegemonic society different from past oligarchies in which power was more visibly concentrated in the form of monarchs, nobles, or the priesthood, is that in today's states power is seen to be largely distributed, and the oligarchic system has a high degree of legitimacy in the eyes of those who are ruled.

Elite legitimacy, today, comes largely from historic concessions, forced through demands from subordinates.[47] This reflects the Life System's ongoing evolution, with oligarchic power continually hemmed in through struggles to re-establish moral community and expand spaces of democracy, human rights, and ecological sustainability. This aspect of modern states speaks to the power of progressive, life-sustaining movements to effect real social change, and to organize at increasing levels of social complexity. However, it is equally true that these movements have not yet succeeded in fundamentally altering political and economic structures, and in overthrowing oligarchy. Modern states remain hegemonic, in which the elite allows limited reforms to co-opt movements, to increase their own legitimacy, and above all else, to maintain their grip on power.

Thus the Canadian government, while engaging in imperialist wars, supporting the socioeconomic status quo, and promoting the tar sands is also, in many people's eyes, the giver of universal health care, the protector of civil rights, and the provider of public education and social services. These life-sustaining institutions, coupled with the universal franchise and reasonably fair and open elections, reinforce perceptions of the state as legitimate guardian of the public good. That every one of these progressive aspects was won through committed activism by subordinate groups, and in defiance of elite and state repression, is generally absent from official histories, and thus from popular consciousness. Modern corporations and wealthy families exhibit similar hegemonic strategies when they support charitable causes. Thus CIBC (Canadian Imperial Bank of Commerce) sponsors the Run for the Cure, McDonald's funds Ronald McDonald houses, Suncor Energy has an Environment Fund, and the Ford, Rockefeller, and Guggenheim names grace prominent public buildings and charitable foundations. All of these sponsorships mask the predatory and ecologically destructive business practices of massive corporations and oligarchic families, and serve to legitimize them in the eyes of the public.

To Gramsci, it is the veil of legitimacy that cloaks oligarchic domination that needs to be torn off if fundamental change is to occur. Once oligarchic legitimacy is reduced to a critical level, then the power of elites is revealed as more dominance than consent – as illegitimate, immoral, and intolerable. At this point, Gramsci argues that a significant number of the 80 per cent who actually don't benefit from oligarchy might then be convinced to push for radical change.[48] The first task of counter-hegemonic movements is thus to delegitimize the actors and institutions of oligarchy, and to reveal their exploitative core. The second task of movements is to organize the opposition to oligarchy, and to build a counter-hegemonic *historic bloc* comprising the diverse groups that experience oppression under the current system.[49]

Gramsci argues that the process of counter-hegemony necessitates a multifaceted struggle within the institutions of *civil society* (churches, media, schools, workplaces, etc.) and also within the state. As a Marxist, Gramsci sees the goal of the counter-hegemonic bloc as overthrowing the capitalist class and seizing state power in the interests of the working class and its allies.[50] Although he thinks it is important that the forces opposing the elite be democratically organized, he believes that the proletariat, the industrial working class, is their natural leader.[51] In this sense, his goal was to replace oligarchic dominance of the capitalist class with oligarchic dominance of the working class and its allies.

In their book *Hegemony and Socialist Strategy*, left intellectuals Ernesto Laclau and Chantal Mouffe rid Gramsci's theory of its lingering essentialism, and argue that there is no historically necessary leader of a counter-hegemonic historic bloc. Laclau and Mouffe maintain that no single group – be it industrial workers, ethnic minorities, students, or women – has a privileged perspective from which to direct resistance to elite domination. Instead, they see the need for an equal and democratic movement of all subordinate groups – a "movement of movements" – that would come together around shared interests in peace, freedom, equality, justice, and ecological sustainability. Such a group might finally have the power, not just to extract concessions from elites, or to replace one oligarchic government for a more benevolent one, but to shatter the oligarchic system completely. This would involve the creation of a post-hegemonic society based on a direct, people's democracy.[52]

Post-Hegemonic Society

It is impossible (and perhaps a bit dangerous) to provide a detailed description of what a modern state freed from the Death System would look like. However, given the characteristics of the Life System identified in the previous chapter, it is possible to sketch a rough outline of what, for lack of a better name, could be called a *democratic, eco-socialist society*. Such a society would embody the basic principles of moral community, the irreducible minimum, and interbeing, and would manifest these principles in political, economic, sociocultural, and ecological subsystems.

Political

In the political realm society would be *democratic*, in which all citizens have access to decision-making power, and in which the rights of all citizens would be protected in law. This system would have the following characteristics:

1. A democratic form of government that largely de-links economic power from political power. This would include:

a. Publicly funded elections (no corporate funding of campaigns at all)
   b. A fully proportional voting system
   c. A ban on the "revolving door" between political office and industry
   d. Independent ombudsmen and transparency offices to strictly control lobbying and other forms of private influence on government
   e. Strong whistle-blower protection
2. Full political participation of all citizens
3. A participatory, or bottom-up, model of representation that includes:
   a. Neighbourhood councils and ward councils
   b. Representative recallability
   c. Participatory budgeting at municipal, regional, and national levels
   d. Referendums on key policy issues
4. An expanded Constitution/Charter of Rights and Freedoms that protects each citizen's human, citizenship, and cultural rights as outlined by the United Nations
5. Settlement of all Indigenous land claims and the establishment of self-governance for Indigenous groups
6. A democratic foreign policy, including:
   a. Strong support for a reformed, democratic United Nations
   b. Withdrawal from military alliances like NATO
   c. Commitment to diplomacy in international relations
   d. Limiting the military to the role of national defence and internationally sanctioned peace keeping
7. An anti-oppressive legal system in which:
   a. Laws are reformed in the interests of individual freedom and social justice
   b. Effective legal representation is affordable by all
   c. Legal sanctions are informed by the principles of restorative justice
   d. Policing is made fully publicly accountable

Economic

In the economic realm society would be *socialist* in character, in which all citizens had access to the means of subsistence, production, and a life well-lived. Characteristics of the economy would include:

1. A mixed economy that combines:
   a. An expanded state sector in which a number of key utilities (energy), services (postal service, schools, hospitals), banks, and primary industries (mining, steel production, etc.) are publicly owned and operated

b. An expanded cooperative and non-profit sector in which businesses and services are operated collectively
   c. A vibrant small-business sector
   d. A private sector in which competition and innovation are directed toward pro-social, ecological ends
2. A guaranteed annual income for all citizens
3. A minimum wage that is indexed to living wage standards
4. Incentives and supports for small businesses
5. Strong legal protection for workers, including support for trade unionization
6. Rewriting of corporate law to remove legal personhood and regulate the ethical conduct of corporations
7. Access for all to free healthcare
8. Access for all to free education
9. Divestment from the global arms industry
10. Significant reform of or withdrawal from neoliberal trade agreements (NAFTA, TPP) and a commitment to fair trade practices

Sociocultural

In the sociocultural realm society would embody the principle of *interbeing*, would foster scientific and creative endeavour, and would ensure equal access for all to cultural resources. Aspects of the culture would include:

1. Promotion of biosphere consciousness by government and education institutions
2. Strong public support for the arts, including school programs and support for working artists
3. Strong public support for scientific research and technological innovation
4. Promotion of anti-oppression, multiculturalism, and the celebration of human behavioural diversity
5. Ensuring the protection of a strong critical culture, including:
   a. Freedom of speech
   b. Freedom of assembly
   c. Freedom of protest and dissent
   d. A free and independent press
   e. Full academic freedom in post-secondary institutions

Ecological

In the ecological realm, all aspects of society would be environmentally sustainable and wild nature and ecosystemic diversity would be protected and expanded. This would include:

1. A zero-growth approach to economics
2. A renewable energy economy powered primarily by solar, wind, hydro, geothermal, and biofuel sources
3. All production and consumption decisions would meet strict standards of environmental sustainability, including:
    a. Industrial processes
    b. Building materials and building codes
    c. Urban design
    d. Transportation
    e. Resource extraction and management
    f. Waste management
4. A sustainable food production system would be created that is:
    a. Local
    b. Organic
    c. Ethically produced
5. Protection of wild nature and ecosystemic diversity that includes:
    a. Expanded wildlife sanctuaries
    b. Remediation of damaged ecosystems

This outline is a very rough approximation of what a democratic, eco-socialist society might actually look like. There are undoubtedly several important aspects that the sketch overlooks, and also considerably more work needed to flesh out many of the listed characteristics. The devil is in the details, as the old saying goes, and the actual contours of a radically transformed social landscape will no doubt change in various places and at different times. In truth, variability is to be encouraged. Enabling local solutions and creative alternatives to thrive is part of what freeing civilization from the oligarchic Death System means. Within the basic principles of democracy, socialism, interbeing, and ecological sustainability, there are countless possible social forms. Movements will develop these forms in light of specific contexts, and most change will be accomplished in stages and through a succession of intermediate forms.

A final point to mention is that some may consider the aspects of a democratic, eco-socialist society that I've presented to be worthwhile, but feel that there is no chance of actually achieving them in practice. Given the forces arrayed against realizing these changes, such cynicism is entirely understandable. Moving from where we are now to something approximating a democratic, eco-socialist society is what I mean by *radical transformation*, and in the final section I will attempt to sketch an equally rough, but hopefully useful, picture of how this change can happen.

Organizing for Radical Transformation

For help with the critical question of how we transform our current oligarchic society into a democratic, eco-socialist society, I return again to Gramsci. As power in hegemonic states is based on perceived legitimacy, then a counter-hegemonic movement of movements must work to delegitimize the rule of elites, while simultaneously building the legitimacy and transformative capacity of the movement. One of the key problems we face is that, because today's governments provide important social services, most of us who are citizens of modern nation-states are rationally averse to the destruction of the current social order. This keeps us from acting decisively to combat its corrupt, authoritarian, and exploitative aspects. To overcome this reluctance, we have to believe that the movement seeking to overthrow the oligarchic power structure is *more legitimate* and a better guardian of moral community than are the oligarchs. This means that movement activists have to take people's intelligence seriously and speak their language, address their concerns, and make programs of change understandable to those who will ultimately carry them out.

In contrast, if movements in opposition are perceived as advocating chaos, violence, and the complete upending of social stability, then they will be *rationally* opposed by the majority of citizens in a hegemonic society.

Life System revolutionaries

To build popular appeal and grow membership, transformative movements need to ground themselves in the existing structural manifestations of the Life System – in terms of institutions, norms, and values. We have to speak and act from a place of sociocultural legitimacy, and to claim ownership over the great motivating concepts of human society – family, community, democracy, freedom, equality, justice, and environmental stewardship. In a hegemonic society these are concepts that are cynically manipulated by oligarchs to keep subject populations in thrall. However, in this elites play a dangerous game, for these concepts speak to deep human aspirations. They are inherently supportive and sustaining of life, and in their true form they represent the very antithesis of oligarchy. The critical task of Life System revolutionaries is to reinterpret and mobilize these concepts, and to manifest them in four strategic areas: resistance, education, solidarity-building, and alternatives-building.

Resistance: Resistance involves directly opposing the destructive and exploitative actions of oligarchs. It means doing as much as possible to jam the gears of the military machine that enables foreign wars of aggression; to confront the corporate and banking interests that pilfer public wealth and impoverish millions; to stop the destructive, fossil fuel powered industrial economy in its mad rush to destroy the biosphere; and to fight the racist, sexist, homophobic, and xenophobic culture that disenfranchises, marginalizes, and murders countless thousands. Resistance of all forms to the destructive manifestations of the Death System is critical in that it slows the rate of destruction and ameliorates harm done to vulnerable populations and to the biosphere. It is also an invaluable tool in educating us about injustice and crisis, and in empowering us to make change. Successful resistance, involving actions that are both strategic and radical, is the engine that drives transformative movement.[53]

Education: The second key task is education, and it directly addresses the problem of consciousness. A critical mass of us will only mobilize to change civilization from collapse to sustainability if we are informed about the crisis we face, its causes, and the ways in which it can be transformed. Education helps with the pivotal task described by sociologist C. Wright Mills, in which people learn that their individual problems and challenges are actually related to the experiences of others, and determined in important ways by larger social structures.[54] Education takes place in many different contexts, including courses taught within traditional secondary and post-secondary institutions, conferences, teach-ins, talks, and workshops. Creative forms of education can also be highly effective, and movements have a long history of using song, theatre, and visual art to tell important stories, to create a sense of collective purpose and identity, and to fortify people to take up the struggle for a better world.

Solidarity-building: Solidarity-building refers to building common understandings and frameworks for collective action among diverse communities – creating what Gramsci terms the *historic bloc*. This process is organic, in that it can't be forced or rushed. Building solidarity between subordinate groups with different identities, experiences, and concerns takes time. It involves listening to others, building trust, and building relationships that are deeper than temporary, issue-focused coalitions. Through solidarity-building, movements create democratic structures of communication, organization, and decision making in which different groups can participate. These structures build unity around shared goals, while protecting space for difference, debate, and disagreement. The ability of diverse groups to act democratically in movement is a precursor to their ability to do so when exercising political power.

Alternatives-building: The final task of alternatives-building occurs at several levels of the social system, and includes reforming existing mainstream institutions, supporting existing alternative institutions, and creating new institutions as needed. Transformative movements will need to work both within established structures, and outside of them. Those working outside have the important task of building new institutions that embody the values of the Life System – organic farms, co-operatives, neighbourhood associations, political organizations, alternative schools, and social enterprises. Those working "within and against" are invaluable in creating democratic openings and strengthened public oversight in institutions of strategic importance such as policing, education, healthcare, and the military. Working within institutions also involves democratizing state power – a topic of some contention among contemporary progressive movements (or what some theorists term "new" social movements, as distinguished from earlier labour and socialist struggles).[55]

Democratizing the state includes making structural changes to the process of electoral politics that increase the representativeness and proportionality of voting and put controls on campaign finance by wealthy individuals and corporations. Other important reforms include introducing elements of direct democracy such as popular referendums, representative recall rights, and participatory budget processes. Strengthening mechanisms of government accountability is also crucial, and includes legislation to make it easier to demand public inquiries, to appoint third-party government accountability positions like ombudsmen and privacy commissioners, and to ensure that oversight mechanisms are strong. Finally, state transformation also entails engaging in electoral politics – whether pushing existing "labour" parties in a more radical direction, or more likely establishing new parties that express the goals of radical democratization and sustainability.

Engaging the critical tasks of movement-building also requires activists to cultivate the skillful understanding and use of emotion. Although oligarchs constantly try to appropriate the symbols and values of the Life System, at its core the Death System is driven by fear, threat, and anger. These emotions divide us, cause us to turn inward, and enable us to be easily controlled. They are the enemies of empathic extension, and tend to reinforce in-group/out-group distinctions and xenophobia. Because of these effects, transformative movements need to carefully consider how they deal with fear and anger internally, and how they express these emotions to those outside of the movement.

Dealing with anger and fear is a balancing act, as these emotions are rational and legitimate responses to the violence, oppression, and ecological destruction that movements oppose. Outrage at injustice can be powerfully motivating, and it is unreasonable to attempt to micro-manage the emotional experience of those resisting the Death System's depredations, or to attempt to cleanse all "negativity" from the movement. At the same time though, it is important to realize the limitations of fear and anger, and the dangers that lurk if they become a movement's primary fuel. Without a positive and affirming emotionality to balance our fear and anger, activists will be hard pressed to create the kind of aspirational politics that will inspire large-scale mobilization. If a counter-hegemonic movement is to be successful, then it is not enough that we fear and despise the Death System. We also have to cultivate the feelings of compassion, solidarity, hope, and even joy, which human beings and human communities need to survive and thrive.

Non-reformist reform

The challenge of a counter-hegemonic movement will be to balance radical analysis and goals, movement legitimacy, and a strategy of successful, yet gradual reform. The actions of Life System revolutionaries must firmly establish the *historic bloc* as true defender of moral community, and must base its direction on the 80 per cent of interests shared between subordinate groups. If the movement of movements is democratically constituted (based on power-with), and not just a number of "peripheral" groups shoe-horned into a political program laid out by a dominant group (such as, those intellectuals speaking on behalf of the industrial working class), then expecting 100 per cent agreement among members is impractical. Human behavioural and cultural diversity are incredible strengths, and democracy, or democratic struggle, does not imply homogeneity of identity, thought, or action. However, through empathic extension and shared experience the 80 per cent of people who are oppressed by oligarchic structures *can* be united by the vision of a renewed moral community – a directly democratic state based on human rights, cultural rights, citizenship rights, economic equality, and ecological sustainability. Creating this unifying vision requires movements to build relationships of solidarity among diverse groups, and to ensure that unity in action does not erase their autonomy. As ecofeminist activist Vandana Shiva says in relation to the broad-based anti-globalization movement, "We are about similar issues; but we are not about *identical* issues."[56]

Because insurrectionism isn't currently viable in states like Canada and the United States, the strategies and tactics used by a counter-hegemonic movement must be based on progressive reforms of social institutions and the state. They must be guided by the radical goal of ending oligarchy and replacing it with direct democracy, and thus must not be "reformist" in character. Anarchist theorist Michael Albert developed a useful, if slightly unwieldy term for this strategy of gradual radicalism – *non-reformist reform*.[57] In *The Trajectory of Change* Albert explains how the strategy works:

> How do we win new gains along the road? We raise the social cost of not granting the gains we seek until we reach the point where those who don't want to give in to our demands have no choice but to do so. Change is a combination of a sequence of reforms or limited victories that string together into a pattern in which we continually change the contours of the world we live in, making ourselves stronger and making those who oppose us weaker until, ultimately, we win basic alterations.[58]

Albert's concept of non-reformist reform helps resolve the argument that has long divided gradualist and insurrectionist theories of change. The position of insurrectionists is that it is impossible to overthrow capitalism, or the deeper system of political oligarchy, through gradual means. They argue that the hegemonic power of elites is so strong that any reform will inevitably fail to confront elite power, and will instead become reformist, and serve to strengthen the hegemony of rulers. This is a valid critique, and in truth many changes to current political and economic systems *do* end up being hegemonic in character. The gains of the civil rights movement during the 1960s and 1970s, while incredibly important, didn't manage to fundamentally transform the racist American culture that continues to sentence so many black and brown men and women to poverty, violence, and incarceration. Similarly, a massive anti-war movement played a significant role in forcing the US military out of Vietnam, but has since done little to disrupt the perpetual war economy. These and others are examples of seemingly radical gains in a hegemonic society being ultimately co-opted by elites, and their potential for fundamental change grounded out in minor concessions.

However, gradualists can point to much historical evidence proving that some reforms of the social system don't just solidify elite hegemonic control, but instead create fundamental changes that expand spaces of democracy and limit oligarchic power.

In chapter 7, I discuss the concept of *structuration*, where successive non-fundamental social changes can, over time, lead to fundamental change. In this sense, reforms can act as an "evolutionary ratchet" in which it becomes incredibly difficult to undo their cumulative systemic effects. These concepts help explain how oligarchy emerged out of successive changes to an originally egalitarian political community, and how this new political formation has been so durable and resistant to change. However, structuration can also work in the direction of democracy, ecological sustainability, and human rights. Some social innovations become "ratchets in reverse," and serve to advance aspects of the Life System that prove remarkably durable in the face of constant oligarchic attack. Some examples of this reverse ratchet effect are state-funded healthcare systems, electoral democracy, the universal franchise, the idea of equal rule of fair and impartial law, the idea of universal civil and human rights, and the notion of ecological stewardship. All of these innovations were won through decades and sometimes centuries of counter-hegemonic struggle, and although their achievement has been at best partial, and not enough to overthrow the Death System, they have created tangible social improvements that increase the well-being and political capacity of subordinate groups.

The constant presence of democratic struggle gives oligarchic polities a seesaw trajectory of development. At times oligarchs are able to crush the democratic urge and its manifest structures and institutions. Yet, this victory is seldom complete, and waits only for the resurgence of power-with in new, more potent forms. While one or the other tendency may be controlling at a given time, the struggle between them is present at all times. Thus in Canada a profoundly undemocratic Conservative Party under Steven Harper was recently responsible for subverting the electoral process, decimating government support for environmental and social justice NGOs, persecuting government whistle-blowers, muzzling government scientists, engaging in foreign wars without popular consent, ramming through a destructive tar sands and pipeline energy policy, and increasing economic inequality.[59] At the same time, the Occupy, Idle No More, and Quebec student movements demonstrate enormous grassroots support for democratic renewal; Fair Vote Canada is building public pressure to deepen electoral democracy; participatory budgeting and neighbourhood association movements are sweeping the country; and a robust local environmentalism based on sustainable food, community gardens, organic produce, public transit, renewable energy, and local economy is deepening its roots.

The United States is no different. The Trump presidency represents a massive step backwards in the character of government, as the state falls even deeper into the grip of the oligarchic class. White supremacists, climate change deniers, crony capitalists and misogynists have all been given an unholy boost through the Republican victory, and the coming four years will see civil society and progressive movements fighting for their very survival. Conversely, the incredible success of Bernie Sanders' campaign for the Democratic nomination shows just how ready the electorate is for truly progressive change. Sanders is no Marxist revolutionary, but the social democratic reforms he campaigned on – free post-secondary education, a $15 minimum wage, strong action on climate change, strengthening worker's rights – are near-revolutionary in the context of current US politics. Equally hopeful is the resurgence of the civil rights movement in Black Lives Matter, the growing movement for climate justice, and the widespread resistance to Trump's presidency.

The internet is another important site of hegemonic struggle in North America today, and despite its dual character, it may well prove to be another reverse ratchet, and a powerful force for dismantling the Death System. As a relatively wide-open conduit of information, the internet can be looked at as embodying the best and worst of human culture. It makes scientific, philosophical, and artistic knowledge more widely available to the general public than at any other time in history. This leap in information accessibility is orders of magnitude greater than that provided by the printing press. The internet radically expands global connections and enables the ideas of human rights, democracy, and citizenship rights to spread worldwide. Because of this massive information network, it is easier than ever for transformative movements to coordinate their actions, and it is harder than ever for oligarchs to hide atrocity and control information.

Of course, it is equally true that the open internet is increasingly colonized by the forces of consumer capitalism, and hemmed in by the control of oligarchic governments. As such, while it enables the freest access to information in human history, it also enables the most widespread and effective forms of government surveillance. All state secret service agencies monitor internet activity – for example, CSIS (Canadian Security Intelligence Service) and the NSA (US National Security Agency) – with Edward Snowden's brave act of whistle-blowing just confirming what many Americans already feared to be true.[60] The internet is also a massive repository of porn, mindless marketing, corporate and government propaganda, deliberately misleading information, and distracting infotainment.

These regressive potentials exist alongside the net's potentials for liberation, and yet despite the clear threat the internet presents to oligarchic dominance, it has thus far proven resilient in the face of attempts to censor or commodify it. This speaks to the importance of the net to billions of people, and particularly to youth, who seem to almost intuitively grasp its transformative potential. If anything can rally the mainstream of North American youth behind the need for progressive change, it will be an attempt by oligarchs to shut down the net. The youth-led movement to preserve net neutrality is currently waging this important struggle, and finding unexpected allies among scientists and even information technology corporations.[61]

The struggle for control being waged over the internet, and within countless other institutions, means that transformative movements will have to engage multiple battlegrounds. In each of these conflict sites the goal remains to delegitimize the position of elites and to build the legitimacy and capacity of resisters. A helpful metaphor for this counter-hegemonic struggle via gradual, yet radical, reforms is to view the matrix of oligarchic control as an elastic. In the face of committed opposition, the hegemonic power of oligarchs will stretch, as they manage the challenges of movements through both coercion and strategic reform. This process can continue, seemingly endlessly, until finally the hegemonic structure snaps.

When hegemony does rupture, and elite dominance is revealed as naked, illegitimate oppression, the strength of a movement receives its deciding test. If it lacks broad-based legitimacy among the state's citizens, then it either accepts a reformist bid from the oligarchic class (a Justin Trudeau or Hillary Clinton) or else is crushed under an authoritarian counter-revolution.

However, if the movement has legitimacy and has sufficiently built its capacity for above and belowground struggle, then it stands a chance of breaking the elite stranglehold on decision making and of once more aligning human evolution with moral community and its democratic, creative, and life-sustaining values.

Standing Rock: A Model for Change?

A movement for radical transformation doesn't yet exist in tangible form; however the recent protest against the Dakota Access Pipeline (DAPL) is an inspiring example of what is possible when movements are grounded in the Life System and committed to strategic, coordinated action. In a dark time in US politics, the Lakota Sioux water protectors are lighting a way forward, and their struggle can teach us important lessons from both its successes and from its set-backs.

The Standing Rock Sioux Tribe have been opposed to a pipeline through their lands since 2014, when the $4 billion DAPL was first proposed.[62] Texas-based Energy Transfer Partners intend the pipeline to move oil from North Dakota oilfields to river ports in Illinois. Under federal law the Sioux had to be consulted about the pipeline's impact on their lands, and especially on the Missouri River, their main source of drinking water. When the tribe was not consulted by Energy Transfer Partners before construction began, a protest was organized in April of 2016. It was quickly followed by legal action based on a violation of treaty rights and environmental law.[63]

The protests were originally held by the Standing Rock Sioux Tribe alone. They called themselves "water protectors," and evoked traditional values of environmental stewardship, protection of the land for future generations, and opposition to the ecological devastation caused by shale oil production and transportation via pipeline.[64] Their concerns were well founded, as the Pipeline and Hazardous Materials Safety Administration (PHMSA) documented more than 3,300 US pipeline leaks and ruptures since 2010.[65] When the Standing Rock protestors were met with state repression and arrests, they put a call out to all Native and non-Native people to come stand with the water protectors and to shut down the pipeline. Incredibly, Native tribes from across North America answered the call, and the global climate change movement endorsed the protest fully, bringing to bear its considerable media and political influence.[66]

In the face of violent assaults by police and national guard, the water protectors responded with prayer, solidarity, and an implacable spirit of resistance. Throughout the struggle the protestors fully embodied the values of the Life System, and as the battle wore on their public legitimacy steadily increased, while the legitimacy of pipeline corporations, police, the Army Corps of Engineers, and the Obama administration steadily declined. In November and December of 2016, a crucial turning point occurred as major politicians like Bernie Sanders started publicly calling to halt construction, numerous celebrities expressed their support, Lakota Sioux elders addressed the United Nations, and over 2,000 US Army veterans journeyed to Standing Rock to act as "human shields" for the water protectors.[67] In the face of this mounting pressure, on December 4, the Army Corps of Engineers decided to deny permits to continue construction of the pipeline under the Missouri River.[68]

The temporary halt to construction was an inspiring victory and shows that a broad-based movement with deep popular legitimacy can stand up against the fossil fuel industry and against the repressive force of the state. The movement is combining militant resistance, masterful public education, and a diversity of transformative strategies. Banks are being pressured to divest, foreign governments are being pressured to boycott, politicians are being pressured to act, and the imagination and will of citizens worldwide is being mobilized.[69]

The transformative potential demonstrated by the Standing Rock resistance is very real, and yet despite its accomplishments, the 2016 election result was catastrophic for the water protectors. The Trump administration is once more pushing the pipeline project forward, and the full weight of state repression is again falling on protestors. The water protectors have skillfully used resistance, solidarity-building and education, but have also revealed the limitations of grassroots movements when they are unaccompanied by a successful strategy to reform the oligarchic state. With Sanders in power, it is likely that Obama's decision to hold construction of the pipeline would have stood. With Trump in power, the resistance movement's success now seems remote.

In this book's introduction I describe the failure of a coalition of activists to save Hamilton's Red Hill Valley from destruction. Experiencing the sting of this defeat caused me to ask: "The next time a conflict like Red Hill happens, how can we save the valley?" At Standing Rock it seems like an answer to this question is within sight, only this time the defenders are attempting to save a major river, a Native community's sovereignty, and hope for a clean energy future. Despite the tragic recommencement of construction, the battle against the DAPL is not over yet, and the larger struggle against expansion of the fossil fuel economy is just beginning. If resistance movements like Standing Rock and political movements like the Sanders campaign ever joined together, then a force capable of challenging oligarchic power might finally be born. The very possibility is great cause for hope.

The Road Ahead

In *Evolution's Arrow*, systems theorist John Stewart states that humanity is at an evolutionary crossroads:

> If humanity is to achieve future evolutionary success, we must not only transform ourselves, we must also transform our societies. Our individual efforts to contribute to the successful evolution of life will be futile without radical changes to our social organization. It is only through the formation of cooperative organizations of larger scale and greater evolvability that humanity can participate successfully in the future evolution of life in the universe.[70]

Stewart's theory of evolving complexity sees a tendency in the evolution of life to produce increasingly more complex and cooperative systems. Through the emergence of *management functions*, the benefits of cooperation are passed on to all participating members in a complex system. He argues that this evolutionary process has led to more complex organisms, to human cultures, and to ever-larger human communities. To Stewart, the great challenge facing civilization today is creating a global democratic management system, in which all human communities are contained within a unifying moral framework.

The concept of *moral community* embodies the systemic management function described by Stewart, as early human cultures structured relationships in the interest of cooperation. Like Stewart, I argue that the only way humanity can meet the challenge of our current crisis is to reassert the pro-social framework of moral community, and to expand its bounds to include all peoples, all nations, and the natural world. Unlike Stewart though, I don't think that this goal represents a predetermined direction to the evolutionary process. The future is fundamentally uncertain, and could lead to the dissolution and collapse of civilization as much as to its democratic transformation. Which path we take is dependent on human imagination, will, and agency. The face of the future depends on the work we do today.

Despite our best predictions, the truth is that it's impossible to know exactly which of the planet's crises will reach tipping points, and when. It is also impossible to know how oligarchs will respond to intensifying crises on a state by state basis – whether through reformism or despotism. It may well be that progressive movements are able to shift social systems enough so that civilization is able to transition to a sustainable form without first experiencing a catastrophic crunch. The potential is certainly there, and would be the best possible outcome. However, it is in no way guaranteed, and it is also possible that the scenario of complete collapse occurs, and that movements are forced to literally fight for their lives and for the life of the biosphere itself. Regardless of which future scenario does play out, the most important work we can do remains building the large-scale democratic counter-power necessary to dismantle the Death System and institute a sustainable, participatory, people's democracy.

Asserting popular control over political decision making is of critical importance, as regardless of the organizing we do, some of the processes already set in motion – like climate change, water depletion, and population growth – will invariably present massive challenges to societies worldwide. There will be difficult debates between accepting immigrants and refugees and maintaining a stable and sustainable domestic population. There will be difficult debates concerning how to phase out fossil fuels and re-orient economies toward zero-growth, sustainable models based on localization and powered by renewable energy. There is no way to immediately resolve these issues, but in each case the best chance we have of resolving them in the interests of a humane and sustainable future is to have in place a directly democratic society in which all available knowledge and expertise can be used to ensure the collective good and preserve individual freedom.

Ultimately, there are three factors that will determine the success or failure of a counter-hegemonic project to transform civilization: context, consciousness, and movement. Context refers to the objective facts of crisis as they appear today in ecological, sociocultural, political, and economic subsystems. As crisis intensifies, the potential for radical change also intensifies, and today the context is bleaker than it ever has been. This creates an opportunity, but unless context translates into an awareness of crisis, its cause, and its possible solution, then worsening objective conditions can fail to spark movement. In recent years we can see widespread evidence that popular consciousness, in countries around the globe, is ripening. The Arab Spring, the Occupy Movement, the global climate justice movement, resistance to austerity in European countries, widespread labour unrest in China, the recent success of insurgent political candidates like Bernie Sanders and Jeremy Corbyn – all of these phenomena reveal mass concern, and a growing understanding of how crisis emerges from inequalities in wealth and political power and from unsustainable economies. Rebellion is in the air, and yet at the present moment it has not been met with the third condition for transformation – an organized, broad-based, and radical movement for democratic socialism and ecological sustainability.

This "movement of movements" will have to boldly speak the truth about our present predicament, and offer a vision of what modern states could be like with the Life System ascendant. The movement will also require a practical, scientifically grounded program of transformation. The protest at Standing Rock is a compelling example of how such a movement can wage an effective counter-hegemonic struggle. If we can learn the lessons of such victories, and combine them with successful strategies for electoral change, then we have a real chance of success.

Reformists want us to make minor adjustments to the state, leaving its oligarchic core intact. Insurrectionists want us to smash the state, in the mistaken assumption that freedom will emerge from societal breakdown. Authoritarians want us to seize the state, and use it to enforce a new oligarchic rule by the party elite. Radical transformation, in contrast, means we must fully *democratize* the state. Success or failure at this task will determine whether human evolution continues its slide into a nightmare world of war, poverty, and ecological collapse, or else leaps forward into a sane, humane, and sustainable future.

Notes

Introduction: Welcome to the Apocalypse

1. Bill Freeman, *Hamilton: A People's History* (Toronto: Lorimer, 2006).
2. Eric Crighton et al., "A Spatial Analysis of Asthma Prevalence in Ontario," *Canadian Journal of Public Health* 103, no. 5 (2012): 384–89.
3. Steven Dutch, "The Niagara Escarpment," last modified June 18, 1999, uwgb.edu/dutchs/GeologyWisconsin/niagesc.htm.
4. Friends of Red Hill Valley, "Red Hill Archives" (July 31, 2004).
5. "City of Waterfalls" accessed February 20, 2017, cityofwaterfalls.ca.
6. Walter Peace, "Farm, Forest and Freeway: Red Hill Creek Valley, 1950–1998," in *From Mountain to Lake: The Red Hill Creek Valley* (Hamilton, ON: W.L. Griffin Printing, 1998), 227.
7. Friends of Red Hill Valley, "Red Hill Archives" (July 31, 2004).
8. Ibid.
9. Nicholas Meyer, *The Day After* (ABC Television Network, November 20, 1983).
10. M. Alex Johnson, "The Culture of Einstein," Msnbc.com, updated April 18, 2005, nbcnews.com.
11. Michael S. Hyatt, *The Millennium Bug: How to Survive the Coming Chaos* (Washington, DC: Lanham, MD: Regnery, 1998).
12. Rachel Carson, *Silent Spring* (Boston, MA: Houghton Mifflin, 1962).
13. Club of Rome, *The Limits to Growth: A Report for the Club of Rome's Project on the Predicament of Mankind*, ed. Donella H. Meadows (New York: Universe Books, 1972).
14. "IPCC Working Group II," accessed February 2017, ipcc.ch/report/ar5.
15. Derrick Jensen, *Endgame*, vol. 1 and 2 (New York: Seven Stories Press, 2006).
16. Jared M. Diamond, *Collapse: How Societies Choose to Fail or Succeed*, rev. ed. (New York: Penguin Books, 2011).
17. James Lovelock, *The Vanishing Face of Gaia: A Final Warning* (New York: Basic Books, 2009).
18. George Monbiot, *Bring on the Apocalypse: Essays on Self-Destruction* (Canada: Doubleday, 2011), contentreserve.com.
19. Bill McKibben, *Eaarth: Making a Life on a Tough New Planet*, rev. ed. (New York: St. Martin's Griffin, 2011).
20. "Free Market Economist Nouriel Roubini: 'Karl Marx had it right. At some point, capitalism can destroy itself. You cannot keep on shifting income from labor to capital without having an excess capacity and a lack of aggregate demand,'" August 16, 2011, WashingtonsBlog.com.
21. Markus Brunnermeier and Martin Oehmke, "Bubbles, Financial Crises, and Sys-

temic Risk," in *Handbook of the Economics of Finance*, vol. 2, part B (North Holland, 2013), 1221–88.
22 Safa Motesharrei, Jorge Rivas, and Eugenia Kalnay, "Human and Nature Dynamics (HANDY): Modeling Inequality and Use of Resources in the Collapse or Sustainability of Societies," *Ecological Economics* 101 (May 2014): 90–102.
23 Trevor Maynard, "Society and Security: Food System Shock: The Insurance Impacts of Acute Disruption to Global Food Supply," 2015, Lloyds.com.
24 Gerardo Ceballos et al., "Accelerated Modern Human-Induced Species Losses: Entering the Sixth Mass Extinction," *Science Advances*, June 19, 2015.
25 P.R. Ehrlich and A.H. Ehrlich, "Can a Collapse of Global Civilization Be Avoided?" *Proceedings of the Royal Society B: Biological Sciences* 280, no. 1754 (March 7, 2013).
26 Roland Emmerich, *The Day After Tomorrow* (20th Century Fox, 2004).
27 Max Brooks, *World War Z: An Oral History of the Zombie War* (New York: Three Rivers Press, 2006).
28 ZombieResearchSociety.com.
29 Noam Chomsky, *Hegemony or Survival: America's Quest for Global Dominance* (New York: Holt Paperbacks, 2004).
30 "Remembering the Social Movements That Reimagined Argentina: 2002–2012," January 17, 2012, Upsidedownworld.org.
31 Joseph A Tainter, *The Collapse of Complex Societies* (Cambridge, UK; New York: Cambridge University Press, 1988 hardcover/1990 paperback).
32 Diamond, *Collapse*.
33 Thomas Homer-Dixon, *The Upside of Down: Catastrophe, Creativity and the Renewal of Civilization* (Toronto: Vintage Canada, 2007).
34 Diamond, *Collapse*, 419–40.
35 Homer-Dixon, *The Upside of Down*, 28.
36 Ibid., 16.
37 Diamond, *Collapse*.
38 Homer-Dixon, *The Upside of Down*, 42.
39 Anne Phillips, "What's Wrong with Essentialism?" *Distinktion: Scandinavian Journal of Social Theory* 11, no. 1 (2010): 47–60.
40 Barry Hindess and Paul Q. Hirst, *Pre-Capitalist Modes of Production*, new ed. (London; Boston: Routledge, 1977).
41 Ernesto Laclau and Chantal Mouffe, "Post-Marxism Without Apologies," *New Left Review*, I, no. 166 (December 1987): 79–106.
42 Lucien van der Walt and Michael Schmidt, *Black Flame: The Revolutionary Class Politics of Anarchism and Syndicalism* (Edinburgh; Oakland: AK Press, 2009).
43 Jensen, *Endgame*, vol. 1 and 2.
44 John Zerzan, *Future Primitive and Other Essays* (Semiotext, n.d./ Autonomedia, 1994).
45 Daniel Quinn, *Beyond Civilization: Humanity's Next Great Adventure* (New York, NY: Broadway Books, 2000).
46 Yves Engler, *The Black Book of Canadian Foreign Policy* (Vancouver: Fernwood, 2009).
47 Nafeez Mosaddeq Ahmed, *A User's Guide to the Crisis of Civilization: And How to Save It* (Pluto Press, 2010).

48 Ernesto Laclau and Chantal Mouffe, *Hegemony and Socialist Strategy: Towards A Radical Democratic Politics*, 2nd ed. (London; New York: Verso, 2014), 133–55.
49 Murray Bookchin, *Philosophy of Social Ecology* (Montreal: Black Rose Books, 1995).
50 Arne Naess, "The Shallow and the Deep, Long-Range Ecology Movement," *Inquiry* 16 (1973): 95–100.
51 Greta Gaard and Lori Gruen, "Ecofeminism: Toward Global Justice and Planetary Health," *Society and Nature* 2 (1993): 1–35.
52 Antonio Gramsci, *Selections from the Prison Notebooks*, ed. Quntin Hoare and Geoffrey Nowell Smith (New York: International Publishers, 1971).

1: Collapse

1 Bart D. Ehrman, *The New Testament: A Historical Introduction to the Early Christian Writings*, 3rd ed. (New York: Oxford University Press, 2004).
2 Tacitus, *The Annals*, The Internet Classics Archive, classics.mit.edu.
3 Derrick Jensen, *Endgame*, vol. 1.
4 *Websters II New Riverside Dictionary* (New York: Houghton Mifflin, 1984).
5 Dictionary.com, "Civilization."
6 Emile Benveniste, *Problems in General Linguistics* (Coral Gables, FL: University of Miami Press, 1973).
7 Cynthia Stokes Brown, "What Is a Civilization, Anyway," *World History Connected* 6, no. 3 (October 2009).
8 V. Gordon Childe, *Man Makes Himself*, 4th rev. ed. (Bradford-on-Avon England: Moonraker Press, 1981).
9 Elman Service, *Primitive Social Organization: An Evolutionary Perspective* (New York, NY: Norton, 1962).
10 William T. Sanders and Barbara J. Price, *Mesoamerica: The Evolution of a Civilization* (New York: Random House, 1968).
11 Eric Wolf, *Europe and the People Without History*, repr. ed. (University of California Press, 1982).
12 Derrick Jensen, *Endgame: The Problem of Civilization*, vol. 1 (Seven Stories Press, 2011).
13 Donald O. Henry, *From Foraging to Agriculture: The Levant at the End of the Ice Age* (Philadelphia: University of Pennsylvania Press, 1989).
14 Elman Rogers Service, *Origins of the State and Civilization: The Process of Cultural Evolution* (New York: Norton, 1975).
15 CubaAgriculture.com, "Cuba Agriculture Information."
16 Spear, Stefanie, "Samso: World's First 100% Renewable Energy-Powered Island Is a Beacon for Sustainable Communities," May 1, 2014, EcoWatch.com.
17 Ludwig von Bertalanffy, *General System Theory: Foundations, Development, Applications* (New York: G. Braziller, 1973).
18 J. Stephen Lansing, "Complex Adaptive Systems," *Annual Review of Anthropology* 32, no. 1 (October 2003): 183–204.
19 "Documentary Tells How Quebec Town Launched Anti-Pesticide Movement," CBC News, updated June 2, 2009, cbc.ca.
20 United States Senate, "Official Declarations of War by Congress," senate.gov.
21 "The Power to Declare War," April 15, 2011, TheWeek.com.

2: Dissociation

1. Annie Leonard and Ariel Conrad, *The Story of Stuff: How Our Obsession with Stuff Is Trashing the Planet, Our Communities, and Our Health – and a Vision for Change.* (New York, NY: Free Press, 2011), 36.
2. Diamond, *Collapse.*
3. Joseph Tainter, *The Collapse of Complex Societies.*
4. Natalie Wolchover, "What Are the Limits of Human Survival?" August 9, 2012, LiveScience.com.
5. Simon Rogers, "US Poverty Mapped – Interactive," *The Guardian*, September 15, 2011, theguardian.com. Brian B Murphy et al., Statistics Canada, and Income Statistics Division, "Low Income in Canada a Multi-Line and Multi-Index Perspective" (Ottawa: Statistics Canada, 2012).
6. "Feds Target Major First Nation Health Problems," *Wawatay News*, accessed August 21, 2014, wawataynews.ca; Canadian Human Rights Commission, *Report on Equality Rights of Aboriginal People*, 2013.
7. Murray N. Rothbard, "Free Market," in *The Concise Encyclopedia of Economics*, Library of Economics and Liberty, econlib.org.
8. Brian Snowdon, "Redefining the Role of the State: Joseph Stiglitz on Building A 'post-Washington Consensus,'" *World Economics* 2, no. 3 (2001): 45–86.
9. John McMurtry, "Myths of the Global Market," *New Internationalist*, June 2007, newint.org.
10. David Harvey, *The Condition of Postmodernity: An Enquiry into the Origins of Cultural Change* (Cambridge, MA: Wiley-Blackwell, 1992).
11. Ibid.
12. Dean Baker, "The Housing Bubble and the Financial Crisis.," *Real-World Economics Review*, no. 46 (May 20, 2008): 73–81.
13. Stephen Spratt, Mary Murphy, and New Economics Foundation, *The Great Transition: A Tale of How It Turned out Right* (London: Nef, 2009).
14. Haudenosaunee Confederacy, accessed August 22, 2014, haudenosauneeconfederacy.com.
15. Anthony Giddens, *A Contemporary Critique of Historical Materialism* (University of California Press, 1981).
16. Marshall McLuhan, *The Gutenberg Galaxy: The Making of Typographic Man* (Toronto: University of Toronto Press, 1962).
17. US Census Bureau, QuickFacts, Celebration CDP, Florida (accessed August 22, 2014); "Celebration, Florida: The Utopian Town That America Just Couldn't Trust," April 20, 2014, Gizmodo.com.
18. Edwards, Adrian, "New UNHCR Report Says Global Forced Displacement at 18-Year High," June 19, 2013, unhcr.org.
19. Serle, Jack, "More than 2,400 Dead as Obama's Drone Campaign Marks Five Years," The Bureau of Investigative Journalism, January 23, 2014, thebureauinvestigates.com.
20. "100 People: A World Portrait," accessed August 22, 2014, 100people.org; Paul Caridad, "If The World Were A Village of 100 People," May 18, 2011, VisualNews.com.
21. Thomas Helbling, "Externalities: Prices Do Not Capture All Costs," Finance & Development, March 28, 2012, imf.org.

22. Sibylla Brodzinsky, "Coca-Cola Boycott Launched after Killings at Colombian Plants," *The Guardian*, July 24, 2003, theguardian.com; "Indian Officials Order Coca-Cola Plant to Close for Using Too Much Water," *The Guardian*, June 18, 2014, theguardian.com.
23. "CoffeeFactSheet.pdf," worldvision.ca, accessed June 5, 2015.
24. Rob Cooper, "Inside Apple's Chinese 'Sweatshop' Factory Where Workers Are Paid Just £1.12 per Hour to Produce iPhones and iPads for the West," Mail Online, January 25, 2013, dailymail.co.uk.
25. Arden Jobling-Hey, "Plastic Water Bottles and the Environment: How Bad, Is Bad?" August 21, 2012, BizEnergy.ca.

3: Complexity

1. Bill McKibben, *The End of Nature* (New York, NY: Random House, 1989), 45–46.
2. Diamond, *Collapse*, 119.
3. Willoughby, Jack, "Burning Up," updated March 20, 2000, Barrons.com.
4. Chris Gaither and Dawn C. Chmielewski, "Fears of Dot-Com Crash, Version 2.0," *Los Angeles Times*, July 16, 2006, articles.latimes.com.
5. "WorldCom Company Timeline," June 26, 2002, washingtonpost.com.
6. Jeff Holt, "A Summary of the Primary Causes of the Housing Bubble and the Resulting Credit Crisis: A Non-Technical Paper," *The Journal of Business Inquiry* 8, no. 1 (2009): 120–29; Dean Baker, "The Housing Bubble and the Financial Crisis, *real-world economics review*, issue no. 46, 20 (20 May, 2008), pp 73–81; Jack Rasmus, "From Global Financial Crisis to Global Recession, part 1," March 27, 2008, zcomm.org.
7. Holt, "A Summary of the Primary Causes of the Housing Bubble and the Resulting Credit Crisis: A Non-Technical Paper."
8. Harvard Joint Center for Housing Studies, "Housing Perspectives: How Helpful Is the Price-to-Income Ratio in Flagging Bubbles?" September 2013, housingperspectives.blogspot.ca.
9. Rasmus, "From Global Financial Crisis to Global Recession, part 1," zcomm.org.
10. David Goldman, "Follow the Money: Bailout Tracker," November 16, 2009, money.cnn.com.
11. Andrew Clark, "Merrill Lynch, the Firm Lost $8bn and the Chief Executive Had to Go – with $159m," *The Guardian*, October 30, 2007, theguardian.com; Michael J. De La Merced and Louise Story, "Nearly 700 at Merrill in Million-Dollar Club," *New York Times*, February 12, 2009, nytimes.com.
12. G. William Domhoff, "Who Rules America: Wealth, Income, and Power," updated February 2013, ucsc.edu.
13. Walden Bello, "The Capitalist Conjuncture: Over-Accumulation, Financial Crises, and the Retreat from Globalisation," *Third World Quarterly* 27, no. 8 (2006): pp 1345–67.
14. Walden Bello, "A Primer on the Wall Street Meltdown," September 26, 2008, commondreams.org.
15. Ibid.
16. "IPCC Working Group II."
17. IPCC "Fourth Assessment Report," 2007, www.ipcc.ch.
18. James Bullard, Christopher Neely, and David Wheelock, "Systemic Risk and the

Financial Crisis: A Primer," *Federal Reserve Bank of St. Louis REVIEW*, September/October (2009): 403–18.

19 National Science Foundation Advisory Committee for Environmental Research and Education, "Transitions and Tipping Points in Complex Environmental Systems," 2009, 28–31, nsf.gov.

20 Homer-Dixon, *The Upside of Down*, 224–31.

4: Stratification

1 Karl Marx, *Karl Marx: Selected Writings*, ed. Lawrence H. Simon (Indianapolis, IN: Hackett, 1994), 61.

2 Kingsley Davis and Wilbert. E Moore, "Some Principles of Stratification," *American Sociological Review* 10, no. 2 (April 1945): 242–49.

3 United Nations Children's Fund (UNICEF), *The State of the World's Children 2014: Every Child Counts: Revealing Disparities, Advancing Children's Rights* (New York, NY: United Nations Children's Fund (UNICEF), 2014).

4 Dave Boyer, "Poverty Level under Obama Breaks 50-Year Record," *Washington Times*, January 7, 2014, washingtontimes.com.

5 Statistics Canada, "2011 National Household Survey: Data Tables," statcan.gc.ca.

6 Irene Ogrodnik, "25 Years since Canada Vowed to End Child Poverty, Where Are We Now?" *Global News*, November 24, 2014, globalnews.ca.

7 National Poverty Centre, University of Michigan, "Poverty in the United States: Frequently Asked Questions," accessed January 23, 2015, npc.umich.edu.

8 Steven Morris, "Poverty Hits Twice as Many British Households as 30 Years Ago," *The Guardian*, June 19, 2014, theguardian.com.

9 Deborah Hardoon et al., "An Economy For the 1%: How Privilege and Power in the Economy Drive Extreme Inequality and How This Can Be Stopped." (Oxford, UK: Oxfam International, January 18, 2016), www.oxfam.org.

10 Oxfam "Wealth: Having It All and Wanting More," *Oxfam Issue Briefing*, January 2015, oxfam.org.

11 Ibid.

12 National Poverty Centre, University of Michigan, "Poverty in the United States: Frequently Asked Questions," npc.umich.edu.

13 "People and Families in Poverty by Selected Characteristics, 2010 and 2009," accessed January 23, 2015, www.infoplease.com.

14 Citizens for Public Justice, "The Burden of Poverty: A Snapshot of Poverty across Canada," October 2014, cpj.ca.

15 Amber Hildebrandt, "Half of First Nations Children Live in Poverty," June 19, 2013, cbc.ca.

16 Tavia Grant, "Canadians Are Feeling the Financial Squeeze," *Globe and Mail*, September 10, 2014, theglobeandmail.com.

17 Armine Yalnizyan, "Study of Income Inequality in Canada: What Can Be Done" (Canadian Centre for Policy Alternatives, April 13, 2013).

18 Murray Dobbin, "Work in the Age of Anxiety," *The Tyee*, September 22, 2014, thetyee.ca.

19 Hope Yen, "4 in 5 in USA Face near-Poverty, No Work," *USATODAY*, September 17, 2013, usatoday.com.

20 Bill Dunphy, "Beasley: Portrait of a Neighbourhood: This Isn't Mr. Rogers' Neighbourhood," *Hamilton Spectator*, January 28, 2006, thespec.com.
21 "Global Profile of Extreme Poverty," October 15, 2012, unsdsn.org.
22 "2014 World Hunger and Poverty Facts and Statistics by World Hunger Education Service," accessed January 23, 2015, worldhunger.org.
23 "Report Finds 400 Million Children Living in Extreme Poverty," October 10, 2010, worldbank.org.
24 Jared Diamond, *Guns, Germs, and Steel* (New York: Norton, 1999), 80.
25 Ibid., 375.
26 Paul Rittman, "Rise and Fall of the British East India Company," paulrittman.com; Bryan Taylor, "The Rise and Fall of the Largest Corporation in History," November 6, 2013, businessinsider.com.
27 Adam Hochschild, *King Leopold's Ghost: A Story of Greed, Terror, and Heroism in Colonial Africa*, repr. ed. (Boston: Houghton Mifflin Harcourt, 1999).
28 Ibid.
29 "Congo Free State Horrors," *New York Times*, November 8, 1901.
30 Benjamin Madley, "Patterns of Frontier Genocide 1803–1910: The Aboriginal Tasmanians, the Yuki of California, and the Herero of Namibia," *Journal of Genocide Research* 6, no. 2 (June 1, 2004): 167–92; Mitchell Smyth, "Beothuk Interpretation Centre Tells Story of Exterminated Newfoundland Natives," culturelocker.com, 2014; Robert M. Poole, "What Became of the Taíno?" *Smithsonian*, October 2011, smithsonianmag.com.
31 Anup Shah, "Effects of Iraq Sanctions," October 2, 2005, globalissues.org.
32 UN Development Programme, "Programme of Assistance to the Palestinian People," accessed January 26, 2015, undp.ps/en/index.html.
33 Canadians for Justice and Peace in the Middle East, "Israel's 'Operation Cast Lead' 1,400 Palestinians Deaths, 5000 Wounded," *Global Research*, June 6, 2010, globalresearch.ca.
34 Engler, *The Black Book of Canadian Foreign Policy*, 82.
35 Ibid., 71–112.
36 Motesharrei, Rivas, and Kalnay, "Human and Nature Dynamics (HANDY)."
37 Ahmed, *A User's Guide to the Crisis of Civilization*, 214–26.
38 Homer-Dixon, *The Upside of Down*, 181.

5: Overshoot

1 Richard Heinberg, "Was Civilization a Mistake?" in *Against Civilization: Readings and Reflections*, ed. John Zerzan (Port Townsend, WA: Feral House Books, 2005), 123.
2 Diamond, *Collapse*, 115–19.
3 William R. Catton, *Overshoot: The Ecological Basis of Revolutionary Change*, new ed. (Urbana: University of Illinois Press, 1982).
4 Ibid.
5 Bible, King James Version (Latus ePublishing, 2014).
6 Edward Grant, *The Nature of Natural Philosophy in the Late Middle Ages* (Washington, DC: Catholic University of America Press, 2010).
7 Carolyn Merchant, *The Death of Nature: Women, Ecology, and the Scientific Revolution*, repr. ed. (New York: HarperOne, 1990).

8 Ibid.
9 Lewis Mumford, *Technics and Civilization* (Chicago: University of Chicago Press, 2010), 51.
10 Michael Perelman, *The Invention of Capitalism: Classical Political Econom and the Secret History of Primitive Accumulation* (Durham: Duke University Press, 2000).
11 James O'Connor, *Natural Causes: Essays in Ecological Marxism* (New York: Guilford Press, 1997), 22–24.
12 Gregory Greene, *The End of Suburbia: Oil Depletion and the Collapse of the American Dream* (Microcinema, 2007).
13 Leslie A. White, *The Evolution of Culture: The Development of Civilization to the Fall of Rome* (London: Thousand Oaks, CA: Left Coast Press, 2007).
14 Robert G. Perrin, "Herbert Spencer's Four Theories of Social Evolution," *American Journal of Sociology* 81, no. 6 (May 1, 1976): 1339–59.
15 W.W. Rostow, *The Stages of Economic Growth: A Non-Communist Manifesto*, 3rd ed. (Cambridge UK; New York: Cambridge University Press, 1991); David E. Apter, *The Politics of Modernization* (Chicago: University of Chicago Press, 1967).
16 United Nations Economic Commission for Latin America and Raoul Prebisch, *The Economic Development of Latin America and Its Principal Problems* (United Nations Department of Economic Affairs, 1950); Theotonio dos Santos, "The Structure of Dependence," *The American Economic Review*, 1970, 231–236.
17 Club of Rome, *The Limits to Growth: A Report for the Club of Rome's Project on the Predicament of Mankind*.
18 Williams E. Rees, Mathis Wackernagel, and Phil Testemale, *Our Ecological Footprint: Reducing Human Impact on the Earth* (Gabriola Island, BC; Philadelphia, PA: New Society Publishers, 1998).
19 "Footprint for Nations," accessed January 19, 2015, footprintnetwork.org.
20 "Energy Use (Kg of Oil Equivalent per Capita)," accessed January 19, 2015, data.worldbank.org.
21 Richard Heinberg, *The Party's Over: Oil, War and the Fate of Industrial Societies*, 2nd ed. (Gabriola Island, BC: New Society Publishers, 2005).
22 Alex Kuhlman, "Peak Oil: The End of the Oil Age," 2007, oildecline.com.
23 Michael T. Klare, "Peak Oil Is Dead, Long Live Peak Oil!" January 9, 2014, commondreams.org.
24 Heinberg, *The Party's Over*.
25 Richard Heinberg, "Renewable Energy Will Not Support Economic Growth," June 7, 2015, commondreams.org.
26 Richard Heinberg, "Searching for a Miracle: 'Net Energy' Limits and the Fate of Industrial Society," Post Carbon Institute, October 2009, postcarbon.org.
27 Charles A. S. Hall, Stephen Balogh, and David J.R. Murphy, "What Is the Minimum EROI That a Sustainable Society Must Have?" *Energies* 2, no. 1 (January 23, 2009): 25–47.
28 Heinberg, "Searching for a Miracle: 'Net Energy' Limits and the Fate of Industrial Society," 9.
29 Jeremy Rifkin, *The Empathic Civilization: The Race to Global Consciousness in a World in Crisis*, (New York: Tarcher, 2009), 476.
30 Joel Achenbach, "Scientists: Human Activity Has Pushed Earth beyond Four of Nine 'Planetary Boundaries,'" *Washington Post*, January 15, 2015.

31. Will Steffen et al., "Planetary Boundaries: Guiding Human Development on a Changing Planet," *Science* 347, no. 6223 (February 13, 2015): 1259855.
32. Eleanor Sterling, "Blue Planet Blues: Demand for Fresh Water Threatens to Outstrip Supply. How Can We Meet the Needs of All of Earth's Species?" *Natural History*, November 2007, 3.
33. Peter H. Gleick, *The World's Water 2008–2009: The Biennial Report on Freshwater Resources* (Island Press, 2008).
34. Mesfin M. Mekonnen and Arjen Y. Hoekstra, "Four Billion People Facing Severe Water Scarcity," *Science Advances*, February 12, 2016.
35. World Bank Group, "High and Dry: Climate Change, Water, and the Economy," 2016, openknowledge.worldbank.org.
36. Stephen Leahy, "Peak Water, Peak Oil . . . Now, Peak Soil?" June 1, 2013, commondreams.org.
37. Tainter, *The Collapse of Complex Societies*, 1990, 45–51.
38. Stephen Leahy, "Peak Soil," Spring 2008, earthisland.org.
39. H.K. Jain, *The Green Revolution: History Impact and Future* (Houston: Studium Press India, 2010).
40. William S. Gaud, "The Green Revolution: Accomplishments and Apprehensions," March 8, 1968, agbioworld.org.
41. R.E. Evenson and D. Gollin, "Assessing the Impact of the Green Revolution, 1960 to 2000," *Science* 300, no. 5620 (May 2, 2003): 758–62.
42. Stephen Leahy, "Peak Water, Peak Oil . . . Now, Peak Soil?" June 1, 2013, commondreams.org
43. Leahy, "Peak Soil."
44. Ibid.
45. Erik Lindquist et al., "Global Forest Land-Use Change from 1990 to 2005," Food and Agriculture Organization of the United Nations, Rome, 2012.
46. "Global Forest Resources Assessment 2010: Main Report" (Rome: Food and Agriculture Organization of the United Nations, 2010), fao.org.
47. Lindquist et al., "Global Forest Land-Use Change from 1990 to 2005.
48. "Millennium Ecosystem Assessment: Ecosystems and Human Well-Being: Synthesis" (World Resources Institute, 2005).
49. Sriyanie Miththapala and IUCN: The World Conservation Union, *Coral Reefs*, Coastal Ecosystems Series, v. 1 (Colombo, Sri Lanka: Ecosystems and Livelihoods Group Asia, IUCN, 2008).
50. Helen Scales, "Oceans Becoming Acidic Ten Times Faster Than Thought," National Geographic Society, November 24, 2008, news.nationalgeographic.com.ion.
51. Ibid.
52. Ibid.
53. Sarah Zielinski, "Ocean Dead Zones Are Getting Worse Globally Due to Climate Change," *Smithsonian*, November 10, 2014, smithsonianmag.com.
54. Christine Dell'Amore, "Species Extinction Happening 1,000 Times Faster Because of Humans?" National Geographic Society, May 30, 2014, news.nationalgeographic.com.
55. W. Steffen, P.J. Crutzen, and R. McNeill, "The Anthropocene: Are Humans Now Overwhelming the Forces of Nature?," *AMBIO: A Journal of the Human Environment* 36, no. 8 (2007): 614–21.

56 Elizabeth Kolbert, *The Sixth Extinction: An Unnatural History* (New York: Henry Holt, 2014).
57 D. Jablonski, "Extinctions in the Fossil Record (and Discussion)," *Philosophical Transactions of the Royal Society of London*, series B, no. 344 (1994): 11–17.
58 Environment Canada Government of Canada, "Wastewater – Water," July 11, 2006, ec.gc.ca.
59 United States Environmental Protection Agency, "2013 TRI National Analysis: Introduction," January 14, 2015, epa.gov.
60 "Municipal Solid Wastes in the United States: 2007 Facts and Figures" (United States Environmental Protection Agency: Office of Solid Waste, November 2008), epa.gov.
61 John Young and Aaron Sachs, *The Next Efficiency Revolution: Creating a Sustainable Materials Economy* (World Watch Institute, 1994), 13.
62 Conference Board of Canada, "Municipal Waste Generation," January 31, 2015, conferenceboard.ca.
63 "40 Facts About Water Pollution," Conserve-Energy-Future, December 23, 2014, conserve-energy-future.com.
64 "Oilsands 101: Alberta's Oilsands," Pembina Institute, January 31, 2015, pembina.org.
65 "Tar Sands and Water," Sierra Club Canada, 2007, sierraclub.ca.
66 "Oilsands 101: Tailings," Pembina Institute, January 31, 2015, pembina.org.
67 "Oilsands 101: Water Impacts," Pembina Institute, January 31, 2015, pembina.org
68 Bob Weber, "Federal Study Says Oil Sands Toxins Are Leaching into Groundwater, Athabasca River," *Globe and Mail*, February 20, 2014, theglobeandmail.com.
69 John Cotter, "Environmental Health Risks of Alberta Oil Sands Likely Underestimated: Study," *Globe and Mail*, February 3, 2014, theglobeandmail.com.
70 "Fracking Myths and Facts: Feb 2012" (Council of Canadians, March 2014), canadians.org.
71 Rebecca Hammer, Jeanne VanBriesen, and Larry Levine, "In Fracking's Wake: New Rules Are Needed to Protect Our Health and Environment from Contaminated Wastewater," *Natural Resources Defense Council* 11 (2012), nrdc.org.
72 Abrahm Lustgarten, "Buried Secrets: Is Natural Gas Drilling Endangering U.S. Water Supplies?" *ProPublica*, November 13, 2008, propublica.org.
73 Josh Fox, *GasLand* (documentary, 2010).
74 Elizabeth Ridlington and John Rumpler, "Fracking by the Numbers: Key Impacts of Dirty Drilling at the State and National Level" (Environment America Research and Policy Center, October 2013).
75 Michelle L. Bell, Devra L. Davis, and Tony Fletcher, "A Retrospective Assessment of Mortality from the London Smog Episode of 1952: The Role of Influenza and Pollution," *Environmental Health Perspectives* 112, no. 1 (October 15, 2003): 6–8.
76 World Health Organization, "Ambient and Household Air Pollution and Health," November 17, 2014, who.int.
77 "Deaths due to Air Pollution to Skyrocket: CMA," CBC News, August 13, 2008, cbc.ca.
78 Pascale Scapecchi, "The Health Costs of Inaction with Respect to Air Pollution," OECD Environment Working Papers, (June 6, 2008), oecd-ilibrary.org.

6: Oligarchy

1. Jean-Jacques Rousseau, *Jean-Jacques Rousseau: The Basic Political Writings* (Indianapolis, IN: Hackett, 1987), 60.
2. Plato, *The Republic* (Mineola, New York: Dover, 2000), 209.
3. Kavitha A. Davidson, "Democracy Index 2013: Global Democracy at a Standstill, the Economist Intelligence Unit's Annual Report Shows," *Huffington Post*, March 21, 2013, huffingtonpost.com.
4. Of course, a significant weakness of democracy in ancient Athens was the fact that few of the city's inhabitants actually qualified for citizenship. Women, foreigners, and slaves were excluded from Athenian democracy. In this sense, modern nation-states are at once more and less democratic than was Athens. More so in that today the franchise and citizenship rights have been extended to a much broader segment of the population. Less so in that the actual form of modern democratic participation (participating in the spectacle of elite-managed elections every few years) is far less meaningful than that of citizens in the ancient Greek city-state.
5. George Orwell, "Politics and the English Language," *Horizon*, April 1946.
6. Hardoon et al., "An Economy For the 1%: How Privilege and Power in the Economy Drive Extreme Inequality and How This Can Be Stopped," *Oxfam Briefing Paper*, January 2016, oxfam.org.
7. Armine Yalnizyan, Canadian Centre for Policy Alternatives, and Canadian Electronic Library (Firm), *The Rise of Canada's Richest 1%* (Ottawa: Canadian Centre for Policy Alternatives, 2011), site.ebrary.com/id/10443636.
8. Hugh Mackenzie, "All in a Day's Work: CEO Pay in Canada" (Ottawa: Canadian Centre for Policy Alternatives, January 2014), policyalternatives.ca.
9. Ibid.
10. Yalnizyan, Canadian Centre for Policy Alternatives, and Canadian Electronic Library (Firm), *The Rise of Canada's Richest 1%*.
11. David Macdonald, "Outrageous Fortune: Documenting Canada's Wealth Gap" (Canadian Centre for Policy Alternatives, April 2014), policyalternatives.ca.
12. G. William Domhoff, "Who Rules America: Wealth, Income, and Power," February 2013, usc.edu.
13. Dwayne Winseck, "The Revolving Door between Telecom-Media-Internet Industries in Canada and Ex-Politicos," *Rabble.ca*, August 16, 2011.
14. Tu Thanh Ha, "Tory Candidate Lobbied Ottawa for U.S. Fighter-Jet Manufacturer," *Globe and Mail*, August 23, 2012, theglobeandmail.com.
15. "Conservative Stronach Joins Liberals," May 17, 2005, cbc.ca.
16. "CBC News Indepth: Paul Martin," March 17, 2006, cbc.ca.
17. "Richest Presidents from Washington to Clinton," *USA TODAY*, March 18, 2013, usatoday.com.
18. Ben Aris and Duncan Campbell, "How Bush's Grandfather Helped Hitler's Rise to Power," *The Guardian*, September 25, 2004, theguardian.com.
19. Tinatin Ninua, "Regulating the Revolving Door" (Germany: Transparency International, 2010).
20. Ibid.
21. Kevin Tomas, "Dollars, Democracy and Disclosure: Should Investors Demand Better Disclosure from Canadian Corporations on Political Spending?"

(Shareholder Association for Research and Education, January 2015), share.ca.
22 Carol Linnitt, "Oil and Gas Industry Requesting Massive Tax Cuts for LNG Terminals in Advance of 2015 Federal Budget," *DeSmog Canada*, February 14, 2015, desmog.ca.
23 Peter Dreier, "The Worst of Wall Street: Meet Donald Trump's Finance Chairman," *The Nation*, May 10, 2016, thenation.com.
24 Jen Wieczner, "Donald Trump: Cabinet Pick Steven Mnuchin Net Worth Is Actually Huge," *Fortune*, January 11, 2017, fortune.com.
25 David A. Graham, "Who Is Jack Lew, Obama's Nominee for Treasury Secretary?" *The Atlantic*, January 9, 2013, theatlantic.com.
26 Matt Taibbi, "The Great American Bubble Machine," *Rolling Stone*, May 5, 2010, rollingstone.com.
27 Robert Weissman and James Donahue, "Sold Out: How Wall Street and Washington Betrayed America" (Essential Information and the Consumer Education Foundation, March 2009), www.wallstreetwatch.org.
28 Peter Cohan, "Today's Financial Meltdown vs. the 1990s S and L Crisis: Which Was Worse?" July 3, 2010, DailyFinance.com.
29 Weissman and Donahue, "Sold Out: How Wall Street and Washington Betrayed America."
30 Taibbi, "The Great American Bubble Machine."
31 Ibid.
32 Walden Bello, "Wall Street Meltdown Primer," September 26, 2008, commondreams.org.
33 Jed Rakoff, "The Financial Crisis: Why Have No High-Level Executives Been Prosecuted?" January 2, 2014, commondreams.org.
34 William Black, "Alan Greenspan and His Disciples Are Intrinsically Terrible Regulators," August 16, 2010, businessinsider.com.
35 David R. Lease, "From Great to Ghastly: How Toxic Organizational Cultures Poison Companies, The Rise and Fall of Enron, WorldCom, HealthSouth, and Tyco International," *Academy of Business Education*, April, 2006, 6–7.
36 Richard Murphy and Tess Riley, "The Cost of Tax Abuse: A Briefing Paper on the Cost of Tax Evasion Worldwide." *The Tax Justice Network*, November 2011, tackletaxhavens.com.
37 Hardoon et al., "An Economy For the 1%: How Privilege and Power in the Economy Drive Extreme Inequality and How This Can Be Stopped."
38 Luke Harding, "What Are the Panama Papers? A Guide to History's Biggest Data Leak," *The Guardian*, April 5, 2016, theguardian.com.
39 Daniel Tencer, "Canadian Names Revealed In Offshore Accounts Leak," *Huffington Post*, May 10, 2016, huffingtonpost.ca.
40 Robert Cribb and Marco Chown Oved, "The Secrecy Specialists behind Panama Papers' Canadian Offshore Dealings," *Toronto Star*, May 9, 2016, thestar.com.
41 "Tax Havens 'serve No Useful Economic Purpose': 300 Economists Tell World Leaders," *Oxfam International*, May 9, 2016, oxfam.org.
42 Gwilym Dodd, "British History in Depth: The Birth of Parliament," BBC History, February 17, 2011, bbc.co.uk.

43 "The Evolution of Parliament," UK Parliament, April 21, 2010, parliament.uk/about/living-heritage/evolutionofparliament/.
44 Centre for Responsive Politics, "Cost of Election," 2016, opensecrets.org.
45 Center for Responsive Politics, "Overall Spending Inches Up in 2014: Megadonors Equip Outside Groups to Capture a Bigger Share of the Pie," October 29, 2014, opensecrets.org.
46 Nicolas Bauer et al., "Democracy Lost: A Report on the Fatally Flawed 2016 Democratic Primaries," *Election Justice USA*, July 2016.
47 Associated Press, "Leaked DNC Emails Reveal Details of Anti-Sanders Sentiment," *The Guardian*, July 24, 2016, theguardian.com.
48 Jamie Brownlee, *Ruling Canada: Corporate Cohesion and Democracy* (Black Point, NS: Fernwood, 2005), 31.
49 Knowlton Thomas, "Canada's Wireless Leaders Form Excessively Lucrative Oligopoly, Reap World-High Profits," July 19, 2010, techvibes.com.
50 Harry McCracken, "A Brief History of the Rise and Fall of Telephone Competition in the US, 1982–2011," March 20, 2011, technologizer.com.
51 Thomas Knowlton, "Is the World's Wealthiest Man Bringing His Wireless Business to Canada?" May 19, 2011, techvibes.com.
52 Ibid.
53 David Olive, "As They Fight to Keep Growing, Our Big Five Could Become the Big Three," *Toronto Star*, July 18, 2014, thestar.com.
54 Ibid.
55 Joan Marques, "Oligopoly Is In!" June 1999, angelfire.com.
56 United Food and Commercial Workers, "Making Change at Walmart," accessed February 18, 2015, changewalmart.org; Ashley Lutz and Mike Nudelman "14 Facts about Wal-Mart That Will Blow Your Mind," October 17, 2013, businessinsider.com; Vincent Trivett, "25 US Mega Corporations: Where They Rank If They Were Countries," June 27, 2011, businessinsider.com.
57 United Food and Commercial Workers, "The Walton Family and Corporate-Style Education Reform," Making Change at Walmart, 2017, changewalmart.org.
58 United Food and Commercial Workers, "An Analysis of Walmart and Walton Family Political Spending," Making Change at Walmart, June 2013, changewalmart.org.
59 United Food and Commercial Workers, "How Rich are the Waltons?" Making Change at Walmart, 2017, changewalmart.org.
60 Tim Dickinson, "Inside the Koch Brothers' Toxic Empire," *Rolling Stone*, September 24, 2014, rollingstone.com.
61 Ibid.
62 Ibid.
63 Howard Zinn, *A People's History of The United States* (New York: Harper Perennial, 2005), 254–57.
64 Ibid., 258–63.
65 Ibid., 258.
66 G. William Domhoff, "Who Rules America: The Corporate Community," October 2013, ucsc.edu.
67 R.L. Zweigenhaft and G. William Domhoff, *Diversity in the Power Elite: How It*

Happens, Why It Matters, 2nd ed. (Lanham, MD: Rowman and Littlefield, 2006); William K. Carroll, "From Canadian Corporate Elite to Transnational Capitalist Class: Transitions in the Organization of Corporate Power," *Canadian Review of Sociology and Anthropology*, August 2007; Brownlee, *Ruling Canada*.
68. Lesley Sklair, *The Transnational Capitalist Class* (Oxford: Blackwell Publishers, 2001); Jerome Klassen and William K. Carroll, "Transnational Class Formation? Globalization and the Canadian Corporate Network," *American Sociological Association* 17, no. 2 (2011): 379–402.
69. Zweigenhaft and Domhoff, *Diversity in the Power Elite: How It Happens, Why It Matters*.
70. Sylvia Bashevkin, "Women's Representation in the House of Commons: A Stalemate?" *Canadian Parliamentary Review* Spring (2011): 17–22.
71. Jerome H. Black, "The 2006 Federal Election and Visible Minority Candidates: More of the Same?" *Canadian Parliamentary Review* Autumn (2008): 7.
72. "Why Does Canada Have so Few Female CEOs?" *Globe and Mail*, October 8, 2010, theglobeandmail.com.
73. "Career Advancement in Corporate Canada: A Focus on Visible Minorities – An Early Preview" (The Diversity Institute in Management and Technology, February 2007), www.ryerson.ca.
74. Joseph F. Fletcher and H.D. Forbes, "Education, Occupation and Vote in Canada, 1965–1984," *Canadian Review of Sociology and Anthropology* 27, no. 4 (1990): 441–61.
75. "Regular Voters, Intermittent Voters, and Those Who Don't: Who Votes, Who Doesn't, and Why" (PEW Research Center, October 18, 2006).
76. Martin Gilens and Benjamin I. Page, "Testing Theories of American Politics: Elites, Interest Groups, and Average Citizens," *Perspectives on Politics* 12, no. 03 (September 2014): 564–81.
77. Veronica Beechey, "On Patriarchy," *Feminist Review* 3, no. 1 (November 1979): 66–82.
78. Peter J. Kareithi, "Hegemonic Masculinity in Media Contents," UNESCO, October 8, 2014, unesco.org.
79. Roxane Gay, "Sorry, the Patriarchy Isn't Dead," September 13, 2013, salon.com; Robert Jensen, "Rape, Rape Culture and the Problem of Patriarchy," April 29, 2014, wagingnonviolence.org.
80. R.W. Connell and James W. Messerschmidt, "Hegemonic Masculinity Rethinking the Concept," *Gender & Society* 19, no. 6 (December 1, 2005): 829–59.
81. Marilyn Waring, *If Women Counted: A New Feminist Economics*, repr. ed. (San Francisco: HarperCollins Canada, 1990).
82. Carl Von Line, *Systema Naturae*, (Netherlands, 1735).
83. Howard Zinn, *A People's History of The United States*, 170.
84. John S. Milloy, *A National Crime: The Canadian Government and the Residential School System* (Winnipeg: University of Manitoba Press, 1999).
85. Jaeah Lee, "Exactly How Often Do Police Shoot Unarmed Black Men?" *Mother Jones*, August 15, 2014, motherjones.com; Craig Benjamin and Jackie Hansen, "The Need for Accurate and Comprehensive Statistics on Missing and Murdered Indigenous Women and Girls," April 15, 2015, amnesty.ca.
86. Joan Bryden, "The Prime Minister Has Not Publicly Uttered One Word of Sup-

port for Canadian Muslims Following Attacks against Canadian Soldiers," *Toronto Star*, November 1, 2014, thestar.com; Christopher Ingraham, "Anti-Muslim Hate Crimes Are Still Five Times More Common Today than before 9/11," *Washington Post*, February 11, 2015, washingtonpost.com.
87 Brownlee, *Ruling Canada*.
88 Martin Thunert, "Conservative Think Tanks in the United States and Canada," in *Conservative Parties and Right-Wing Politics in North America* (Springer, 2003), 229–52, link.springer.com.
89 Daniel Tencer, "U.S. Tea Party Billionaires Funding Tories' Favourite Think Tank," *Huffington Post*, April 26, 2012, huffingtonpost.ca.
90 People for the American Way, "American Enterprise Institute," August 2006, rightwingwatch.org.
91 People for the American Way, "Heritage Foundation," December 2006, rightwingwatch.org.
92 Nancy Scola, "Exposing ALEC: How Conservative-Backed State Laws Are All Connected," *Atlantic*, April 14, 2012, theatlantic.com.
93 Alejandro Chafuen, "We See Thee Rise: Canada's Emerging Role In Policy Leadership," *Forbes*, August 6, 2013, forbes.com.
94 Engler, *The Black Book of Canadian Foreign Policy*.
95 Munk School of Global Affairs, Our Founding Donors," accessed February 22, 2015, munkschool.utoronto.ca.
96 "Munk Out of UofT: Stop the Corporate Takeover," 2011, munkoutofuoft.files.wordpress.com.
97 "Scientist Calls U of C Energy Centre a Failure," January 28, 2013, cbc.ca.
98 Nick Turse, "Wrestling the Military-Academic Complex," AlterNet, May 1, 2004, alternet.org.
99 Naomi Oreskes and Erik M. Conway, *Merchants of Doubt: How a Handful of Scientists Obscured the Truth on Issues from Tobacco Smoke to Global Warming*, repr. ed. (New York: Bloomsbury Press, 2011), 10–25.
100 Ibid., 32–35.
101 H.S. Karagueuzian et al., "Cigarette Smoke Radioactivity and Lung Cancer Risk," *Nicotine and Tobacco Research* 14, no. 1 (September 27, 2011): 79–90.
102 Janine K. Cataldo, Judith J. Prochaska, and Stanton A Glantz, "Cigarette Smoking Is a Risk Factor for Alzheimer's Disease: An Analysis Controlling for Tobacco Industry Affiliation," *Journal of Alzheimer's Disease* 19, no. 2 (2010): 465–80.
103 S. Nassir Ghaemi, Arshia A. Shirzadi, and Megan Filkowski, "Publication Bias and the Pharmaceutical Industry: The Case of Lamotrigine in Bipolar Disorder," *Medscape Journal of Medicine* 10, no. 9 (September 10, 2008): 211.
104 Jeremy Hsu, "Dark Side of Medical Research: Widespread Bias and Omissions," LiveScience.com, June 24, 2010.
105 Joel Lexchin et al., "Pharmaceutical Industry Sponsorship and Research Outcome and Quality: Systematic Review," *British Medical Journal* 326, no. 7400 (May 29, 2003): 1167–70.
106 Hsu, "Dark Side of Medical Research."
107 Nate Raymond and Jessica Dye, "Merck Agrees to Proposed $27.7 Million Settlement over Fosamax Lawsuits," Reuters, December 9, 2013, reuters.com.

108 Martha Rosenberg, "7 Drugs Whose Dangerous Risks Emerged Only After Big Pharma Made Its Money," January 2, 2014, alternet.org.
109 Bob Grant, "Merck Published Fake Journal," *The Scientist*, April 20, 2009, the-scientist.com.
110 American Society for Nutrition, "Our Sustaining Members," accessed March 1, 2015, nutrition.org.
111 Rebekah Wilce, "Science Media Centre Spins Pro-GMO Line," April 29, 2014, commondreams.org.
112 Michele Simon, "And Now a Word From Our Sponsors: Are America's Nutrition Professionals in the Pocket of Big Food?" January 2013, eatdrinkpolitics.com.
113 "Researchers Uncover Multiple Sources of Bias in GMO Risk Assessments," Bioscience Resource Project, February 25, 2014, bioscienceresource.org.
114 Wilce, "Science Media Centre Spins Pro-GMO Line."
115 European Network of Scientists for Social and Environmental Responsibility (ENSSER), "No Scientific Consensus on Safety of Genetically Modified Organisms: Scientists Release Statements as World Food Prize Goes to Monsanto and Syngenta," October 21, 2013), ensser.org.
116 "Monsanto: A Corporate Profile," *Food and Water Watch*, 2013, documents.foodandwaterwatch.org.
117 Chris Parker, "The Monsanto Menace," *Village Voice*, July 24 2013, villagevoice.com.
118 Josh Sager, "Monsanto Controls Both the White House and the US Congress," *Global Research*, May 24, 2014, globalresearch.ca.
119 Ibid.
120 Oreskes and Conway, *Merchants of Doubt*.
121 "Dealing in Doubt: The Climate Denial Machine vs. Climate Science," Greenpeace USA, September 2013, greenpeace.org/usa.
122 Amanda Fallin, Rachel Grana, and Stanton A Glantz, " 'To Quarterback behind the Scenes, Third-Party Efforts': The Tobacco Industry and the Tea Party," *Tobacco Control*, February 20, 2013, 1–10.
123 "Dealing in Doubt: The Climate Denial Machine vs. Climate Science," Greenpeace USA, September 2013, greenpeace.org.
124 Mark Prigg, "23% of Americans Do Not Believe Global Warming Is Happening," Mail Online, January 17, 2014, dailymail.co.uk.
125 "Vast Majority Accept Climate Change," Forum Poll, July 23, 2014, poll.forumresearch.com.
126 Brad Plumer, "Scott Pruitt Could End up Being One of Trump's Most Consequential Cabinet Picks," February 17, 2017, vox.com.
127 Michael Bolen, "Average Canadian Climate Denier Is an Evangelical Man from Alberta Who Votes for the Tories," *Huffington Post*, July 25, 2014, huffingtonpost.ca.
128 Madeleine de Trenqualye, "Climate Change Politics in the Age of Trudeau and Trump: What's Next?" *The Tyee*, December 16, 2016, thetyee.ca.
129 John Dupuis, "The Canadian War on Science: A Long, Unexaggerated, Devastating Chronological Indictment," Confessions of a Science Librarian, October 24, 2014, scienceblogs.com/confessions.

130 Edward S. Herman and Noam Chomsky, *Manufacturing Consent: The Political Economy of the Mass Media* (New York: Pantheon, 1988), 306.
131 Herman and Chomsky, *Manufacturing Consent*.
132 "Media and Internet Concentration in Canada, 1984–2013," Canadian Media Concentration Research Project, November 26, 2014, cmcrp.org.
133 Ashley Lutz, "These 6 Corporations Control 90% Of The Media In America," *Business Insider*, June 14, 2012, businessinsider.com.
134 Edward Helmore, "Trump's Media War Threatens Journalists Globally, Protection Group Warns," *The Guardian*, February 25, 2017, theguardian.com.
135 Tom Cahill, "Media Coverage of the Primaries Was Awful, Harvard Study Confirms," June 14, 2016, usuncut.com.
136 "Americans' Views on Income Inequality and Workers' Rights," *New York Times*, June 3, 2015, nytimes.com.
137 Public Citizen Press Room, "Voters Overwhelmingly Want More Enforcement of Laws and Regulations, New Poll Shows," October 1, 2014, citizen.org/pressroom.
138 Nicholas Confessore and Megan Thee-brenan, "Poll Shows Americans Favor an Overhaul of Campaign Financing," *New York Times*, June 2, 2015.
139 Maureen Brosnahan, "Canada's Prison Population at All-Time High," CBC News, November 25, 2013, cbc.ca.
140 Nick Wing, "Here Are All of the Nations That Incarcerate More of Their Population Than the U.S.," *Huffington Post*, August 13, 2013, huffingtonpost.com.
141 Alex Altman, "Person of the Year 2014 Runner-Up: Ferguson Protesters," *Time*, December 10, 2014, time.com.
142 Jon Swain, "Baltimore Freddie Gray Protests Turn Violent as Police and Crowds Clash," *The Guardian*, April 26, 2015, theguardian.com.
143 Andrew Grossman, Alison Fox, and Sean Gardiner, "Wall Street Protesters Evicted from Camp," *Wall Street Journal*, November 16, 2011, wsj.com; Obert Modano, "Quebec Police Unleash Violence on Anti-Austerity Protesters," *The Canadian Progressive*, March 27, 2015, canadianprogressiveworld.com; "Police Brutality," January 21, 2015, blacklivesmatter.com; Gloria Galloway and Jane Taber, "N.B. Protesters Plan More Protests after Violent Clash with RCMP over Shale-Gas Project," *Globe and Mail*, October 18, 2013, theglobeandmail.com.
144 CBS News, "Human Rights Watch: 297 Killed in Egypt Protests," CBS News, February 7, 2011, cbsnews.com.
145 Jules Dufor, "The Worldwide Network of US Military Bases," *Global Research*, July 1, 2007, globalresearch.ca.
146 William Blum, *Killing Hope: U.S. and C.I.A. Interventions Since World War II – Updated through 2003*, 2nd ed. (Common Courage Press, 2008).
147 Engler, *The Black Book of Canadian Foreign Policy*.
148 Matthew White, "Source List and Detailed Death Tolls for the Primary Megadeaths of the Twentieth Century," February 2011, necrometrics.com.
149 Ibid.
150 Z. Obermeyer, C.J.L. Murray, and E. Gakidou, "Fifty Years of Violent War Deaths from Vietnam to Bosnia: Analysis of Data from the World Health Survey Programme," *British Medical Journal* 336, no. 7659 (June 28, 2008): 1482–86.

151 Allan Hyde, "New Analysis 'Confirms' 1 Million + Iraq Casualties," Opinion Research Business, January 28, 2008.
152 David North, "The War against Iraq and America's Drive for World Domination," October 4, 2002, wsws.org.
153 Dwight D. Eisenhower, "Eisenhower's Farewell Address to the Nation," January 17, 1961, informationclearinghouse.info.
154 "U.S. Federal Budget 2016 Fiscal Year: Where Your Money Really Goes" (New York, NY: War Resisters League, February 2015), warresisters.org.
155 Sam Perlo-Freeman and Carina Solmirano, "Trends in World Military Expenditure, 2013," SIPRI Fact Sheet (Stockholm International Peace Research Institute, April 2014), books.sipri.org.
156 "CCPA Report: Canadian Military Spending Highest since WW2," March 9, 2011, ceasefire.ca.
157 Robert Hunziker, "America's Deep State: Tells the Facts, Names the Names," February 25, 2014, counterpunch.org.
158 Ibid.
159 Nick Turse, "The Special Ops Surge: America's Secret War in 134 Countries," January 16, 2014, commondreams.org.
160 Nick Turse, "America's Black-Ops Blackout," July 1, 2014, commondreams.org.
161 Tom Engelhardt, "The National Security State as a Criminal Enterprise," December 15, 2014, commondreams.org.
162 Richard Heinberg, "Oil Depletion and the Fate of the World" (Post Carbon Institute, 2004).
163 Shane Harris, "Water Wars," *Foreign Policy*, September 18, 2014, foreignpolicy.com.

7: The Death System

1 Mumford, *Technics and Civilization*, 311.
2 Thomas Hobbes, *Leviathan* (Indianapolis, Indiana: Hackett, 1994), 59.
3 Ibid., 76.
4 Brian Ferguson, "The Birth of War," *Natural History* July/Aug 2003 (2003): 28–35; Brian Ferguson, "Born to Live: Challenging Killer Myths," in *Origins of Altruism and Cooperation*, ed. R.W. Sussman and C.R. Cloninger, Developments in Primatology: Progress and Prospects (Springer, 2011).
5 Polly Wiessner, "The Vines of Complexity: Egalitarian Structures and the Institutionalization of Inequality among the Enga," *Current Anthropology* 43, no. 2 (April 2002): 235.
6 James Woodburn, "Egalitarian Societies," *Man* 17 (1982): 431–51.
7 Ibid., 434.
8 Christopher Boehm, "Conflict and the Evolution of Social Control," *Journal of Consciousness Studies* 7, no. 1–2 (2000): 79–101.
9 Ibid.
10 Woodburn, "Egalitarian Societies."
11 Elizabeth Marshall Thomas, "Management of Violence Among the Ju/Wasi of Nyae Nyae: The Old Way and A New Way," in *Studying War: Anthropological Perspectives*, ed. S.P. Reyna and R.E. Downs, vol. 2, War and Society (Amsterdam: Gordon and Breach, 1994), 69–84.

12 Clive Finlayson, *The Humans Who Went Extinct: Why Neanderthals Died out and We Survived*. (Oxford: Oxford University Press, 2009).
13 Peter J. Richerson and Robert Boyd, "Institutional Evolution in the Holocene: The Rise of Complex Societies," in *The Origin of Human Social Institutions* (British Academy/Novartis Foundation, W.G. Runciman, 2000), 33.
14 Frans B.M. de Wall, "The Antiquity of Empathy," *Science* 336 (May 18, 2012): 874–76.
15 Peter J. Richerson and Robert Boyd, *Not by Genes Alone* (Chicago: University of Chicago Press, 2006), 195–97.
16 Daniel H. Mann et al., "Life and Extinction of Megafauna in the Ice-Age Arctic," *Proceedings of the National Academy of Sciences*, November 2, 2015.
17 Faye Flam, "The Evolution of Sex Roles Anthropologists Are Looking at How Prehistoric Tasks Were Divided, Perhaps Indicating the Moment When We Became Truly Human," Philly-Archives, April 2, 2007, articles.philly.com.
18 Virginia Hughes, "Were the First Artists Mostly Women?" *National Geographic*, October 9, 2013, news.nationalgeographic.com.
19 Josh Clark, "Prehistoric Dads Helped with Child Care," Msnbc.com, March 17, 2010, nbcnews.com.
20 P.A. Spikins, H.E. Rutherford, and A.P. Needham, "From Hominity to Humanity: Compassion from the Earliest Archaic to Modern Humans," *Time and Mind* 3, no. 3 (November 2010).
21 Paul Radin, *The World of Primitive Man* (New York, NY: Dutton, 1971), 106.
22 Murray Bookchin, *The Ecology of Freedom: The Emergence and Dissolution of Hierarchy* (Oakland, CA: AK Press, 2005), 218.
23 Robert Wallace, "Revolutions and a New Order in Solonian Athens and Archaic Greece," in *Origins of Democracy in Ancient Greece*, ed. Kurt A. Raaflaub, Josiah Ober, and Robert Wallace (University of California Press, 2007), 49–82.
24 Gonzalo Alvarez, Francisco C. Ceballos, and Celsa Quinteiro, "The Role of Inbreeding in the Extinction of a European Royal Dynasty," *PLoS ONE* 4, no. 4 (April 15, 2009): e5174.
25 Peter J. Richerson and Robert Boyd, *The Origin and Evolution of Cultures* (Oxford: Oxford University Press, 2005), 10.
26 Bookchin, *The Ecology of Freedom*, 121–23.
27 Kenneth M. Ames, "On the Evolution of the Human Capacity for Inequality and/or Egalitarianism," in *Pathways to Power: New Perspectives on the Emergence of Social Inequality*, ed. Douglas T. Price and Gary M. Feinman (New York: Springer, 2010), 15–44.
28 Woodburn, "Egalitarian Societies."
29 Thich Nhat Hanh, "Clouds In Each Paper," Awakin.org, March 25, 2002, awakin.org.
30 Jeremy Rifkin, "'The Empathic Civilization': Rethinking Human Nature in the Biosphere Era," *Huffington Post*, March 18, 2010, huffingtonpost.com.
31 Bookchin, *The Ecology of Freedom*, 143–72.
32 Douglas T. Price and Gary M. Feinman, eds., *Pathways to Power: New Perspectives on the Emergence of Social Inequality*, Fundamental Issues in Archaeology (New York: Springer, 2010).
33 Stewart Clegg and James Bailey, *International Encyclopedia of Organization Studies:*

Agency-Structure Debate (Thousand Oaks, California: SAGE Publications, 2008).
34. Anthony Giddens, *The Constitution of Society: Outline of the Theory of Structuration*, Berkeley, University of California Press, 1986.
35. Bookchin, *The Ecology of Freedom*.
36. T.D. Price and O. Bar-Yosef, "Traces of Inequality at the Origins of Agriculture in the Ancient Near East," in *Pathways to Power: New Perspectives on the Emergence of Social Inequality* (New York: Springer, 2010), 147–68.
37. Tina L. Thurston, "Bitter Arrows and Generous Gifts: What Was a 'King' in the European Iron Age?" in *Pathways to Power: New Perspectives on the Emergence of Social Inequality* (New York: Springer, 2010), 193–254.
38. Brian Hayden and Suzanne Villeneuve, "Who Benefits from Complexity? A View from Futuna," in *Pathways to Power: New Perspectives on the Emergence of Social Inequality* (New York: Springer, 2010), 95–145.
39. Mark Aldenderfer, "Gimme That Old Time Religion: Rethinking the Role of Religion in the Emergence of Social Inequality," in *Pathways to Power: New Perspectives on the Emergence of Social Inequality* (New York: Springer, 2010), 77–94.
40. Robert. L Carniero, "A Theory of the Origin of the State," *Science* 169 (1970): 733–38.
41. Kenneth M. Ames, "The Archaeology of Rank," in *Handbook of Archaeological Theories*, ed. R.A. Bentley, H.D.G. Maschnner, and C. Chippendale (Lantham: Alta Mira Press, 2007), 487–513.
42. Ibid.
43. R. Brian Ferguson, "The General Consequences of War: An Amazonian Perspective," in *Studying War: Anthropological Perspectives*, ed. S.P. Reyna and R.E. Downs, vol. 2 (Amsterdam: Gordon and Breach, 1994), 85–111.
44. Thurston, "Bitter Arrows and Generous Gifts: What Was a 'King' in the European Iron Age?"
45. S.P. Reyna, "A Mode of Domination Approach to Organized Violence," in *Studying War: Anthropological Perspectives*, ed. S.P. Reyna and R.E. Downs (Amsterdam: Gordon and Breach, 1994), 29–65.
46. Joanna Macy, *Coming Back To Life* (Gabriola Island, BC, Canada; Stony Creek, CT: New Society Publishers, 2009).
47. Hayden and Villeneuve, "Who Benefits from Complexity? A View from Futuna."
48. Gramsci, *Selections from the Prison Notebooks*.
49. Hayden and Villeneuve, "Who Benefits from Complexity? A View from Futuna."
50. Wiessner, "The Vines of Complexity: Egalitarian Structures and the Institutionalization of Inequality among the Enga."
51. Raymond Williams, *Marxism and Literature* (Oxford: Oxford Paperbacks, 1995), 112.
52. Gramsci, *Selections from the Prison Notebooks*, 60–61.
53. Ibid., 321–34.
54. Hayden and Villeneuve, "Who Benefits from Complexity? A View from Futuna."
55. T.D. Price and Bar-Yosef, "Traces of Inequality at the Origins of Agriculture in the Ancient Near East."

56 Bruce Trigger, *Understanding Early Civilizations* (New York, NY: Cambridge University Press, 2003), 203.
57 Reyna, "A Mode of Domination Approach to Organized Violence."
58 Friedrich Engels, *The Origin of the Family, Private Property and the State*, ed. Eleanor Burke Leacock, trans. A. West, rev. ed. (London: Lawrence & Wishart Ltd, 1972), 231.
59 Trigger, *Understanding Early Civilizations*, 142–46.
60 Ibid., 244–47.
61 Ibid., 142–54.
62 Karl Marx, *Capital*, Oxford's World Classics (Oxford: Oxford University Press, 1995), 361–62.
63 John McMurtry, *The Cancer Stage of Capitalism: From Crisis to Cure*, 2nd ed. (Winnipeg: Fernwood, 2013).
64 J. Haas, *Evolution of the Prehistoric State* (New York: Columbia University Press, 1982), 212.
65 Shmuel N. Eisenstadt, *The Political Systems of Empires*, rev. ed. (New Brunswick, USA: Transaction Publishers, 1993), 317–42.
66 Ferguson, "The General Consequences of War: An Amazonian Perspective."
67 Joyce Marcus, "The Peaks and Valleys of Ancient States: An Extension of the Dynamic Model," in *Archaic States* (Santa Fe, NM: School of American Research Press, 1998), 59–94.
68 Trigger, *Understanding Early Civilizations*, 142–60.
69 Tainter, *The Collapse of Complex Societies*, 1990.
70 Tainter, *The Collapse of Complex Societies*, 1988, 118–23.
71 Thomas L. Friedman, "Foreign Policy by Whisper and Nudge," *New York Times*, August 24, 2013, nytimes.com.
72 Mikael Colville-Andersen, "The 20 Most Bike-Friendly Cities on the Planet," *Wired*, June 2, 2015, wired.com.
73 Dupuis, "The Canadian War on Science."
74 Eric Bradner, "Trump Picks Scott Pruitt to Head EPA," CNN, December 8, 2016, cnn.com.
75 Annie Leonard, "Story of Stuff, Referenced and Annotated Script," *Journal of Occupational and Environmental Health* 13, no. 1 (2007); Giles Slade, *Made to Break: Technology and Obsolescence in America* (Cambridge, MA: Harvard University Press, 2007).
76 Paul Kennedy, *The Rise and Fall of the Great Powers: Economic Change and Military Conflict from 1500 to 2000* (London: Unwin Hyman, 1988), xvi.
77 Tainter, *The Collapse of Complex Societies*, 1990, 71–73.
78 Seth Cline, "The Other Symbol of George W. Bush's Legacy," US News & World Report, May 1, 2013, usnews.com.
79 Matthew Fisher, "Photos: Harper Lauds Troops on Surprise Afghanistan Visit," *National Post*, May 30, 2011, news.nationalpost.com/news.
80 "A Million Europeans Enslaved," *Washington Times*, March 10, 2004, washingtontimes.com.
81 Rose Troup Buchanan, "Coptic Christians: Who Are They – and Why Have They Been Targeted by Isis in Beheading Video?" *The Independent*," February 16, 2015, independent.co.uk.

82 Chase Peterson-Withorn and Jennifer Wang, "The Definitive Net Worth of Donald Trump," *Forbes*, September 28, 2016, forbes.com; Tom McCarthy, "Trump's Cabinet Picks: Here Are All of the Appointments so Far," *The Guardian*, December 14, 2016, theguardian.com.
83 Pew Research Centre, "The Politics of Financial Insecurity," Pew Research Center for the People and the Press, January 8, 2015, people-press.org.
84 Daisy Grewal, "How Wealth Reduces Compassion," *Scientific American*, April 10, 2012, scientificamerican.com; Wency Leung, "Yes, the Rich Really Are Different from the Rest of Us," *Globe and Mail*, September 20, 2012, theglobeandmail.com; Kathleen Blanchard, "Power Robs the Brain of Empathy," August 10, 2013, digitaljournal.com; "Exploring the Psychology of Wealth, 'Pernicious' Effects of Economic Inequality," PBS NewsHour, June 21, 2013, pbs.org.
85 Thorstein Veblen, *The Theory of the Leisure Class*, new ed. (New York: Dover Publications, 1994).
86 Wallace, "Revolutions and a New Order in Solonian Athens and Archaic Greece."
87 Noam Chomsky, "The U.S. Behaves Nothing like a Democracy" August 17, 2013, salon.com.
88 Wallace, "Revolutions and a New Order in Solonian Athens and Archaic Greece."
89 Richard Sanders, "Wall Street's Fascist Plot to Seize the White House," *Coalition to Oppose the Arms Trade*, August 2004, coat.ncf.ca.
90 Terry Eagleton, *Ideology: An Introduction* (London; New York: Verso, 1991), 47.
91 Leung, "Yes, the Rich Really Are Different from the Rest of Us."
92 Benjamin J. Newman, Christopher D. Johnston, and Patrick L. Lown, "False Consciousness or Class Awareness? Local Income Inequality, Personal Economic Position, and Belief in American Meritocracy," *American Journal of Political Science* 59, no. 2 (February 1, 2015): 326–40.
93 Michael Barkun, *A Culture of Conspiracy: Apocalyptic Visions in Contemporary America* (Berkeley, Calif: University of California Press, 2006).
94 Gayle MacDonald, "Lights, Camera, Apocalypse!" *Globe and Mail*, March 20, 2009, theglobeandmail.com.
95 Harvey, *The Condition of Postmodernity*; Joseph A. Schumpeter, *Capitalism, Socialism, and Democracy*, 3rd ed. (New York: Harper Perennial Modern Classics, 2008).
96 John Pilger, "South Africa: The Liberation's Betrayal," October 2, 2008, johnpilger.com.
97 R.D. Hare, "Psychopathy: A Clinical Construct Whose Time Has Come," *Criminal Justice and Behaviour* 23, no. 1 (1996): 25–54.
98 Paul Babiak and Robert D. Hare, *Snakes in Suits: When Psychopaths Go to Work* (New York: HarperBusiness, 2007).
99 Mark Achbar and Jennifer Abbott, *The Corporation* (documentary, 2004).

8: Toward a System of Life

1 Rousseau, *Jean-Jacques Rousseau: The Basic Political Writings*, 70.
2 Trigger, *Understanding Early Civilizations*, 203.
3 Bill McKibben, *Deep Economy: The Wealth of Communities and the Durable Future* (New York, NY: St. Martin's Griffin, 2008), 213–32.

4 David Suzuki, Amanda McConnell, and Adrienne Mason, *The Sacred Balance: Rediscovering Our Place in Nature*, 3rd ed. (Vancouver: Greystone Books, 2007), 293–308.
5 Jed Greer and Kenny Bruno, *Greenwash: The Reality Behind Corporate Environmentalism* (Penang: Rowman & Littlefield Publishers, 1997).
6 "Interface Sustainability," 2008, interfaceglobal.com/sustainability.aspx.
7 Zinn, *A People's History of the United States*, 329–98.
8 Ibid., 399–401.
9 Matthew Behrens and the Canadian Foundation for Labour Rights, eds., *Unions Matter: Advancing Democracy, Economic Equality, and Social Justice* (Toronto: Between the Lines, 2014).
10 Kimberle Crenshaw, "Demarginalizing the Intersection of Race and Sex: A Black Feminist Critique of Antidiscrimination Doctrine, Feminist Theory and Antiracist Politics," *University of Chicago Legal Forum*, 1989, 139–67.
11 Derrick Jensen, Aric McBay, and Lierre Keith, *Deep Green Resistance: Strategy to Save the Planet* (New York: Seven Stories Press, 2011), 77–78.
12 Murray Bookchin, "Listen, Marxist!" in *Post-Scarcity Anarchism*, 2nd ed. (Montreal; Buffalo: Black Rose Books, 1986), 195–244.
13 Marx, *Capital*, 363–77; Perelman, *The Invention of Capitalism*.
14 Karl Marx and Friedrich Engels, *The Communist Manifesto*, ed. Gareth Stedman Jones, trans. Samuel Moore, rep. ed. (Penguin Classics, 2015).
15 Ibid.
16 Philippe Rekacewicz, "Environmental Disaster in Eastern Europe," *Le Monde Diplomatique*, English version, 2000, July edition.
17 Tomasz Sommer and Marek Chodakiewicz, "Average Joe: The Return of Stalin Apologists," *World Affairs Journal*, January/February 2011, worldaffairsjournal.org; James Marson, "The Left Must Face up to Stalin's Evil," *The Guardian*, August 24, 2009, theguardian.com.
18 Massimo Livi-Bacci, "On the Human Costs of Collectivization in the Soviet Union," *Population and Development Review* 19, no. 4 (December 1, 1993): 743–66; "Collectivization and China's Agricultural Crisis in 1959–1961," *Journal of Political Economy* 98, no. 6 (December 1, 1990): 1228–52.
19 Gramsci, *Selections from the Prison Notebooks*, 56–58, 235, 244, 248.
20 Vladimir Ilyanovich Lenin, *What Is to Be Done?* (1902).
21 Andrew Feenberg, "Paths to Failure: The Dialectics of Organization and Ideology in the New Left," in *Race, Politics, and Culture Critical Essays on the Radicalism of the 1960s*, 1986, 119–44; Karl-Erik Tallmo, "On the Question of the Guilt of the New Left . . .," 2011, art-bin.com/art/arenegadeeng.html.
22 Noam Chomsky, "Domestic Terrorism: Notes on the State System of Oppression," *New Political Science* 21, no. 3 (1999): 303–24; "Spy-Watchers Urge a Shorter Leash for CSIS," *Globe and Mail*, August 23, 2012, theglobeandmail.com.
23 Aric McBay, "DGR and Transphobia," May 14, 2013, aricmcbay.org.
24 Michelle Matisons and Alexander Reid Ross, "Deep Green Resistance – a Critique," *Earth First! Newswire*, May 18, 2015, earthfirstjournal.org.
25 Jensen, *Endgame*, vol. 1 and 2 (New York: Seven Stories Press, 2006).
26 Jensen, McBay, and Keith, *Deep Green Resistance*, 11.
27 Ibid., 16.

28 Ibid., 33.
29 Ibid., 438.
30 Adam Hochschild, *Bury the Chains: Prophets and Rebels in the Fight to Free an Empire's Slaves*, rep. ed. (Boston: Mariner Books, 2006).
31 "A History of the American Suffragist Movement, Timeline," accessed June 8, 2015, suffragist.com/timeline.htm.
32 Sasha Lilley, "Great Chaos Under Heaven: Catastrophism and the Left," in *Catastrophism: The Apocalyptic Politics of Collapse and Rebirth* (Toronto: Between the Lines, 2012), 71–76.
33 Michigan Technological University, "Let It Snow! Solar Panels Can Take It," October 24, 2012, sciencedaily.com.
34 Jensen, McBay, and Keith, *Deep Green Resistance*, 23.
35 Monte Paulsen, "Step Inside the Real Home of the Future: Passivhaus," *The Tyee*, January 25, 2011, thetyee.ca; Ottmar Edenhofer et al., eds., *Renewable Energy Sources and Climate Change Mitigation: Special Report of the Intergovernmental Panel on Climate Change* (New York: Cambridge University Press, 2012).
36 "Radically Sustainable Buildings," *Earthship Biotecture*, June 15, 2015, earthship.com.
37 C.J. Bearman, "An Examination of Suffragette Violence," *English Historical Review* 120, no. 486 (April 1, 2005): 365–97.
38 Ibid.
39 Katherine Connelly, *Sylvia Pankhurst: Suffragette, Socialist and Scourge of Empire* (London: Pluto Press, 2013).
40 Jensen, McBay, and Keith, *Deep Green Resistance*.
41 "Clayoquot Sound," *Canadian Encyclopedia*, accessed May 19, 2015, thecanadianencyclopedia.ca.
42 "The Burnt Church Crisis," October 16, 2014, criminalizingdissent.wordpress.com; Krystalline Kraus, "Grassy Narrows Wants Justice for Destructive Logging and Mercury Poisoning," Rabble.ca, November 5, 2013, rabble.ca; Chelsea Vowel, "The Majority of Canadians Have Been Woefully Under-Informed about What Is Really Going in Elsipogtog," *Toronto Star*, November 14, 2013, thestar.com; "First Nations Say They Will Fight Oilsands, Pipeline," March 20, 2013, cbc.ca; Meg Borthwick, "Northern Gateway: Resistance Continues," Rabble.ca, June 18, 2014, rabble.ca.
43 Josh Lederman, "Obama Vetoes Keystone XL Pipeline Bill," Global News, February 24, 2015, globalnews.ca.
44 Mario Blaser, Harvey A. Feit, and Glenn McRae, *In the Way of Development: Indigenous Peoples, Life Projects and Globalization* (New York: Zed Books, 2004).
45 Thorkild Jacobsen, "Primitive Democracy in Ancient Mesopotamia," *Journal of Near Eastern Studies* 2, no. 3 (1943): 159–72; Benjamin Isakhan and Stephen Stockwell, eds., *The Secret History of Democracy*, rep. ed. (Basingstoke: Palgrave Macmillan, 2012).
46 Gramsci, *Selections from the Prison Notebooks*, 57.
47 Ibid., 59.
48 Ibid., 60–61.
49 Ibid., 137.
50 Ibid., 229–39.

51 Ibid., 56.
52 Laclau and Mouffe, *Hegemony and Socialist Strategy*, 159–77.
53 Stephen D'Arcy, *Languages of the Unheard: Why Militant Protest Is Good for Democracy* (Toronto: Between the Lines, 2013).
54 C. Wright Mills and Todd Gitlin, *The Sociological Imagination*, 40th anniv. ed. (Oxford, UK; New York: Oxford University Press, 2000).
55 Lorna Weir, "Limitations of New Social Movement Analysis," *Studies in Political Economy* 40, no. Spring (1993): 73–102.
56 Jill Friedberg and Rick Rowley, *This Is What Democracy Looks Like* (documentary, 2000).
57 Michael Albert, *The Trajectory of Change: Activist Strategies for Social Transformation* (Cambridge, MA: South End Press, 2002), 2.
58 Ibid., 41.
59 "Harper Watch," May 18, 2015, harperwatch.wordpress.com; Yves Engler, *The Ugly Canada – Stephen Harper's Foreign Policy* (RED Publishing, 2012).
60 David Cole, "The NSA on Trial," December 21, 2013, commondreams.org; David Sirota, "Pentagon and NSA Officials Say They Want Snowden Extrajudicially Assassinated," January 17, 2014, commondreams.org.
61 Alex Wilhelm and Cat Zakrzewski, "Google, Other Leading Internet Companies Support Net Neutrality, Call For Extension To Mobile Providers," TechCrunch, July 14, 2014, social.techcrunch.com.
62 Justin Worland, "What to Know about the Dakota Access Pipeline Protests," *Time Magazine*, October 28, 2016, time.com.
63 Meyer Robinson, "The Legal Case for Blocking the Dakota Access Pipeline," *Atlantic*, September 9, 2015, theatlantic.com.
64 Julia Carrie Wong, "'This Is an Awakening': Native Americans Find New Hope after Standing Rock," *The Guardian*, December 8, 2016, theguardian.com.
65 Worland, "What to Know about the Dakota Access Pipeline Protests."
66 Julia Carrie Wong, "Dakota Access Pipeline: US Denies Key Permit, a Win for Standing Rock Protesters," *The Guardian*, December 5, 2016, theguardian.com.
67 Charlie May, "'We Beg for Your Forgiveness': Veterans Join Native Elders in Celebration Ceremony," December 5, 2016, salon.com.
68 Chas Danner, "Protesters Declare Victory after Construction of Dakota Access Pipeline Halted," *Daily Intelligencer*, December 2016, nymag.com.
69 Edward Helmore, "Standing Rock Protesters Unfurl Banner over Field at Minneapolis NFL Game," *The Guardian*, January 1, 2017, theguardian.com; Sam Levin and Julia Carrie Wong, "Standing Rock Activists Eye Pipeline Finances to Cement Dakota Access Win," *The Guardian*, December 29, 2016, theguardian.com.
70 John Stewart, *Evolution's Arrow: The Direction of Evolution and the Future of Humanity* (Chapman Press, 2000), 158.

Index

accumulation, 180; capital, 72, 81, 103, 133; of profit, 50, 62, 164; wealth, 113, 157
adaptive culture, 143–44
adroit usurpation, 179
Afghanistan: invasion of, 54–55, 74, 128, 129, 133; NATO mission in, 153; Soviet war, 115
African Americans, 115, 192
age: advanced, 141; marginalization based on, 185; status differences concerning, 139, 147
agency: despotic, 149; human intelligence and, 193; structure vs., 148
aggression, 136, 145
agrarian states, 160
agribusiness, 75
agricultural economy, 38
agricultural exhaustion, 89–90
agricultural expansion, 40
agriculturalists, 138
agriculture, 150, 154, 161; impact of on natural systems, 89–90; industrial, 39, 81, 90; intensification of, 90; urban, 40
Ahmed, Nafeez: *A User's Guide to the Crisis of Civilization*, 22, 75
air quality, 3, 94–95
Albert, Michael: *The Trajectory of Change*, 209
Alberta: tar sands in, 89–87, 93–94, 102, 124, 133, 194, 200, 210
Allende, Salvador, 117
alpha males, 139, 150, 175–76, 189
Al Qaeda, 54, 128
alternatives-building, 31, 207
American Academy of Nutrition and Dietetics (AND), 121
American Enterprise Institute (AEI), 116
American Indian Party, 190
American International Group (AIG), 118
American Legislative Exchange Council (ALEC), 116

Americans for Prosperity, 123
American Society for Nutrition (ASN), 121
anarchism, 18–19, 183, 188
anarcho-primitivism, 20
Anderson, Ray, 182
Anglia Ruskin University: Global Resource Observatory, 8
Anthropocene epoch, 92, 95
anthropocentrism, 26, 79
anti-Arab sentiment, 115
anti-austerity, 198–99, 216
anti-civilization, 20–21, 25–27, 36, 39, 188, 190
anti-colonialism, 23
anti-globalization, 198, 208
anti-monarchism, 23
anti-Muslim sentiment, 115
anti-oppression, 202, 203
anti-war movement, 189, 209
apartheid, 194–95
apocalypticism, 6–7, 9–10, 29, 173
Apter, David, 83
Arab-Israeli war, 115
arable land, disappearance of, 89–90, 159
Arab Spring, 30, 127, 198, 216
archaeology, 24, 137–41, 150
Argentina, 11–12
aristocracy, 160, 175
Aristotle, 79
arms industry, 129, 164, 203
arts, public support for, 203
al-Assad, Bashar, 167
asset bubbles, 59–63
Association of American Universities (AAU), 118
AT&T, 108
Athabasca River, 93–94
atmospheric carbon, 88, 92
Augustine, 24, 137
Australia: life expectancy for Indigenous peoples in, 69; political power in, 29

242

authoritarianism, 9, 156, 187, 205, 216; and communism, 186; elite, 24; left, 189; in Marxism, 19; and militarized states, 126–31; and revolution, 198, 212; social control and 25; and state power, 29
autonomy, 5, 25, 141, 146, 178, 208

Bacon, Francis, 79–80; *Advancement of Learning*, 80
Bakunin, Mikhail, 20, 24
Bangladesh, energy use in, 84
banking sector, 65, 108, 173, 175. *See also* financial collapse
Barrick Gold, 75, 117
Beachy, Roger, 122
Belgium, colonial occupation by, 73
Bell/Bell CTV, 108, 125
Bello, Walden, 62–63
Benveniste, Emile: "Civilization," 37
Beothuk people, 74
Berlusconi, Silvio, 169
beverage sector, 109
big pharma, 120–21
big tobacco, 118–20, 123
Bilderberg Group, 173
Bin Laden, Osama, 54
biodiversity: decline in, 91; ocean, 91–92
biological agents, 14
biosphere, 78, 82, 88, 160, 180, 182, 191, 215; as collection of nested systems, 66; consciousness, 147, 203; degradation of, 82, 132, 186, 190–91, 206; pressures on, 7–8, 93
biotechnology, 101, 120–22
Bismarck, Otto von, 73
Black Lives Matter, 30, 127, 199, 211
blackness, 168, 175
Black Panther Party, 185, 190
Blum, William: *Killing Hope*, 128
Boehm, Christopher, 139
Bolivia, radical government in, 199
Bonaparte, Napoleon, 198
Bond and Co., 105
Bookchin, Murray, 26, 39, 144; *The Ecology of Freedom*, 141–42, 147
bourgeoisie: alienation of, 81; as force of history, 18
Brazil, 63, 188
Brenner, Robert, 62
Britain: biotechnology, 121; history of parliamentary democracy, 106–7; influence of, 17; Labour Party, 184; poverty, 68; Science Media Centre (SMC), 121

British East India Company, 73
Brown, Lester, 18
Brown, Michael, 127
Brown Brothers Harriman, 101
Brownlee, Jamie: *Ruling Canada*, 108, 115–16
Brown Lives Matter, 127
Brzezinski, Zbigniew, 173
"bubblenomics," 63
bureaucracy, 11, 38, 161
Burma, 98
Bush, George H.W, 101, 116, 130, 167–69
Bush, George W., 55, 101, 118, 124, 169
Bush, Prescott, 101, 170

Cacerolazos, 11–12
Cambodia, 172
Cameron, David, 105
campaign finance, 107
Canada: air pollution, 95; banking sector, 108; democracy, 98–99; elections, 112; electoral process, 210; energy use, 84–85; environmental defence, 197; First Nations, 49, 69, 115, 197; greenhouse gases, 124; Green Party, 184; incarceration rates, 126; income gap, 99–100; Indian Act, 115; influence of, 17; insurrection, 188, 208; lobbying, 102; macro-systems model, 22; media revenues, 125; military expenses, 130; New Democratic Party (NDP), 184, 199; NGOs, 210; oligopoly, 108; political doublespeak, 128; radicalism, 196; RCMP, 189; revolution, 28; revolving door in, 101; social movements, 30; tax evasion, 105; unions, 183; waste generation, 93; women, 113–15, 167; women in Parliament, 112
Canada Steamship Lines (CSL), 101
Canadian Centre for Policy Alternatives (CCPA), 99
Canadian Chamber of Commerce (CCC), 115
Canadian Council of Chief Executives (CCCE), 115
Canadian Energy Research Institute (CERI), 117
Canadian Federation of Independent Business (CFIB), 115–16
Canadian International Development Agency (CIDA), 117
Canadian Manufacturers and Exporters Association, 115
Canadian Medical Association, 95

Canadian Security Intelligence Service (CSIS), 211
Canadian Taxpayers Association, 116
Canisius, Edgar, 73–74
capital: accumulation of, 72, 81, 103, 133; concentration of, 64; post-war compromise between labour and, 63, 157; rate of turnover of, 51–52, 62
capitalism, 5, 7, 15, 19, 49, 52, 78, 175, 180, 184; consumer, 83–84, 211; contradictions within, 62; crony, 210; economic life-blood of, 50; emergence of, 81; global, 22, 55, 58, 62, 64; Golden Age of, 63; green, 133; mercantile, 72–74; overthrow of, 183; vs. oligarchy, 185–86; vs. socialism, 187. *See also* industrial capitalism
Carnegie, Andrew, 111
Carneiro, Robert, 149
Carson, Rachel: *Silent Spring*, 7
catagenesis, 13
Cato Institute, 116
Catton, William, Jr.: *Overshoot*, 78, 84
C.D. Howe Institute, 116
Ceballos, Gerardo, 8
Celebration (Florida), 56
Center for Strategic and International Studies, 116
Cheney, Dick, 17, 116
chiefdoms, oligarchic, 158, 160
Childe, V. Gordon, 37–38; *Man Makes Himself*, 38
children, 67, 193; infant mortality, 68; labour, 172; and poverty, 49, 68–69, 71–72
Chile, 117
China, 39, 128, 187; economic growth of, 63; influence of, 17; labour unrest in, 216; revolution in, 188, 198; water scarcity in, 89
Chomsky, Noam, 10, 176; *Manufacturing Consent*, 124–25
CHOP (Clear Hamilton of Pollution), 3–4
Christianity, 168, 173; fundamentalist, 19
circumscription, 149, 153; political, 159; resource, 159
cities, 38–39, 82; sustainable vs. unsustainable, 40–41
Citigroup Alternative Investments, 102
Citizens for a Sound Economy (CSE), 110, 123
civilization: analysis of using systems, 41–45; challenges of, 46–57; characteristics of, 38; as collection of nested subsystems, 43; definition of, 36–41; colonial European and modern industrial, 37; as gigantic organism, 42; human impact of, 67; industrial capitalist, 39–41, 44, 46–57, 58–59, 65–66, 75, 78, 95, 99, 113–14, 131–32, 159; limits on, 78; popular use of term, 99; as problem-solving organization, 181; totalizing definitions of, 39; unsustainable nature of, 40–41; vs. non-civilization, 37
civilization collapse, 13, 22, 25; fascination with, 8–9. *See also* collapse
civil rights, 11, 21, 23, 44, 115, 126–27, 183, 189, 200, 209–11
civil society, 166, 201, 210
class conflict, 17–18. *See also* conflict
class inequality, 27, 30, 188. *See also* socioeconomic class
classism, 112, 172
Clayoquot Sound (British Columbia), 197
clear-cut logging, 53, 197
Cleaver, Eldridge, 185
climate change, 8, 14–15, 20, 30, 35, 90, 127, 149, 215; activism and, 171–72; as crisis point, 22, 82, 133; denial of, 122–24, 164, 173, 210; and destruction of past societies, 46, 160; global warming, 7, 64–66, 88, 92, 95; and species extinction, 140
climate justice, 199, 216
climatology, 64
Clinton, Bill, 103, 118
Clinton, Hillary, 107–8, 125, 212
Club of Rome: *Limits to Growth*, 7
coal, 64, 86–87, 133, 194
coercion, 145, 151–53, 157, 186
Cold War, 6, 128–29, 187
collapse, 8–17, 19–20, 25–27, 32, 34–45, 58–59, 66, 75, 77–78, 131–33, 178, 181, 183, 187, 191–92, 206, 215; of oligarchy, 156, 158–61, 165, 170; systemic, 50. *See also* ecological collapse; financial collapse
Colombia, 75, 117
colonialism, 5, 37, 39, 72–74, 81, 114–15
commodification, 78, 81–82, 182, 211
communism, 183, 186, 187, 188
competition, 144–46; corporate, 170; excess, 63; internal, 170–72; oligarchic, 165
Competitive Enterprise Institute (CEI), 123
complex adaptive systems (CAS), 42
complexity, 38, 42, 46, 58–66, 67, 82, 83, 95, 131–32, 143, 154, 174, 179, 198;

Index 245

energy vs., 16; increasing, 13, 15, 23, 26, 214; vs. oligarchy, 161–65. *See also* social complexity
conceptual modelling, 42
Conference Board of Canada, 116
conflict, 23, 25, 40, 67, 127–28, 132–33, 139, 144–45, 149–50, 171. *See also* class conflict
Congo, Belgian colonial occupation of, 73
Congo Free State, 73
Congress of Industrial Organizations (CIO), 183
conquest, 35, 37, 74, 155, 157, 158, 180
Conrad, Joseph: *Heart of Darkness*, 73
consciousness, 216; oligarchic, 169–70
conscription, 154
consensus, 153; rigged, 152; value, 156
conservation, 1–5, 6, 180
conspiracy: culture of, 172; system vs., 172–75
consumer culture, disposable, 144
consumer economies, 75, 184
consumer lifestyle, 83–84
consumption, 49–51, 54, 81; conspicuous, 170
context, 216
Conway, Erik: *Merchants of Doubt*, 119
cooperation, 113, 140–41, 145–46, 155, 189, 214–15; democratic, 136
Coors empire, 116
Copenhagen (Denmark): cycling in, 163
coral reefs, 91
Corbyn, Jeremy, 30, 199, 216
corporate power, 9, 115–16
corporate sponsorship, 117, 200
corporate time, 50–51, 53
corruption and criminality, 103–8
counter-hegemony, 29, 158, 197–201, 205, 208, 210, 212, 216
counter-power, 140
counter-revolution, authoritarian, 212
creative intelligence, 140–41, 145, 146, 150, 191
Cribb, Robert, 105
critical development studies, 83
critical-race theory, 17
Crutzen, Paul, 92
Cuba, 39, 40, 128; revolution in, 188, 194–95
cultivation, extensive vs. intensive, 89
cultural adaptation, 154
cultural information, access to, 146
culture, 14; adaptive, 143–44; cooperative, 150; industrial, 82

Dakota Access Pipeline (DAPL), 199, 212–14
dam-building, 75
Day, Stockwell, 101
The Day After Tomorrow, 8
dead zones, ocean, 92
Death System, 23, 32, 136–77, 180, 185, 188–89, 215; contradictions of, 198; founding myth of, 199; and Life System, 24–25, 29, 180; logic of, 190; overthrow of, 199, 201, 204, 206, 208, 210–11
debt, 63, 69
decision making, 145, 148–49, 151, 161–64, 181, 183, 201, 215
deep collapse, 66
deep ecology, 26, 28
Deep Green Resistance (DGR), 190–96, 197
deep state, 130
deep-water wells, 162
defeatism, 193
deforestation, 7, 64, 88, 89, 90–91
democracy, 23–25, 28, 29, 43, 128, 142, 152, 187, 191, 193, 200, 204–12, 214–16; and adaptive culture, 143–44; and cooperation/community, 136, 140, 146, 176; direct, 30, 39, 151, 198, 201, 209, 215; discourse of, 98–100; electoral, 210; genesis, 106–7; participatory, 181; people's, 215; protection of, 127; pushback, 154; and revolution, 23; struggle, 23, 198, 208, 210
de-regulation, 2; financial, 103
Descartes, René, 79–80
despotism, 141, 215
Devonshire Initiative, 117
dialectical naturalism, 26
Diamond, Jared, 18, 180–81; *Collapse*, 7, 13–16, 23, 46, 58–59, 77, 161; *Guns, Germs and Steel*, 72
dictatorship, 97, 128, 153, 156, 186
direct action, 19, 183, 196–97
disease, 46; infectious, 49, 72
disenfranchisement, 107, 179, 206; Indigenous, 75; middle class, 11
dishonesty, 145
dispensationalism, 173
dispute resolution, 149
dissociation, 46–57, 131, 143, 179
distributed power generation, 194
Dofasco, 1, 3
Dole, Bob, 110
Domhoff, G., 112

domination, 151, 153–54, 156, 175, 180, 186, 191
"dot-com" bubble, 59–60
droughts, 89
Du Pont family, 170
Dutch East India Company, 73
dynamics, 59; destructive/dysfunctional vs. healing/generative/transformative, 41; fundamental, 133; group, 144–46
dysfunction, 6, 12, 35–36, 66–67, 174, 186; anti-human/anti-ecological, 164. *See also* ecological dysfunction; economic dysfunction; social dysfunction

Earth First!, 190
Earth Liberation Front, 190
Easter Island, 58–59, 77, 159
ecocentrism, 79
eco-feminism, 26, 28
economic bailouts, 61
ecological collapse, 7, 22, 46, 178, 186–87, 194, 208, 216. *See also* collapse
ecological deficit, 82
ecological dysfunction, 35, 66, 82
ecological footprint, 84, 88, 100, 140
ecological overshoot, 20, 159, 174
ecological stewardship, 210
ecological stress/instability, 8, 14
ecological symbiosis, 146
ecological system, 59; subsystems, 201
economic contraction, 88
economic crisis (2008), 7, 61–63, 65
economic dysfunction, 35, 66
economic equality, 143, 208
economic instability, 22, 35, 66, 75
economic sanctions, 154
economic stagnation, 54
economic stimulus spending, 61
Economist Intelligence Unit: *Report on the State of Global Democracy* (2013), 98
eco-socialism, 201–5
ecosystem collapse, 91, 95–96, 160
ecosystemic degradation, 15, 77, 91–92, 95, 127, 133, 178, 180
ecosystemic diversity, 204
ecosystem viability, 66, 89
eco-technologies, 163
Ecuador, mine resistance movements in, 75
Edison, Thomas, 111
education, 31, 49, 203, 206, 214
egalitarianism, 25, 138, 139–40, 141–45, 147–49, 151, 160, 188
Egypt, 167, 168; revolution in, 188
Ehrlich, Anne, 8

Ehrlich, Paul, 8
Einstein, Albert, 6
Eisenhower, Dwight, 129
Eisenstadt, Shmuel, 156, 165
Election Justice USA: *Democracy Lost*, 107–8
electoral fraud, 106–8
electoral process, subversion of, 210
electricity, 48
electronic communications, 39
elites, 31, 53, 61, 97, 106–8, 112, 115–18, 127, 131, 137, 144, 151, 163, 181, 183, 189, 196; aggrandizing goals of, 156; aristocratic, 24; authority, 152; consensus, 116; control, 23, 98, 178, 184, 186, 212; corporate, 55, 99–100, 165; culture, 170; de-legitimization of, 156; economic, 49, 61–62, 81, 115, 118, 125, 173, 187; exploitation by, 143, 166, 187; financial, 103–4; and hegemony, 154; ideology and policy, 116; legitimacy of, 199–200; military, 165; and oligarchy, 154–59, 165–76, 188; opposition to, 201, 205, 209, 212; political, 49, 55, 81, 99, 115, 125, 165–66, 173, 187; power of, 153, 179, 200, 206, 209; reformist strategy of, 157; rule, 136, 167, 205, 216; and subordinates, 156; wealth, 116
empathic displacement, 47, 54–57
empathy, 145–46, 150, 191, 198
empire, European ideology of, 37
empire-building, 37
empiricism, 80
Enbridge, 118
energy: alternative sources of, 86–87; availability of, 8, 14, 22; consumption of, 82–83, 161–62; depletion, 82–88; efficiency, 40, 83, 162; intensiveness, 83; per country, per capita use of, 84–85; renewable, 40, 87, 204, 215; scarcity of, 160, 163; sources of, 83; strategic resources, 85
energy return on investment (EROI), 86–87
Energy Transfer Partners, 212
Engels, Friedrich: *Communist Manifesto*, 185; *Origin of the Family, Private Property and the State*, 154–55
Engler, Yves: *The Black Book of Canadian Foreign Policy*, 117
Enlightenment, 81
Enron, 105
environmental degradation, 14, 159, 196–97; human-made, 58–59, 77, 160

environmentalism, 20, 27, 127, 172, 183, 196; local, 210; reformist, 21
environmental resources, cost of, 50
environmental standards, 2, 63, 100
environmental worldview, 79
Environment America Research and Policy Center, 94
equality of unequals, 142
essentialism, 18, 155, 201; class, 170; gender, 113–14
ethics, 47; consumer choice and, 182
Ethiopia, 115
ethnicity, 48, 112, 114, 167, 184–85, 198; and politics, 175; and poverty, 68
ethnocentrism, 36–37, 99, 114
ethnographic research, 137–39, 141, 150
eugenics, 114
European Network of Scientists for Social and Environmental Responsibility (ENSSER), 122
Eurozone countries: democracy in, 98–99; macro-systems model in, 22; political power in, 29; resistance to austerity in, 30
evolution, 15, 214–15; cultural, 144
evolutionary time, 53
exceptionalism, 170
exploitation, 81, 154, 156, 160, 170, 175, 179, 186, 191; of child/sweatshop labour, 172; corporate, 196; ecological, 85, 159; elite, 143, 166, 187; maximization of, 180; of subordinate classes, 155
externalities, 57, 179
extinction rates, 88, 91–92, 160
Exxon Mobil, 123

fair trade, 182, 203
Fair Vote Canada, 210
false consciousness, 99, 152
famine, 35
Fannie Mae, 60, 62
Fanon, Frantz, 178
fascism, 158, 186–87
feedback, 42, 49, 52–53, 58–59, 140, 156, 178; ecosystemic, 143–44; empathic, 144; loop, 42, 65–66; positive, 150; signal, 42; social, 144
Feldstein, Martin, 118
femininity, 113
feminism, 17, 23
fertilizers, 88, 93
feudalism, 154
financial collapse, 7–8, 61–62, 65, 104. *See also* banking sector; collapse
Financial Crisis Inquiry Commission, 104

financialization, 63
first humans, 138–39
First Nations. *See* Indigenous peoples
fishing: industrial, 53; rights, 197
Fletcher, Joseph F., 112
Flint Sit-down Strike, 183
food: adequate, 141–43; insecurity, 22, 69, 71; prices of, 8, 71–72; production of, 54, 88, 89, 149; shortages of, 8, 46; sustainable production of, 204
food industry, 121–22
foragers, immediate-return, 138–39
Forbes, H.D., 112
Ford, Henry, 51
foreclosures, 61
foreign policy, 49, 129; American, 55, 132, 173; democratic, 202; militarization of, 22, 127; and oligarchy, 128
foreign species, introduction of, 59
forest systems, 65–66
fossil fuels, 49, 64, 87, 93, 133, 163, 194, 215; depletion of, 7, 30, 39, 83, 86, 88, 95, 162; unconventional, 162
fracking, 87, 93–94, 133
France, 27, 36; banking sector in, 108; influence of, 17; Vichy, 153
franchise, universal, 210. *See also* women: suffrage
Fraser Institute, 116, 123
Freddie Mac, 60, 62
freedom of (assembly, press, etc.), 202–3
FreedomWorks, 123
free market, 49–50; competition, 108
free trade, 2
French Revolution, 198
fresh water depletion. *See* water: shortages
Friends of Red Hill Valley (FORHV), 4
functionalism, 16, 181

Gaddafi, Muammar, 133
Galileo, 80
Gasland documentary, 94
Gates, Bill and Melinda, 171–72
Gaud, William, 90
Geithner, Timothy, 102
gender, 17, 48, 112, 139, 141, 147, 184–85, 198; equality, 141; essentialism, 113–14; and poverty, 68; socialization, 17. *See also* women
gene/culture/environment co-evolution, 139–40
Genesis, Book of, 79
genetically engineered seeds, 95, 122
genetically modified organisms (GMO), 121–22

genocide, 172, 176; Indigenous, 75, 115; Rwandan, 15
George C. Marshall Institute, 122
Germany: banking sector in, 108; Fascist coup in, 158
Giddens, Anthony, 55, 148
Gilens, Martin, 112
GlaxoSmithKline (GSK), 120
Gleick, Peter: *The World's Water 2008-2009*, 89
global banking system, 61–62
global capitalism, 22, 55, 62, 64
Global Climate Coalition (GCC), 123
global economic meltdowns, 59–64, 65
global financial markets, 51, 61; crisis in, 53, 61–63, 65
globalization, 63; capitalist, 51–52
global justice, 23, 191
global village, 55–56
global warming, 7, 65, 88, 92, 95; deniers, 123. *See also* climate change
GoldCorp, 75
Goldman, Emma, 17
Goldman Sachs, 102–4
Gore, Al, 18, 171–72; *An Inconvenient Truth*, 65
governance, 10, 21; oligarchic, 23, 99, 156, 161, 174; popular, 23; structures of, 31, 98, 126, 131, 153
government regulation, 52, 104, 109, 119
gradualism, 209
Gramsci, Antonio, 28–29, 152–53, 199–201, 205, 206; *The Prison Notebooks*, 152
Gray, Freddie, 127
Great Chain of Being, 114
Great Depression, 61, 103–4
Great Men of History, 10–11
Great Smog (1952), 94–95
Great Whale hydroelectric development, 197
Green, Larry, 4
green anarchy, 20
greenhouse gases, 64, 100
Greenpeace, 65, 123, 197
Green Revolution, 90
Greenspan, Alan, 103–4
greenwashing, 182
Greystar Corp., 117
guaranteed annual income, 203
Guatemala, mine resistance movements in, 75
guerilla movements, 194–96
Gunnlaugsson, Sigmundur Davíð, 105

Haas, Jonathan, 156
habitat destruction, 82, 91–92
Haiti, 128, 199
Hall, Stuart, 28
Hamilton (Ontario), 1–4, 70–71. *See also* Red Hill Valley
Hampton, Fred, 17
HANDY (Human and Nature Dynamics), 8, 75
Harper, Stephen, 116, 124, 163, 168, 210
Harvey, David: *The Condition of Postmodernity*, 51–52, 175
Haudenosaunee, 53–54
Hayden, Brian, 152
health care, 200, 203, 210
hegemony, 152–54, 184, 188, 211–12; and balance, 157; and counter-hegemony, 197–201; and negotiation, 157; power and, 27–29, 156, 205, 209
Heinberg, Richard, 77; *The Party's Over*, 85, 132–33; *Searching for a Miracle*, 86–87
Hermand, Edward: *Manufacturing Consent*, 124–25
Heritage Foundation, 116
hierarchies, 144, 147, 150, 154, 160, 161, 168–69, 186
Hilbeck, Angelika, 121
historical time, 53–54
historic bloc, 206, 208
Hitler, Adolf, 165
Hobbes, Thomas, 24, 136–37, 141, 151, 154, 180
Hoekstra, Arjen, 89
Holling, Crawford, 65–66
Homer-Dixon, Thomas, 18; *The Upside of Down*, 13–16, 22, 65, 75
homosexuality, 113
Honduras, revolution in, 188
Hoover, Herbert, 101
horticulturalists, 138, 149
House of Saud, 133, 167
housing, Indigenous peoples and, 69
housing bubble (2007), 53, 60–61, 103–4
humanism, enlightened, 141
human nature, 136–40
human rights, 6, 10, 30, 117, 126, 167, 171, 187, 191, 200, 202, 208, 210–11
hunter-gatherer communities, 137–39, 141, 143, 160
Huntington, Samuel, 173
Hussein, Saddam, 128
hydraulic fracturing, 87, 93–94, 133
hyper-compression, 51
hyper-masculinity, 113

ice-albedo effect, 65
Iceland, 68, 84, 90
Icke, David, 172
identity: collective, 166, 206; homogeneity of, 208; oligarchic, 170; politics, 30; religious, 168; sexual, 21, 198; shared, 154; social, 185; women's, 113
ideological manipulation, 154
Idle No More, 30, 127, 210
Illuminati, 173
immigration, and refugees, 215
imperialism, 114, 187, 200; over-extension, 164
incarceration, 49, 70, 126–27
income gap, 9, 49, 61, 99–100. *See also* inequality: income
India: British Raj, 63, 89, 153
Indigenous peoples, 37, 39, 67, 69, 73–75, 115, 172, 179, 212–14; disenfranchisement and genocide of, 73–75; internal colonization of, 115; land claims, 202; and poverty, 56, 69; resistance by, 197; status of, 49; theft of land from, 9; treaty rights, 213; women, missing and murdered, 115
individuality, 141, 146
industrial capitalism, 2, 15, 17, 22–23, 28, 39, 50, 53, 72, 114, 132–33, 160, 178, 183, 193; collapse of, 160; contradictions, 22; creative power of, 186; culture of, 164; domination of nature, 26, 51; globalized forms of, 58; impact of, 67, 76, 83, 91, 190; mercantilism and, 74; stratification caused by, 71; triumph of, 82; vulnerability of, 7. *See also* capitalism
industrialism, 78, 81, 184; ecological impacts of, 83
industrialization, 5, 15, 49, 81, 94, 132; legacy of, 2; and poverty, 68
industrial revolution, 174
Industrial Workers of the World (IWW), 183
inequality, 67, 126, 136, 148, 160, 187; class, 188; global, 68; income, 61, 72, 99–100, 183, 210; power, 67, 173–74; property, 155; racialized nature of, 69; social, 8, 17, 54, 75; wealth, 67, 69, 144, 147, 150, 155, 173–74
inhumanity, dynamics of, 22
innovation, 141; cultural, 154
institutional analysis, 173–74
insurrectionism, 19, 187–89, 191, 197, 208–9, 216
interbeing, 146–47, 204

Interface, 182–83
Intergovernmental Panel on Climate Change (IPCC), 7, 64, 123
interlocking directorates, 111
International Union for the Conservation of Nature (IUCN), 91
internet, 211–12
intersectional power, 166–69
investment, 50, 60–63, 103
invisibility, 49, 70
IPOs (initial public offerings), 104
Iran, 115, 128, 133, 167, 198
Iraq, US invasions of, 11, 16–17, 54–55, 74, 115, 128–29, 133, 162, 165, 187
Ireland, independence movement, 194–95
irreducible minimum, 141–43, 146–47, 201
Israel, 74, 153
Italy, 108, 158

Jackson, Andrew, 101
Jacobs, Norm, 4
James Bay Cree, 197
Japan, 29, 68, 95
Jefferson, Thomas, 101
Jensen, Derrick, 1, 20–21, 39; *Deep Green Resistance*, 190–96; *Endgame*, 7, 20, 36–37, 39–40, 41, 190; *Endgame: Resistance*, 190
John Birch Society, 109, 172
John of Patmos, 35, 131
Jones, Alex, 172
JP Morgan Chase, 102
Ju/Wasi, 139

Kalnay, Eugenia, 8
Keating, Charles, 104
Keith, David, 117–18
Keith, Lierre, 184–85; *Deep Green Resistance*, 190–96
Keltner, Dacher, 169
Kennedy, John F., 101
Kennedy, Paul: *The Rise and Fall of the Great Powers*, 164–65
Kenney, Jason, 116
Kerry, John, 169
Keystone XL pipeline, 197
kinship structures, 153, 155
Kissinger, Henry, 173
Kissinger and Associates, 102
Klare, Michael: *The Race for What's Left*, 86
Koch family, 109–11, 116
Koch Industries, 109–10, 123

Kolbert, Elizabeth: *The Sixth Extinction*, 92
Kropotkin, Peter, 20, 24
Kyoto Accord, 124

labour: division of, 148; gendered division of, 155; laws, 2; post-war compromise between capital and, 63, 157; slave, 180; struggles, 2; wage, 154, 180
Laclau, Ernesto, 28; *Hegemony and Socialist Strategy*, 201
laddering, 104
LaHaye, Tim, 173
Lakota Sioux water protectors, 212–14
landfill sites, 93
LaRouche, Lyndon, 172
Lay, Kenneth, 116
laziness, 145
leadership, 144–46; oligarchic, 145; prestige, 145; transparency and accountability of, 146
Leahy, Stephen, 90
Lebanon, 115
left: crisis and, 184–97; critical tradition, 12, 17–21, 22, 165; political, 2
Left Behind, 173
Leibniz, Gottfried, 80
Lenin, Vladimir, 189
Leonard, Annie: *The Story of Stuff*, 46
Leopold II, King, 73
leveraging/deleveraging, 64
Lew, Jacob "Jack," 102
Lexchin, Joel, 120
Libertarian Party, 110
Libya, 115, 128, 133, 168; revolution in, 188
life expectancy, 49, 68–69
Life System, 24–27, 29, 32, 146–47, 154, 210; and Death System, 180; emerging, 140–46; revolutionaries, 205–8; toward, 178–216
limits, 46–47; on human civilization, 78; systemic, 67
Lloyds: *Food System Shock*, 8
lobbying, 102, 116, 202
localization, 215
Lockheed Martin Aeronautics, 101
logging, 75, 90, 197
Lovelock, James, 7

MacKay, Peter, 168
MacMillan Bloedel, 197
Macy, Joanna, 151
Madison, James, 101
Magna Carta, 106
Magna Corporation, 101

Malthus, Thomas, 78
management functions, 214
manufacturing, 63
Mao Zedong, 189
Marcellus Shale deposit, 94
Marcus, Joyce, 158, 165
marginalization, 74; political, 70
"mark to market" schemes, 105
Martin, Paul, Jr., 101
Marx, Karl, 24, 51, 67, 151, 165; *Communist Manifesto*, 185
Marxian theory, 22, 62–63
Marxism, 17–19, 63, 99, 152–53, 186, 201
masculinity, 113, 167; hyper-aggressive, 140; stereotypical, 113
mass media, 124–26
material deprivation, 72
material sustenance, 141
McBay, Aric: *Deep Green Resistance*, 190–96
McKibben, Bill, 7, 18; *Deep Economy*, 181–82; *The End of Nature*, 58
McLuhan, Marshall, 55–56
McMurtry, John: *The Cancer of Stage of Capitalism*, 155
mechanistic worldview, 79–80
mega cities, 82
Mekonnen, Mesfin, 89
mental illness, 141; police shootings and, 126
mercantilism, 72–74, 81
Merchant, Caroline: *The Death of Nature*, 80
Merck and Company, 120–21
Merrill Lynch, 61, 102
Mexico: American Movil, 108
Meyer, Hartmut, 121
middle class, 11, 70, 169, 188
militarization, 22, 43, 75
militarized spending, 129–31
militarized states, 126–31
military: expansion of, 11, 35; technology, 72
military-industrial-academic complex, 118
military-industrial complex, 127–29
millenarianism, 173
Mills, C. Wright, 206
minimum wage, 203
mining, 75, 93, 101, 117, 172
minorities, police shootings and, 126
misogyny, 112, 210
mission civilatrice, 37
Mnuchin, Steven, 102
modernization theory, 83

modified organisms, 88
monarchy, absolutist, 27
Monbiot, George, 7, 18
Monsanto, 101, 121–22
moral community, 140–47, 191, 200, 201, 205, 208, 215
morality, 47, 189
Morgan, J.P., 111, 170
Mossack Fonseca, 105
Motesharrei, Safa, 8
Mouffe, Chantal, 28; *Hegemony and Socialist Strategy*, 201
movement of movements, 29–31, 201, 216
Mubarak, Hosni, 127
Mulroney, Brian, 2, 100
multiculturalism, 203
multinational corporations, 30
Mumford, Lewis: *Technics and Civilization*, 80, 136
Munk, Peter, 117; School of Global Affairs/Centre for International Studies, 117
Mussolini, Benito, 152

narcissism, 171
NASDAQ, 60
National Citizens Coalition, 116
nationalism, 125, 167, 174, 187
NATO, 202
natural gas, 86–87
Natural Law, 79
natural resources: commodification of, 81; depletion of, 82, 88–91
nature: devitalization of, 80–81, 82; as external and alien, 79; humans' relationship with, 78–82; mechanistic conception of, 82; survival of, 95; as a woman, 80
neighbourhood councils, 202, 210
neocolonialism, 9, 83
neo-conservatism, 24
neoliberalism, 2; restructuring, 63; trade agreements, 203
neo-Malthusianism, 14
Nepal, energy use in, 84
net energy, 86
neuronal mirroring, 169
New Left, 185
Newton, Huey, 185
Newton, Sir Isaac, 80
new world order, 174–75
nihilism, 26, 29
nitrogen, 88
Nixon, Richard, 125
non-human environment, 140

Nortel, 60
North Korea, 39, 98, 128, 198
nuclear disasters, 95
nuclear power, 83, 86
nuclear war, threat of, 6–7, 14

Obama, Barack, 17, 104, 118, 122, 124, 130, 167, 197, 213–14
obsolescence, planned and perceived, 164
Occupy Movement, 30–31, 127, 199, 210, 216
ocean acidification, 7, 88, 91–92
ocean biodiversity, 91–92
offshore tax havens, 105–6
oil, 101, 133, 162, 179; "easy," 86–88; prices, 63; scarcity of, 85, 133; unconventional sources of, 87, 162; wealth, 165
oil shale, 87
oligarchic imperative, 154, 157, 160, 172, 175, 180–81
oligarchy, 19, 23, 27–28, 46, 97–134, 136–37, 144–45, 148, 150–55, 178–80, 182, 184, 187–89, 191, 195, 210–12, 215; and authoritarian/militarized states, 126–31; benevolence of, 179; capitalism vs., 185–86; and collapse, 160–61; complexity vs., 161–65; and concentration of wealth, 99–100; consciousness, 169–70; constitution of, 165–77; and control over science/technology, 115–26; and corruption/criminality, 103–8; crisis of, 131–34; definition of, 97; dismantling of, 28–29, 198–200, 205, 209; ecological contradiction of, 158–60; emergence of, 136, 147, 149–50; myth of, 179; and oligopoly/political influence, 108–12; and patriarchy/white supremacy, 112–15; questioning of, 182; and revolving door, 100–103; social contradiction of, 155–58; as system/class, 166; vs. psychopathology, 175–77
oligopoly, political influence and, 108–12
O'Neal, Stan, 61
OneWest Bank, 102
OPEC (Organization of the Petroleum Exporting Countries), 63, 85, 115
oppression, 132, 156, 178–79, 195, 208; female, 167; racial, 176
Oreskes, Naomi: *Merchants of Doubt*, 119
organic societies, 144
organizational complexity, 13
Orwell, George: *Politics and the English Language*, 98

Oved, Marco Chown, 105
over-accumulation, 51, 62
over-fishing/grazing/planting, 89–91
over-leveraging, 103
over-production, 51–52, 62, 90
overshoot, 46, 77–96, 132, 159, 174, 179–80
Oxfam, 68–69, 105–6

Page, Benjamin, 112
Pakistan, 167
Palaniappan, Meena: *The World's Water 2008–2009*, 89
Palestine, 74, 115, 186, 186
Panama Papers, 105–6
panarchy, 66
participatory budgeting, 210
participatory representation, 202
pastoralism, 138
patriarchy, 17, 167; and white supremacy, 112–15
Paulson, Henry, 102
peace activism, 55
peacekeeping, 128
peak oil, 20, 85, 88
peak soil, 89
The People of the Valley, 4–5
Perot, Ross, 169
Peru: mine resistance movements in, 75; Spanish conquest of, 72, 75
pesticides, 93, 95
pharmaceutical industry, 120–21
"philosopher-king" model, 10
phosphorous, 88
physical handicap, 141
Piff, Paul, 169
Piketty, Tomas, 105; *Capital in the Twenty-First Century*, 106
Pinochet, Augusto, 117
Pizarro, Francisco, 72
planetary boundaries, 88
Plato, 10, 24, 137; *Republic*, 97
pogroms, 176
police: forces, 114, 179; states, 156; violence, 126–27, 213
political doublespeak, 128
political economy, 39
political influence, 121; oligopoly and, 108–12
political instability, 22, 75, 132, 159–60, 170
political organization, 39, 54, 143, 175, 191
political participation, 38, 142, 166–67, 202

political structure, 38, 97–134, 181, 201–2
Ponzi schemes, 103
population, 14; growth of, 8, 14, 25, 40, 78, 81, 89, 153, 215; impact of industrial capitalism on, 67; size, 149; stable, 140; urban, 81–82
Poroshenko, Petro, 105
positive feedback loops, 65
possible worlds, 25–31
post-hegemonic society, 201–5
poverty, 9, 48, 67–72, 74, 95, 155, 179; child, 49, 68–69, 71–72, 216; extreme, 71; Indigenous, 56; lived experience of, 69–70; police shootings and, 126; relative, 71; voting and, 112
power: concentration of, 164; decision-making, 16–17, 27, 112, 148, 183, 201; economic, 9, 12, 15, 17–18, 22, 100, 107–8, 115, 121, 129, 151, 163, 167, 174, 199, 201; elite, 156, 174, 198, 200, 209; exploitative, 154; and hegemony, 27–29, 153; intersectional, 166–69; political, 5, 9, 12, 15, 17–18, 22, 29, 50–55, 97–134, 147, 151, 163, 167–68, 174, 183–84, 199, 201, 207, 216; productive, 154; relationships of, 17, 181; wealth-distributing, 148
power-over, 140, 151, 153, 156
power-to, 153, 156
power-with, 140, 151
prejudice, 17
pre-state societies, 138
Price, Barbara, 38
primordial adaptive complex, 137, 144–46
private property rents, 50
privilege, 17
production, 49–52, 54, 81, 146; agricultural, 161; capitalist modes of, 155; costs of, 63; economic, 149, 159; industrial mass, 39; methods of, 59; state control of, 187; technological innovation in, 51; vs. profitability, 63–64
profit: accumulation of, 50; maximization of, 62
profitability, crisis in, 63–64
proletariat, 184, 187, 201; alienation of, 81; as force of history, 18
Project for a New American Century, 116
Proudhon, Pierre-Joseph, 20
psychologizing, 165–66
psychopathology, 175–77, 191
Putin, Vladimir, 105

Quebec: student movement, 30, 127, 210
Quebecor, 100, 125
Quinn, Daniel, 20, 39

race, 17, 114, 184–85, 198; and politics, 175
racialized minority status, and poverty, 68
racism, 17, 95, 112, 114–15, 172; biological, 24; systemic, 115
radicalism, 18, 21–22, 199, 209
radical transformation, organizing for, 205–12
Radin, Paul, 141
Rakoff, Jed, 104
RAND Corporation, 116
rationalism, 80
Reagan, Ronald, 2, 102, 116, 118
realism, 137
realpolitik, 128
rebellion, 54, 153–54, 156, 170, 186, 216
recallability, representative, 202
Red Hill Valley, 1–5, 11, 12, 22, 35, 82, 178, 214
Rees, William, 84; *Our Ecological Footprint*, 84
referendums, 202
reform, non-reformist, 208–12
reformism, 18, 20–21, 26, 181–84, 209, 215–16
Regan, Don, 102
reification, 155
religion, 17, 147–48, 153, 167, 174, 184–85
repression, 163, 188; capability for 158; elite, 200; military, 115; state, 126, 135, 200, 213–14; violence and, 156, 160, 195–96
resistance, 30–32, 75, 195, 198–99, 206, 213–14, 216; to elites/oligarchy, 154, 156, 184, 201; Indigenous, 197; militant, 192, 196–96
resources: extraction of, 59, 63, 75, 81, 161; over-exploitation of, 156
restorative justice, 202
Revelation, Book of, 34–35, 131
revolutionary movements, 28, 185, 187–89, 198
revolving door, 100–103, 166, 202
Reyna, Stephen: *Studying War*, 151
Rice, Condoleezza, 167
Rifkin, Jeremy" *The Empathic Civilization*, 87–88
rigged consensus, 152
rights, 201, 208, 211; citizenship, 30, 202, 208, 211; corporate, 111; cultural, 202, 208; ecological, 117 equal, 29; fishing, 197; fundamental, 141; of oligarchy, 167; recall, 207; safety and security, 141; treaty, 213; workers', 126, 183, 192, 211. *See also* civil rights; human rights
Rinehart, Georgina, 171–72
Riquetti, Victor de, 37
Ritter, Michael, 105
Rivas, Jorge, 8
Robber Barons, 111
Roberts, Pat, 172
Rockefeller, John D., 111, 170
Rogers, Ted, 171
Rogers Communications, 101, 108, 125
role specialization, 144, 148
Roman Empire, 35; rise and fall of, 13, 16
Romanow, Roy, 101
Romney, Mitt, 169
Roosevelt, Franklin D., 170
Rostow, Walt, 83
Rothschild family, 173
Roubini, Nouriel, 7
Rousseau, Jean-Jacques, 24, 97, 179
Rubin, Robert, 103
rule of law, 98, 126; fair and impartial, 210
Russia, 27, 128, 133, 187; influence of, 17; revolution in, 188, 198
Rwanda, 15

Sachs, Jeffrey, 106
Samso (Denmark), 40
Sanders, Bernie, 30, 107–8, 125, 184, 199, 211, 213–14, 216
Sanders, William, 38
Saudi Arabia, 98, 133, 167
savings and loan institutions, 103–4
scale, and complexity, 25, 28, 59, 64–66, 67, 132, 143, 174, 179, 198
Schumpeter, Joseph, 175
science, 78, 80–81, 143; control over, 115–26; public support for, 203
scientific revolution, 80–81
sedentary living, 150
Seitz, Frederick, 122
self-fulfillment, 146
self-identity, 146
selfishness, 136–37, 145
September 11 attacks, 6, 54
Serbia, revolution in, 188
Service, Elman, 38
sexism, 95, 185, 206; biological, 24
sexuality, 184; alternative, 141; identity, 21, 198

shadow government, 130
shale gas/oil, 85–86, 94, 162, 213
Shareholder Association for Research and Education, 102
Sharp, Fred, 105
Shaw Communications, 125
shelter, adequate, 141–43
Shiva, Vandana, 208
Siddiqui, Islam, 122
Sierra Leone, life expectancy in, 68
Six Nations Confederacy, 4, 53–54
slavery, 73, 114–15, 154, 176, 179, 192
Slim, Carlos, 108
small business, 203
Snowden, Edward, 211
social change, 187–88, 198–99
social complexity, 25, 38, 137, 144, 149–50, 153, 161, 186. *See also* complexity
social control, 25, 146
social Darwinism, 114
social dynamics, 12, 137
social dysfunction, 12, 17, 35, 66, 137, 173–74, 182, 187
social ecology, 26, 28
social evolution, 83
social instability, 54
socialism, 19, 23, 183, 202, 204; capitalism vs., 187; democratic, 216
sociality, 146, 150, 191
social justice, 6, 131, 183, 202, 210
social learning, 140
social movements, 2, 10–11, 29–32, 182, 188, 192, 207, 216
social roles, 150
social sanctions, 154
social scale, 25, 38
social security, 63
social stability, 66, 157, 189, 205
social stratification, 38, 67, 149, 150, 173, 184. *See also* stratification
social structure, 23, 54, 75, 147–48, 150, 160, 206; egalitarian, 139; psychopathic, 176
social system, 9, 27, 47, 59, 99, 133, 174–75, 207, 209, 196, 215; American, 162; authoritarian/militarized, 126; dysfunction in, 173, egalitarian, 140; macro-level, 43; oligarchic, 172
social unrest, 88
socioeconomic class, 17, 160; divisions, 148, 198; formation, 176; status quo, 200
socioeconomic status, 48, 69, 167
sociological time, 52–54

soil erosion, 89–90
solar power, 86–87, 162, 204
solidarity, 198; norm of, 142; solidarity-building, 31, 206–7, 214
Soros, George, 171
South Africa, 175, 186, 194–95
Spain, Fascist coup in, 158
spatial displacement, 47–50, 56
species extinction, 7, 91–92
Spencer, Herbert, 83
Sprint, 108
Sri Lanka, 167
Standard Oil, 111
Standing Rock Sioux, 197, 212–14, 216
status, 138–39, 141, 143–45, 150, 171, 174; inequality, 147–48; obsession with, 170; subordinate, 168
Steffen, Will, 88
Stelco, 1–3
stereotypes, 113–14
Stewart, John: *Evolution's Arrow*, 214–15
stock market crash (1929), 103
stratification, 46, 67–76, 99, 132, 165, 174, 176, 179. *See also* social stratification
Stronach, Belinda, 101
structuration, 148, 176, 209–10
Students for a Democratic Society (SDS), 185
Stuenicki, Daviken, 75
Sturgeon, Raymond, 101
subprime mortgages, 60–62
subsistence, 37, 90, 146, 159, 202; economy, 39, 139
suburbs, 82
suicide, 49
Summers, Larry, 118
super-PACs (political action committees), 107
surveillance, 154, 156, 211
sustainability, 10, 27, 41, 187, 191, 207; from collapse to, 15, 25, 133, 183, 192, 206; convenience vs., 144; ecological, 22, 84, 131, 146, 171, 188, 200–201, 204, 208, 210, 216; threats to, 161
sustainable growth, 133
Suzuki, David, 18; David Suzuki Foundation, 65; *The Sacred Balance*, 181–82
synchronic cultural evolution, 83
synchronous failure, 15
Syria, 115, 128, 133, 167, 168; revolution in, 188
system, vs. conspiracy, 172–75
systemic risk, 65–66

Index   255

systems theories, 12, 13–17, 21–22; analysis of civilization using, 41–45

Taibbi, Matt, 103–4
tailings ponds, 94
Taino people, 74
Tainter, Joseph, 18, 180; *The Collapse of Complex Societies*, 13–16, 22, 23, 89–90, 161–65
tar sands extraction, 86–87, 93–94, 124, 133, 194, 200, 210
Tasmania, aborigines of, 74
taxation, 154
tax evasion, 105–6
Tea Party, 123
technology, 37, 78, 82, 163; and agriculture, 90; creation of, 137; emancipatory, 191; innovation in, 51, 75, 86, 174, 203; military, 72; science and, 81, 194
tech sector stocks, 60, 103–4
teleology, 18–19
Telus, 101, 108, 125
temporal displacement, 47, 50–54, 56, 62
the Terror, 198
terrorism, 7, 8, 22, 75, 128; political, 35
Thatcher, Margaret, 17
The Advancement of Sound Science Coalition (TASSC), 123
theocratic states, 167, 186
Thermidorian reaction, 198
think tanks, 115–16
Thomas, Elizabeth, 139
350.org, 65
Thyssen, Fritz, 101
time-space distanciation, 55
tipping points, 65–66, 91, 133
tobacco industry, 118–20, 123
Tobacco Industry Research Committee, 119
topsoil, degradation of, 89–90
Toronto, 40–41
Torstar, 101
Tory, John, 101
totalitarianism, 27, 172
totalizing categories, 184–85
toxic chemicals/waste, 2–3, 7, 82, 88, 93–95
trade unions, 2, 52, 63, 157, 183, 203
transegalitarianism, 148, 151–53
Transnational Capitalist Class, 111
Transparency International, 102
transportation, 63; collapse of, 88
tribalism, 147, 160, 170–71; from band level to, 149

Trotsky, Leon, 189
Troubled Asset Relief Program (TARP), 61
Trudeau, Justin, 124, 212
Trump, Donald, 124–25, 164, 169, 210–11, 213–14
Twain, Mark: *King Leopold's Soliloquy*, 73

Ukraine, revolution in, 188
ultra-radicalism, 189
unemployment, structural, 71
UNESCO, 4
unilineal cultural evolution, 83, 154
Union Banking Corporation, 101
United Nations, 173, 202; Food and Agriculture Organization (FAO), 71, 90
United States: Army Corps of Engineers, 213; banking sector, 108; campaign finance, 107; child poverty, 68–69; Citizens United decision (2010), 107; Clean Air Act, 110; COINTELPRO, 189; Democratic Party, 108, 125, 184; Department of Defense, 118, 130; Department of the Treasury, 102, 130; energy use, 84, 162; Environmental Protection Agency (EPA), 93, 110, 164; Farm Bill (2012; Monsanto Protection Act), 122; Federal Reserve Bank, 61, 102; Food and Drug Administration (FDA), 101, 122; food industry, 121; Glass-Steagall Act (1933), 62, 103; Homeland Security/Advisory System, 7, 130; incarceration rates, 126–27; income gap, 100; influence of, 17; macro-systems model, 22; media revenues, 125; military budget, 129; National Institutes of Health, 118; National Science Foundation, 118; National Security Agency (NSA), 211; NGOs, 116; Office of Naval Research, 118; oligopoly, 108; Pentagon, 130; Pipeline and Hazardous Materials Safety Administration (PHMSA), 213; police shootings, 127; poverty, 68–69; revolution, 28; revolving door, 101; Securities and Exchange Commission (SEC), 102; Special Operations (Northern) Command (SOCOM/SOCNORTH), 130; State Department, 130; Strategic Defense Initiative (SDI), 122–23; tax evasion, 105; warfare, 43–44; wealth, 69
United Steel Workers of America (USWA), 2
universities, 117–19
Uruguay, radical government in, 199

vanguardism, 189–96, 197–98
Veblen, Thorstein, 170
Venezuela, 128, 133; radical government in, 199
Verizon, 108
Vietnam War, 165, 209
violence, 21, 56, 70, 75, 136, 175, 179, 191, 205, 208; alpha male, 176; against biosphere, 78; for compliance, 151–52; and conquest, 157; direct, 20; elites and, 31, 154, 158; human, 25; inter-group, 138; and masculinity, 167; police, 126–27, 213; and racism, 115, 209; repressive, 156, 160, 172, 195; and revolution, 19; structural, 20, 71; against women, 113
visible minorities: overrepresentation of in prisons and among poor, 49; police shootings and, 126; in political office, 112; poverty rates for, 69; voting and, 112
voluntarism, 189
voting system, 202

Wackernagel, Mathis, 84; *Our Ecological Footprint*, 84
wages: disparity in, 99; higher rates of, 63; suppression of, 52
Walmart, 109; Political Action Committee, 109
Walton Family Foundation, 109, 111
war/warfare, 35, 37, 39, 40, 43–44, 46, 74–75, 88, 132, 138, 149, 157–60, 165, 175, 176, 180, 210, 216
Waring, Marilyn: *If Women Counted*, 113–14
warrior culture, 114, 150, 167
Washington, George, 101
waste: production and disposal of, 48, 93, 100, 194
water, 48; absolute scarcity of, 89; industrial use of, 53; quality of, 93–94; shortages, 7, 8, 88–89, 133, 215; stress, 89
wealth, 68–69, 158, 171; accumulation of, 157; concentration of, 99–100; creation and distribution of, 72; extraction of, 164; inequality, 67, 69, 144, 147, 150, 173–74; maximization of, 169; oil, 165; redistribution of, 187
wealth disparity, 75
weapons of mass destruction, 129
Weather Underground, 190
welfare state, 29, 188
West, Cornel, 28
whistle-blowing, 202, 210, 211
White, Leslie, 83
whiteness, 167–68, 175
white supremacy, 210; patriarchy and, 112–15
Wiessner, Polly, 138
WikiLeaks, 108
wildlife, 204; loss of, 82, 91–92
Williams, Raymond, 171; *Marxism and Literature*, 153
Wilson, Darren, 127
wind power, 86–87, 162, 194, 204
Winkler-Koch, 109
Wolf, Eric, 38
women: Indigenous, missing and murdered, 115; patriarchy and feminism, 112–14; subordination of, 67, 167; suffrage, 194–95. *See also* gender
women's movement, 189
Woodburn, James, 138–39
worker protection, 203. *See also* rights: workers'
working class, 2, 11, 47, 72, 112, 167, 169, 171, 184–85, 201, 208; immiseration of, 155; women of, 167
WorldCom, 60, 105
World Resources Institute: *Millennium Ecosystem Report*, 91
World War II

xenophobia, 145

youth: internet and, 211–12; voting and, 112
Y2K scare, 6
Yuki people, 74

Zerzan, John, 20–21
Zinn, Howard: *A People's History of the United States*, 111
zombies, 9
Zweigenhaft, R.L., 112